HENRY PIERS'S
CONTINENTAL TRAVELS, 1595–1598

HENRY PIERS'S
CONTINENTAL TRAVELS, 1595–1598

edited by
Brian Mac Cuarta SJ

CAMDEN FIFTH SERIES
Volume 54

CAMBRIDGE
UNIVERSITY PRESS

FOR THE ROYAL HISTORICAL SOCIETY
University College London, Gower Street, London WC1 6BT
2018

Published by the Press Syndicate of the University of Cambridge
University Printing House, Shaftesbury Road, Cambridge CB2 8BS, United Kingdom
One Liberty Plaza, Floor 20, New York, NY 10006, USA
477 Williamstown Road, Port Melbourne, VIC 3207, Australia
C/Orense, 4, Planta 13, 28020 Madrid, Spain
Lower Ground Floor, Nautica Building, The Water Club,
Beach Road, Granger Bay, 8005 Cape Town, South Africa

First published 2018

A catalogue record for this book is available from the British Library

ISBN 9781108496773 hardback

SUBSCRIPTIONS. The serial publications of the Royal Historical Society, *Royal Historical Society Transactions* (ISSN 0080-4401) and Camden Fifth Series (ISSN 0960-1163) volumes, may be purchased together on annual subscription. The 2018 subscription price, which includes print and electronic access (but not VAT), is £195 (US $325 in the USA, Canada, and Mexico) and includes Camden Fifth Series, Volumes 54 and 55 and Transactions Sixth Series, Volume 28 (published in December). The electroniconly price available to institutional subscribes is £163 (US $272 in the USA, Canada, and Mexico). Japanese prices are available from Kinokuniya Company Ltd, P.O. Box 55, Chitose, Tokyo 156, Japan. EU subscribers (outside the UK) who are not registered for VAT should add VAT at their country's rate. VAT registered subscribers should provide their VAT registration number. Prices include delivery by air.

Subscription orders, which must be accompanied by payment, may be sent to a bookseller, subscription agent, or direct to the publisher: Cambridge University Press, University Printing House, Shaftesbury Road, Cambridge CB2 8BS, UK; or in the USA, Canada, and Mexico: Cambridge University Press, Journals Fulfillment Department, One Liberty Plaza, Floor 20, New York, NY 10006, USA.

SINGLE VOLUMES AND BACK VOLUMES. A list of Royal Historical Society volumes available from Cambridge University Press may be obtained from the Humanities Marketing Department at the address above.

Printed in the UK by Bell & Bain Ltd.

CONTENTS

ACKNOWLEDGEMENTS

I wish to express my gratitude to those who have supported the research which this edition has entailed. At the Royal Historical Society, Andrew Spicer has been a calm and efficient series editor, while the readers of the proposal offered serious and fruitful suggestions. I am grateful to the staff at Cambridge University Press for their care in preparing the manuscript for publication, and Miranda Bethell's close and attentive reading of the text deserves special mention. My thanks to David Cox and Matthew Stout who prepared the maps. The insights and expertise of others have enriched my understanding of Henry Piers and his world. Máire Kennedy has been generous in sharing her expert knowledge of the Gilbert materials in the Dublin City Library. The staff at the Bodleian in Oxford; Special Collections, Christ Church College; the National Library of Ireland; and Trinity College Dublin have made the materials in their care available in a professional and courteous manner.

I thank those who have responded to queries of various kinds: Bruce Barker-Benfield, Mauro Brunello, Pascual Cebollada SJ, Ben Hazard, Victor Houliston, Gerard Kilroy, Marc Lindeijer SJ, Martin Murphy, Cristina Neagu, Patrick Riordan SJ, and Maurice Whitehead, archivist at the Venerable English College, Rome, who also gave me a guided tour of the college. Simon Ditchfield made valuable recommendations on the Italian context while Thomas McCoog SJ kindly read through the entire draft, and shared his expert knowledge of the English Jesuits; Declan Mac Cuarta alerted me to verbal infelicities; the work is stronger thanks to their contributions. Any remaining errors, and stylistic lapses, are mine.

Without a sabbatical from Archivum Romanum Societatis Iesu, Rome, this work would not have reached completion; I am grateful to Father General Arturo Sosa, and to my colleagues at ARSI, especially Raúl González SJ. The Irish province of the Society of Jesus has been most supportive; I would like to thank Tom Layden SJ and Leonard Moloney SJ, successive provincials of the Irish Jesuits. I have been fortunate in being able to spend time in Campion Hall, Oxford, a warm and hospitable academic community; Peter Davidson's knowledge and enthusiasm have been a regular source of encouragement, while Wilma Minty helped me navigate bibliographical challenges.

My brother Declan Mac Cuarta has provided his customary interest and support. In particular he instigated a lengthy odyssey to Tristernagh by car one August evening, with several stops to ask for ever more precise location details, culminating in a visit to the ruins of Henry Piers's home (and the family chapel), from where his travels began.

ABBREVIATIONS

AVCAU	Archivum Venerabilis Collegii Anglorum de Urbe, Rome
Cal. S.P. Dom. 1595–1597	*Calendar of State Papers, Domestic Series, 1595–1597: Preserved in the Public Record Office* (London, 1869)
Cal. S.P. Ire.	*Calendar of the State Papers relating to Ireland, 1571–1608: Preserved in the Public Record Office*, 13 vols (London, 1867–2010)
Cal. S.P. Spanish 1587–1603	*Calendar of Letters, Despatches, and State Papers relating to English Affairs, 1587–1603: Preserved Principally in the Archives of Simancas* (London, 1899)
DIB	James McGuire and James Quinn (eds), *Dictionary of Irish Biography*, 9 vols (Cambridge, 2009)
Diccionario Histórico de la Compañía de Jésus	Charles O'Neill and Joaquín Domínguez (eds), *Diccionario Histórico de la Compañía de Jésus Biográfico-Temático* (Rome and Madrid, 2001)
'Discourse'	'A discourse of HP his travelles written by him selfe', Oxford, Bodleian Library, Rawlinson MS D. 83
Dizionario Biografico degli Italiani	Published by *Istituto dell'Enciclopedia Italiana, Treccani* (Rome, 1960–); online resource
Miranda, *The Cardinals of the Holy Roman Church*	*The Cardinals of the Holy Roman Church*, a digital resource created and produced by Salvador Miranda consisting of the biographical entries of the Cardinals from 494 to 2015

Foley, *Records*, VI	Henry Foley (ed.), *Records of the English Province of the Society of Jesus*, Vol. VI (Supplemental Volume): *The Diary of the English College, Rome, from 1579 to 1773, With Biographical and Historical Notes; The Pilgrim-Book of the Ancient English Hospice Attached to the College from 1580 to 1656, with Historical Notes* (London, 1880)
ODNB	H.C. Matthew, Brian Harrison, Lawrence Goldman (eds), *Oxford Dictionary of National Biography*, (Oxford, 2004–)
OED	*Oxford English Dictionary*
SJ	Society of Jesus

MAPS

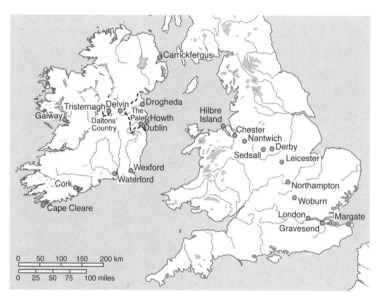

Map 1. Ireland and England: Henry Piers's world.

Map 2. Europe, west: places mentioned in text.

Map 3. Europe, central: places mentioned in text.

INTRODUCTION

The following memoir by an Irishman (of English parents settled in Elizabethan Ireland) recounts his journey from Dublin to Rome in 1595, through the Low Countries, Germany, and northern Italy. He lists many of Rome's churches, and describes religious processions together with some of the city's antiquities, and includes an account of the battle of Lepanto (1571) before relating his journey north towards Genoa, giving a detailed presentation of the pilgrimage site of Loreto. Arriving in Alicante in Spain, he proceeded to Valladolid, and thence to Seville, from where he returned to Ireland in late 1598.

At one level, therefore, this work may be located within the genre of Elizabethan travel literature featuring the Continent, particularly Italy.[1] However, the present text is distinguished by its explicitly Catholic perspective, a rare example within that literary corpus.[2] For the author's motivation in undertaking the journey, as he relates, was spiritual. Piers was brought up in the established church, a denominational identity reinforced by a marriage alliance with a leading Protestant family in colonial Ireland. Moved by doubts arising from what he experienced of the diversity among Protestant groupings, he was encouraged to explore Catholicism by encounters with some Catholic laymen. Leaving wife, lands, and a position as seneschal, he decided to travel to Rome, helped by recusant connections spanning the Irish Sea. His conversion to Catholicism on arrival in Rome, his sojourn in the city, and his subsequent movements in Spain occurred within the network of the English Jesuit exiles on the Continent.

---

[1] For an overview of this literature as regards Rome, see Thomas Frank, 'Elizabethan travellers in Rome', in Mario Praz (ed.), *English Miscellany: A Symposium of History Literature and the Arts*, 4 (Rome, 1953), 95–132, reference to Piers at 127. See also Edward Chaney, ' "Quo vadis?" Travel as education and the impact of Italy in the sixteenth century', in Edward Chaney, *The Evolution of the Grand Tour: Anglo-Italian Relations since the Renaissance* (London, 1998), 58–101; on the Elizabethan era, see 72–86.

[2] In 1581, the English priest Gregory Martin composed a description of Rome, devotional and apologetic in tone, based on his stay there in 1576–1578; treating of churches, relics, and processions, followed by religious houses, colleges, and hospices; the text remained unpublished until 1969, Gregory Martin, *Roma Sancta (1581): Now First Edited from the Manuscript*, ed. George Bruner Parks (Rome, 1969); Gregory Martin (?1542–1582), *ODNB*.

A leitmotiv of the memoir is gratitude to God for blessings received, and especially for the author's embracing of Catholicism. Thus the text may be viewed as a Catholic conversion narrative. In line with this genre, he relates relationships through which that new denominational adherence came about; in describing various situations he loses no opportunity to make a polemical defence of Catholicism against the objections of the reformers.[3] This narrative includes his struggle to overcome Roman suspicions regarding his English and heretical family background, resulting in an appearance before the Inquisition.

Describing his life in the English College from 1595 to 1597, the memoir affords a layman's view from the epicentre of one of Elizabethan Catholicism's long-standing internal disputes. In the details of daily life in the college, his account complements the anti-Catholic perspective of another young Elizabethan, Anthony Munday, who lived there for over two months in 1579. There is no clear evidence that Piers engaged with the earlier work; however, as a Catholic loyalist, Piers was at pains to refute the assertion, widespread in England, and strongly represented in Munday's portrayal, that the English scholars in Rome were engaged in traitorous conversation against the Elizabethan regime.[4]

The memoir concludes with the relatively shorter narrative of his year in Spain (1598), which illuminates the stresses and tensions experienced by Irish and English merchants living there during the Anglo-Spanish War (1585–1604).

Henry Piers's Irish Background

In order to introduce the travel memoir of Henry Piers (1567–1623),[5] it is necessary to situate him within the political and cultural context

---

[3] For a discussion of this genre, together with a guide to the secondary literature, see Molly Murray, ' "Now I ame a Catholique": William Alabaster and the early modern conversion narrative', in Ronald Corthell et al. (eds), *Catholic Culture in Early Modern England* (Notre Dame, IN, 2007), 189–215.

[4] Anthony Munday, *The English Roman Life*, ed. Philip Ayres (1582; 1590; citations from Oxford, 1980), 22, 44, 65; Anthony Munday (1560–1633), *ODNB*; for a reading of this work in terms of the situation of Catholics in England, see Donna Hamilton, *Anthony Munday and the Catholics, 1560–1633* (Aldershot and Burlington, VT, 2005), 47–51; 'A discourse of HP his travelles written by him selfe' (Bodleian, Rawlinson MS D. 83) [henceforth 'Discourse'], 118–119; for William Allen's rebuttal of this negative representation of the exiles, see Mark Netzloff, 'The English colleges and the English nation: Allen, Persons, Verstegen, and diasporic nationalism', in Corthell et al., *Catholic Culture*, 240–244.

[5] Henry Piers (1567–1623) is to be distinguished from his near-contemporary namesake, Henry Piers (Pierse) (d.1638), who served as secretary to Lord Deputy Chichester, and was

of late Elizabethan Ireland. He was born of an English military officer settled in Ireland since the mid sixteenth century, and his English wife, and until about 1574 the family was living in Carrickfergus, in north-east Ulster, where Henry's father, William, was constable of the castle. From about 1580 they were resident on the property of a dissolved monastery at Tristernagh in Co. Westmeath, located just beyond the Pale, on the southern border of Ulster.[6] Thus far the family's profile fits that of the New English, those recent arrivals from England and Wales, usually Protestant, who served the expanding Tudor state in Ireland both in central government and, chiefly as military figures, in various localities hitherto little touched by anglicization.

While Piers spent time in England as a young man, there is no documentary evidence that he frequented one of the inns of court, or attended Oxford or Cambridge.[7] Although his parents were English, adherents of the established church, the evidence of his memoir suggests that Henry himself identified with the old-established colonial community in Ireland, who traced their origins to the twelfth-century conquest, and who into the sixteenth century designated themselves as 'the English of Ireland'. As a youth, Piers came under the influence of the leading magnate in his area, Christopher Nugent, 14th Baron Delvin,[8] head of one of the foremost English noble families of Ireland, who himself had studied at Cambridge in the mid 1560s, and at that time composed an Irish grammar for Queen Elizabeth. Writing not long after the baron's death, Piers expressed his appreciation of his wide culture, prudence, hospitality, and Catholic faith; their acquaintance dated to when Henry was aged about eighteen, for in late 1585 the peer returned from confinement in England to live in his castle in Delvin, Co. Westmeath, which lay on the route between the Piers house and Dublin; Piers may have spent some time in the Nugent household.

granted lands in Co. Cavan under the Ulster Plantation, Henry Piers, *DIB*, sub nomine; a descendant of the Tristernagh family, yet another Henry Piers, wrote 'A chorographical description of the county of Westmeath' in 1682, published in Charles Vallancey, *Collectanea de Rebus Hibernicis* (Dublin, 1786), 1–126.

[6] Petition of William Piers to Queen Elizabeth, n.d. [*c.* July 1574], *Cal. S.P. Ire., 1571–1575*, 627–628; William Piers acquired a lease of the property in 1562, A. Gwynn and R. Hadcock, *Medieval Religious Houses: Ireland* (London, 1970), 196–197.

[7] There is a reference to one 'Henry Peers' who at Easter 1585 matriculated from Jesus College, Cambridge; while the author was about 17 by that date, and had spent some time in England as a young man, it is not possible to link this reference with certitude to the subject, John Venn and J.A. Venn, *Alumni Cantabrigienses*, Part I, Vol. III (Cambridge, 1924), 328.

[8] Christopher Nugent, 14th Baron Delvin (1544–1602), *DIB*; on Delvin's Irish grammar, see Denis Casey, *The Nugents of Westmeath and Queen Elizabeth's Irish Primer* (Dublin, 2016).

The Pale marcher areas were Irish-speaking; while pursuing education in England and cherishing humanist culture, the Nugent family
was renowned for involvement in Gaelic literary life; the baron had a
library, to which he was devoted; in a reform treatise from the mid
1580s he decried the lack of a university in Ireland.[9] In this magnate,
Piers encountered a model of learned civility, colonial loyalism, and
devotion to the old faith that the young man found attractive; doubtless Nugent's example encouraged him on the road to Catholicism.
Piers's admiration for the Nugent lineage prompted him, while he
was in Rome, to visit Francis Nugent, the Capuchin friar, who
arrived in the city in about September or October 1596.[10]

Young Piers also acquired the musical education which was standard at this social level in contemporary England, and enjoyed singing and could perhaps play the lute: while travelling through Padua
in September 1595, captivated by 'verie sweete musicke' he heard by
chance at a doorway, he was invited inside to spend an evening of
song with the household, indicating that he was used to singing madrigals.[11] Passing through Bologna he encountered John Dowland, the
Elizabethan musician, though Piers made no reference to this meeting.[12] His delight in music was further in evidence when in Rome,
where on occasion he noted how he was moved by the choirs he
heard.

Growing up in the marcher area straddling south Ulster and the
northern Pale, he also had direct exposure to the Gaelic world.
Down to the onset of peace in 1603, the Piers were the solitary
New English family of any standing settled on the north-western
marches of the Pale. County Westmeath, though originally part of
the medieval colony, by the mid sixteenth century had become gae-
licized.[13] Outside a narrow social elite, knowledge of English was rare.

---

[9] On the political and literary worlds of the Nugent family in the late 16th century,
linked via the Fitzgeralds to a kin network in England, see the biography of William
Nugent (1550–1625), brother of Christopher Nugent, 14th Baron Delvin, Basil Iske, *The
Green Cockatrice* (Meath, 1978); on the family's bilingualism, see Vincent Carey, ' "Neither
good English nor good Irish": Bi-lingualism and identity formation in sixteenth-century
Ireland', in H. Morgan (ed.), *Political Ideology in Ireland, 1541–1641* (Dublin, 1999), 45–61.

[10] 'Discourse', 72–73.

[11] 'Discourse', 25; madrigals were sung by four voices, each voice reading from the part-
book, in a domestic setting, Alfred Einstein, *The Italian Madrigal* (Princeton, NJ, 1949), 244–
245.

[12] John Dowland to Robert Cecil, 10 Nov 1595, from Nuremberg, Historical
Manuscripts Commission, *Calendar of the Manuscripts of … Marquess of Salisbury*, 24 vols
(London, 1883–1976), V, 447.

[13] Their landed neighbours in the mid 1590s in the barony of Moygoish, Co. Westmeath,
included the Tuite, Nangle, and FitzGerald families, Anglo-Norman names, 'A perambulation

Irish was the normal language. While serving in north-east Ulster
over many years, Captain William Piers (Henry's father) functioned
in a Gaelic environment; he continued to draw on that skill on moving to Co. Westmeath, and inculcated it in his son. The Gaelic lordship of the O'Farrells lay just a few miles west of the Piers house. As a
boy Henry was fostered there with the family of Gerald O'Farrell and
his wife Elizabeth Tankard.[14] An echo of that early upbringing was
his joy in meeting Brian McFargus O'Farrell, then a clerical student,
when Piers was staying in the English College in Valladolid.[15] That
Piers noted this encounter was itself significant, all the more so in
that he expressed his appreciation of Brian as a man of learning
who had died by the time Piers was writing his memoir.

In 1590, then aged about 22 or 23, Piers acquired the position of
seneschal of 'Daltons' Country', a territory in Westmeath adjacent
to the Piers estate. The seneschal role, a crown appointment,
involved assembling the inhabitants for defence, and some judicial
responsibilities, and in return the septs were to contribute levies in
kind to cover the seneschal's expenses.[16] It implied an ability to
engage with the local population, and was clearly linked to the military and official standing of his father in the eyes of the crown.
Young Henry was thus fully integrated into the social, political,
and cultural world of this marcher area west of the Pale.

Piers displayed a sensitivity to the varying identities within the
Elizabethan world. In the 'Discourse', he differentiated between
Irish and English in referring to the people he met from the Tudor
realms. In presenting himself to the English College in Rome, he indicated that he was Irish, but of English parents.[17] Thus he fully identified
with the land of his birth, referring to 'this realme of Eirland', 'this
commonwealth', and 'oure contrimen'.[18] His focus was on religious
issues in question between the confessions, and, apart from a brief
note on his disputing the religious motivation of the Irish revolt (on
his arrival in Rome), he made no explicit reference to the Irish political

of Leinster, Meath and Louth, of which consist the English Pale' [1596], *Calendar of the Carew
Manuscripts*, 6 vols (London, 1867–1873), III, 188–196, at 192.
[14] Elizabeth Hickey, 'Some notes on Kilbixy, Tristernagh and Templecross and the family of Piers who lived in the abbey of Tristernagh in Westmeath', *Ríocht na Midhe* 7 (1980–
1981), 52–76.
[15] 'Discourse', 199.
[16] 'Fiants Ireland, Elizabeth', No. 5431 (1 July 1590), *Sixteenth Report of Deputy Keeper of the
Public Records of Ireland* (Dublin, 1884), Appendix, 120.
[17] 'The Pilgrim-Book of the English College', in Henry Foley SJ (ed.), *Records of the English
Province of the Society of Jesus*, Vol. VI (London, 1880) [henceforth Foley, *Records*, VI], 567–568
(gives 19 names for 1595). This designation rendered him eligible for admission, which the
college statutes specified was reserved to those of English parentage.
[18] 'Discourse', 2, 4, 13.

scene.[19] His outlook was defined by English culture and loyalty to the crown, in common with his family, which included the connections in the Irish military represented by his father; in the 1580s and 1590s Piers senior was a trusted government figure in Westmeath, and was one of the most prolific writers of treatises on Tudor Ireland.[20]

Reinforcing the family's New English identity, by about 1593 Henry had married Jane, a daughter of Thomas Jones (1550–1619), who became Church of Ireland bishop of Meath and member of the Irish Privy Council in 1584.[21] By this marriage Henry became part of a broad and influential network of mainly New English families in late sixteenth-century Ireland, for Jones himself was married to a sister-in-law of his predecessor as prelate and chancellor, Adam Loftus.[22] In the years of Piers's conversion to Catholicism, his father-in-law was noted as a consistent advocate of a severe anti-recusant policy. Family pressures against embracing the old faith were real. However, in terms of political identity, Piers clearly opposed Tyrone's campaign in the 1590s, a stance that caused him grief on arrival in Rome. His lands and properties in Co. Westmeath suffered the depredations associated with intensification of the war in the wake of Tyrone's military success at the Yellow Ford in August 1598. Thereafter the midlands region was engulfed in military strife, as the Irish attacked the homes of leading English loyalists.[23]

A formative experience in shaping his religious outlook was his exposure through preaching to the varieties of English Protestantism in the later Elizabethan period. His stay in England (at some stage from the mid 1580s to the early 1590s) coincided with the appearance of radical preachers, especially in London, as dissatisfaction with the limited nature of the Anglican reform coalesced into the various puritan groupings.[24] It was a theme which interested him; open-air preaching was a lively if not rowdy popular

---

[19] 'Discourse', 31.

[20] One of his tracts, c.1594, is reproduced in David Heffernan (ed.), *'Reform' Treatises on Tudor Ireland* (Dublin, 2016), 323–325.

[21] Thomas Jones became archbishop of Dublin and lord chancellor of Ireland in Nov. 1605, *DIB*.

[22] The Loftus connection included the military families of Bagenal, Colley, and Warren, together with the Usshers, a prominent Dublin family, Adam Loftus (1533/4–1605), *DIB*.

[23] 'Discourse', 210–211; on the attack on the home of one midland settler family at this time, see B. Mac Cuarta (ed.) 'Sir John Moore's Inventory, Croghan, King's County, 1636', *Journal of the County Kildare Archaeological Society* 19 (2000–2001), 206–217.

[24] Proclamation against unlicensed preachers in London, 26 Mar. 1589, Robert Steele, *A Bibliography of Royal Proclamations of the Tudor and Stuart Sovereigns … 1485–1714*, 2 vols (Oxford, 1910), I, 89; on how laity engaged with preaching, see Arnold Hunt, *The Art of Hearing: English Preachers and their Audiences, 1590–1640* (Cambridge, 2010), especially ch. 2, 'The art

occasion; he became conversant with the range of conflicting views on church and theology. In this regard, later, in summer 1595, while travelling through the town of Naarden in the Low Countries, he noted the presence of various English sects (he referred to the followers of Robert Browning, and Henry Barrow, leaders of Independency, and Congregationalism, persecuted in the early 1590s) who had fled to the Netherlands and found refuge there. This clash of religious positions left him unsettled, and he sought a locus of ecclesial unity; from these experiences he was drawn to the Roman church.

Writing some years after his return to Ireland from the Continent, Piers offered several motives for why he continued his spiritual exploration by means of the journey to Rome. His reflections exemplified some of the social pressures within the New English community in the 1590s against converting to Catholicism. His extensive family network was almost exclusively Protestant, and his father-in-law was the powerful Thomas Jones, subsequently archbishop of Dublin, and lord chancellor of Ireland. Piers was conscious of the power exercised by this connection, and their strong opposition to any move towards Catholicism on his part. That these fears were not groundless was indicated by developments in the years after Piers's return home. At the end of the 'Discourse', he referred to 'the troubles crosses or damadges wch I have sustained since I came into this land [1598] for that they are alreadye sufficiently knowen to moste of this contrie'. He was alluding in part to the fractious relationship with his father-in-law regarding the religious upbringing of the young couple's children.[25]

This sense of isolation and disapproval within the extended family was reinforced when he considered his public role. As a prominent crown appointee within his own locality (seneschal of Daltons' Country), which placed him among the elite of county society, Piers shared the concern, widespread among men of rank, of losing their office as a consequence of becoming Catholic. As a result, as Piers observed, in Ireland men of this condition deferred their conversion so as to avoid the loss of position and prestige. A third motive

of hearing'. On situating contemporary theological disagreement, especially on predestination, in a preaching context, see ibid. 342–372.

[25] In 1607–1608, Thomas Jones was attempting to win control of the Tristernagh properties, having ensured that the couple's eight children were being brought up in his own house, Archbishop Jones to Salisbury, 1 June 1607; same to same, 24 Feb. 1608, *Cal. S.P. Ire., 1606–8*, 155, 425; on 5 Dec. 1608 Jones acquired a royal grant of the priory, J. Erck (ed.), *A Repertory of the Inrolments on the Patent Rolls of Chancery in Ireland* (Dublin, 1852) I, Part II, 513; the subsequent legal title is unclear, but Tristernagh remained in the possession of the Piers family.

adduced for not wanting to explore his leanings towards Catholicism while in Ireland was the little credibility, in his view, of the majority of Catholics (lay and clerical) he encountered there. The scandal of their lives, so he reasoned, would inhibit him from embracing Catholicism.

Henry Piers and a Recusant Network: England and Ireland

However, Piers initially found Catholicism attractive in some laymen of his acquaintance in Ireland; these too were actively supportive of his desire to travel to Rome. As already noted, the life, conversation, intellectual curiosity, and Catholic piety of Christopher Nugent, Baron Delvin made an impression on the young Piers. A more intimate and continuous influence, as he relates, derived from his sister Mary's marriage with 'a Catholicke gentleman', Thomas Jans. From the late 1580s, once Piers turned about twenty years of age, he was drawn through this connection into the extended English recusant community, which was decisive in leading him towards Catholicism. Against the backdrop of the Anglo-Spanish war (1585–1604), and arising from increasing government pressure on recusants in England, a support network was emerging, involving families and clergy, and spanning the Irish Sea. In the 1580s, individual English Catholics, occasionally with families, began moving to Ireland (often for a limited duration), because anti-recusant measures were less severe there.[26]

One key figure in facilitating this migration was James Jans, a prominent Dublin merchant and alderman, who had served as the city's mayor in 1593–1594; his brother Thomas had married Mary Piers, Henry's sister. The alderman's father Robert Jans had moved from England to Dublin by the 1540s, and the family maintained contact with their English kin. Their household in Dublin was a centre of new-style recusant Catholicism, where returned missionary clergy were sheltered; in this setting converts among English people residing in Ireland were made.[27] Here also refugee Catholics from England were welcomed. While the measures against recusants were less severe

---

[26] David Edwards, 'A haven of popery: English Catholic migration to Ireland in the age of plantations', in A. Ford and J. McCafferty (eds), *The Origins of Sectarianism in Early Modern Ireland* (Cambridge, 2005), 95–107.

[27] On the Jans household as recusant centre, see Thomas [Jones], bishop of Meath, to Sir Robert Cecil, 23 Oct. 1599, *Calendar of the Manuscripts of … Marquess of Salisbury*, IX, 375–376; James Jans (d.1610), Dublin alderman from 1588, 'Prosopography of aldermen, 1550–1620', in Colm Lennon, *The Lords of Dublin in the Age of Reformation* (Dublin, 1989), 258.

in Ireland than in England, the alderman experienced imprisonment for his Catholic activities: Piers relates that James Jans suffered 'a longe imprisonment to his great hinderance' for helping with Henry's travel arrangements, and he was probably one of those Dublin aldermen who refused to attend the established church as requested by the Ecclesiastical High Commission in the winter of 1602–1603, and who were imprisoned briefly as a result.[28] The marriage in the late 1580s of Mary Piers to Thomas Jans, brother of the alderman, brought Henry into regular contact with this vibrant recusancy, with strong English connections; on Piers's visit to England at about this time, he may have furthered his acquaintance with recusants there through the Jans connection.[29] The alliance between these two families contributed to making north Westmeath into a particularly dynamic centre of revived Catholicism, for in the early years of the seventeenth century the alderman facilitated the renewal of the Franciscan presence in their convent of Multyfarnham, not far from the Piers house at Tristernagh.[30]

In this clandestine world, there existed the risk of infiltration by informers. Like other Catholic families with relations in both countries, the Jans family in Dublin had their own cross-channel network based on their English kin, who could validate the identity of those arriving in Ireland. In the case of some exiles, however, recognized recusant figures in England provided letters of recommendation.[31] Visiting English recusant clergy, though few in number, were active in households of the elite, and Piers was doubtless exposed to their preaching and conversation; he may have met the English priest Richard Haddock (whom he later encountered in Rome) on one of Haddock's pastoral visits to families in Ireland. By their English culture, and continental theological formation, these priests (rather than the clergy then active in Ireland) were more suited to engaging with individuals of Piers's English background.

---

[28] 'Discourse', 3; lord deputy and council to Privy Council, 24 Feb. 1603, *Cal. S.P. Ire., 1601–3*, 569; in May 1606 Jans was one of three Dublin aldermen fined for their recusancy in the court of castle chamber, Jon Crawford, *A Star Chamber Court in Ireland: The Court of Castle Chamber, 1571–1641* (Dublin, 2005), 488–489.

[29] After the death of Thomas Jans, Mary Piers married firstly Gilbert Gardener, and then one Lannen, 'Memoirs of the family of Sir Henry Piers of Tristernagh in the County of Westmeath', National Library of Ireland, MS 2563.

[30] Piers, 'A chorographical description of the county of Westmeath', in Vallancey, *Collectanea*, 68–69.

[31] Among those who provided recommendations for English recusants travelling to Ireland in the mid 1590s were Henry Garnet SJ ('Father Whalley'), superior (leader) of the Jesuit mission, and George Blackwell, archpriest, *Cal. S.P. Dom., 1595–1597*, 14.

After arrival in the east-coast ports of Dublin or Drogheda, the exiles had to be assigned to suitable households. Through his mercantile contacts, and the high status he enjoyed as a Dublin alderman, James Jans was ideally placed to allocate new arrivals to families in the Pale and adjacent territories. Thus it happened that the Piers house in the former priory at Tristernagh, Co. Westmeath – a particularly remote and inaccessible location in the marcher area beyond the Pale – became part of the nexus of gentry and noble households which sheltered recusants from England.[32] Reflecting this temporary migration, in 1595 a young Englishman, Philip Draycott, then aged about 22, had been placed as a servant with Henry Piers in Ireland. From a staunchly recusant gentry family in east Staffordshire (with properties in adjoining counties), by spring 1595 Draycott had decided to enter the English College in Rome (founded 1579), to become a missionary priest.[33] He had just spent some time at the recently established English Jesuit college for boys in St Omer (founded 1593), in the Spanish Netherlands.[34] Given this schooling, and Draycott's intention to proceed to a continental seminary, a Jesuit in England (possibly the superior, Henry Garnet) may have been involved in directing the young man, and in facilitating the travel arrangements. Thus it would appear that Philip's Irish sojourn with Henry Piers, in the short interval between finishing at St Omers, and proceeding to the English College, Rome, was organized with travel to Rome in mind.

Draycott's decision to follow a seminary formation, and Piers's resolution to explore Catholicism free from the pressures of his home environment, drew them both to travel to Rome. Acquaintances formed over several years with those he had met through the Jans connection helped prompt Piers's Roman journey and his formal conversion once he arrived there. These influences, however

---

[32] Piers's services to refugee Catholics were noted by Cardinal Sega: report on visitation of English College, Rome, 1596, in Foley, *Records*, VI, 45.

[33] John Dracot (or Draycott) was one of the leading Staffordshire Catholics; the family featured repeatedly in government anti-recusant measures from the mid 1570s onwards, and in 1601 both John and his son Philip were suspected of harbouring priests, William R. Trimble, *The Catholic Laity in Elizabethan England* (Cambridge, MA, 1964), 76–80, 139, 144, 159, 172; for the late 1580s, see Timothy McCann (ed.), *Recusants in the Exchequer Pipe Rolls 1581–1592*, Catholic Record Society, 71 (1986), 53; for the 1590s, see M.M.C. Calthrop (ed.), *Recusant Roll No 1, 1592–3*, Catholic Record Society, 18 (1916), 301–8; and Hugh Bowler (ed.), *Recusant Roll No. 3 (1594–1595) and Recusant Roll No. 4 (1595–1596)*, Catholic Record Society, 61 (1970), index, sub nomine; Anthony Draycote, an archdeacon who had been deprived by 1560, when he was imprisoned, was also of this connection, Joseph Gillow, *A Literary and Biographical History, or, Bibliographical Dictionary of the English Catholics*, 5 vols (London and New York, 1885–87), II, 105.

[34] Geoffrey Holt (ed.), *St Omers and Bruges Colleges, 1593–1773: A Biographical Dictionary*, Catholic Record Society, 69 (1979), 89.

compelling, were not sufficient for Piers to go against his family, and
break with the established church by embracing the Roman denomination. This resolve arose from his religious restlessness over the past
number of years, together with a realization that his life in Ireland
did not offer a suitable setting for his inner quest. Aged 27, married
with a young family, and heir to a sizeable estate, and holding a
prominent position in local government, Henry Piers decided to
travel to Rome. In this decision he could draw on the advice and support of lay Catholics he respected. In particular Alderman James
Jans, drawing on his continental mercantile experience, was helpful
in facilitating travel details, and in the financing of the journey.[35]

It was arranged that Piers and Draycott were to travel together: thus
the 'Discourse' is also in part an account of how one Elizabethan seminarian travelled from England to Rome.[36] Draycott, travelling as
Piers's servant so as to deflect the attention of the authorities, probably
accompanied Piers from the beginning of the journey in Dublin.
Proceeding across England from Chester to London, among the stag-
ing posts was the home of Draycott's father, in Sedsdale [Sedsall],
Derbyshire;[37] henceforth, as Piers himself noted, the young man's status changed from Piers's servant to travelling companion.

The journey overland from Ireland to Rome took several months
(for Piers and Draycott, from 9 June to 25 September 1595), and was
hazardous, with a real risk of robbery and other mishaps. From
England they travelled via the Netherlands, Germany, and Austria,
so as to avoid France, then in the throes of the wars of religion. The
support and solidarity of trusted companions was desirable. For
young men destined for Catholic centres on the Continent, within
the recusant community informal systems were in place to facilitate
travel. Beyond the normal hazards, in England in the 1590s youths

[35] In 1595, before his departure, in the case of several townlands in Co. Westmeath,
Henry Piers sold the tithes in corn for that year's harvest ('forty couples of tithe corn')
to Alderman James Jans, presumably in view of financing his continental journey,
Chancery pleadings, National Archives of Ireland, I, 166.

[36] Under a proclamation of 1581 against seminary education, it was illegal to travel
abroad without special licence, Steele, *Bibliography of Royal Proclamations*, I, 81; for Piers
and Draycott, no record survives of any licence to travel sought or issued, for the registers
of the Privy Council are not extant for the period 26 Aug. 1593–1 Oct. 1595, J.R. Dasent,
Acts of the Privy Council of England, NS, 46 vols (London, 1890–1964), XXIV [1592–1593], pref-
ace; for another account of a journey by English seminarians, see Martin Murphy (ed.),
'William Atkins, A Relation of the Journey from St Omers to Seville, 1622', in Royal
Historical Society, Camden 5th ser., Miscellany XXXII (London, 1994), 191–288.

[37] In the mid 1590s a messuage in Sedsall, in Derbyshire, was among the properties of
Philip Draycott, of Cheadle, Staffordshire; Sedsall is located on the River Dove, on the
border with Staffordshire, about a mile south of Rocester; this holding was occupied by
Philip Draycott, son of George Draycott, gentleman, Bowler, *Recusant Roll*, 40, 43.

travelling to and from the Continent for Catholic education also faced
the added threat of scrutiny by the authorities and exposure by informers. Those setting out on the journey were doubtless schooled on how
to reply to prying officials.[38] For young Draycott, it was advantageous
to have a master and patron for this long journey.[39] As befitted Piers's
standing as a gentleman, the pair travelled with several pieces of luggage, and each had a pistol. A man of independent means, Piers
had access to sufficient funds for horses and waggons at various stages
of the journey, in addition to accommodation at inns.

Arrival in Rome, September 1595

The English College in Rome was their destination. The college was
constituted in 1579 as a seminary for the training of Englishmen
(including Welsh students) as priests who would serve on the mission
in their homeland. However, the English presence in this location
was much older. Founded in 1362, the English Hospice in via di
Monserrato had been sheltering English pilgrims to Rome for over
two hundred years. The hospice had decayed in the mid sixteenth
century, as a consequence of the volatile ecclesial situation in
England. Because of growing numbers at the English seminary established in 1568 in Douai, in the Spanish Netherlands, a new educa-
tional establishment was deemed necessary. Thus in 1579 the
English College in Rome emerged, and the premises of the hospice
were assigned by papal decree to the newly established college. In
addition to its role as a seminary, the college assumed the functions
of the existing hospice for visiting English pilgrims.[40] Established by a
group of exiles from the college in Douai and endowed with a charter
by Gregory XIII, by 1595 the college in Rome was staffed by Jesuits
and had been preparing English and Welsh students for service as
priests on the English mission for some years.
    In undertaking their journey, Piers and Draycott were transgress-
ing the war-time Elizabethan ordinances against travel to Rome

[38] On the discovery by officials of English recusant schoolboys travelling to the
Continent via Ireland in the 1590s, see Edwards, 'A haven of popery', 95–96; Piers and
Draycott, faced with questioning on their religion from an innkeeper in Jena, 'because
he was no magistrate we refused to answeare directly to any of his questions',
'Discourse', 15–16.
[39] Reflecting on bonds forged during their travel together and strengthened by both
adhering to the loyal minority in the English College disturbances, Piers referred to
Draycott's 'offices of gratitude and faithfulness towards myself', 'Discourse', 163.
[40] On the transition from medieval hospice to Tridentine seminary, see Anthony Kenny,
'From hospice to college', in 'The English Hospice in Rome', *The Venerabile Sexcentenary Issue*
(May 1962), 218–273.

and Spanish-held territories, which contributed to the paucity of English visitors to the city, relative to the numbers visiting other Italian regions to the north.[41] Catholic authorities, too, created inhibitions on English travel to Rome. By the early 1590s, an indication of the suspicion surrounding newcomers from the Tudor and Stuart realms on their arrival in Rome were the procedures required for entry into the English College, whether as pilgrims in the hospice, or as students.[42] In the wake of the papal excommunication of Elizabeth in 1570, it was considered necessary to protect against English government spies: several agents posing as students had gained access to the college, with devastating consequences for the mission in England. Because of this risk, no one could be received at the college without letters of recommendation, or they had to be known personally by some English or Irish residents of Rome. It regularly happened that those without the requisite recommendation were refused admission.[43]

Thus on arrival in the city on 25 September 1595 in the company of some Italian gentlemen, one of these accompanied Piers and Draycott to the English College. Not having letters of recommendation, the English Jesuit whom they met sent them to an Irish priest, Dr Fagan, native of Waterford, so that Fagan could vouch for them. There they met Richard Haddock, an English priest who in the 1580s had spent regular sojourns among the older colonial community in Ireland; thus Haddock and the newly arrived Piers had acquaintances in common. The English priest was delighted to meet Piers (they may have met in Ireland), and asked after his friends there, naming in particular one Gerard Dillon, who was among those with whom he stayed. Haddock then facilitated the admission of Draycott and Piers as pilgrims in the hospice of the English College, for the customary period of eight days.

During these days the two newcomers followed the conventional programme for pilgrims: they were reconciled with the Catholic

---

[41] On the considerable numbers of Elizabethan Englishmen who studied at Padua, see Jonathon Woolfson, *Padua and the Tudors: English Students in Italy, 1485–1603* (Cambridge, 1998); on the place of travel in shaping English Catholic identity in the Elizabethan era, see the perceptive essay by Netzloff, 'The English colleges and the English nation', 236–259.

[42] On English visitors to Rome in the later 16th century, see Frank, 'Elizabethan travellers in Rome', 95–132; for a succinct overview of society and infrastructure in 16th-century Rome, see Mark Girouard, *Cities and People: A Social and Architectural History* (New Haven, CT, and London, 1985), 115–136.

[43] In 1616, Francis Lea, of Yorkshire, was not admitted as a pilgrim, but received food and alms; similarly in 1626, Patrick Swetman of Northamptonshire, 'being unknown' was not admitted, but received alms, Foley, *Records*, VI, 595, 603.

Church, and went to confession in St Peter's; they received holy communion; and they visited the seven major ancient churches of Rome (the devotion known as the *Sette Chiese*). Writing almost ten years after the event, Piers recalled the powerful experience of the sacrament of reconciliation by means of the designated confessor for English-language pilgrims, Father Richard Coolinge SJ, member of the multi-national community of Jesuit confessors in Rome.[44]

Henry Piers and the Roman Inquisition

Notwithstanding these rites of conversion, Piers's early days in Rome gave evidence of the routine suspicion of Protestantism with which individuals of English background (together with Welsh and Scots) were regarded. The taint of heresy, inconvenient at least, and bearing the possibility of an appearance before the Roman Inquisition, was intensified in Piers's case by the ingrained mutual antipathy which characterized Irish and English Catholics in exile.[45] News of Piers's arrival in the city spread quickly. Within about a week he was experiencing opposition from a section of the Irish in the city: tensions arising from the revolt of the Ulster lords against the crown were threatening to disrupt his stay. By autumn 1595 the war in Ireland had been underway for over a year; in June 1595 Hugh O'Neill, earl of Tyrone, had been proclaimed a traitor, and he had just taken over as leader of the confederate forces. Already some of the Irish in Rome, partisans of Tyrone, were highlighting the confessional motivation of the struggle, framing it for a Roman audience in terms of the contemporary religious wars in France.[46]

---

[44] Richard Coolinge SJ (1562–1618), 'Cowlinus', served as English-language confessor in the 'Collegio Penitentiariorum' at St Peter's, 1593–1596, and lived in the English College. Thomas McCoog (ed.), *Monumenta Angliae: English and Welsh Jesuits*, 3 vols (Rome, 1992–2000), I, 99–100; II, 277–278.

[45] On tensions between English and Irish Catholic exiles on the Continent in the late 16th century, see Christopher Highley, *Catholics Writing the Nation in Early Modern Britain and Ireland* (Oxford, 2008), 119–121.

[46] This grouping inspired a tract, published in Rome in 1596, recounting the Irish military victories in 1595, highlighting Tyrone's defeat of Sir John Norris, south of Armagh, in September; the confederate army was always referred to as the 'Catholic League', *Relatione della Guerra d'Hibernia, tra la Lega de'Catholici di quel regno, e l'asserta Reina d'Inghilterra. Dove s'intende i progressi maravigliosi fatti da essa Lega contro gli heretici, Dal principio dell'anno presente 1595. Che presero l'armi, fino al mese d'Ottobre. Et particolarmente una segnalata vittoria, ottenuta dal Conde di Tyron Generale di detta Lega, contro Giovan Noris Generale d'Inghilterra. A di 19 di Settembre* (Roma, 1596); the tract is listed in Douglas Hyde and D.J. O'Donoghue (eds), *Catalogue of the Books and Manuscripts … of Sir John Gilbert* (Dublin, 1918), 687.

Lacking a firm institutional base (in contrast to the hospice and college of the English community) the Irish presence in the city at the end of the sixteenth century remains shadowy. There was a small grouping on Piers's arrival there in September 1595. The most significant cluster was associated with the cardinal protector of the Irish, Girolamo Mattei (1547–1603), dating from some time after his creation as cardinal in November 1586. By 1595, if not before, there was an informal college of Irish priests and students ('scholars') living in commodious premises adjacent to the church of Santa Lucia, and close to the cardinal's palace.[47] Those at Santa Lucia were ecclesiastics, including students, and diocesan priests, some of whom may have been functionaries in various curial institutions. One of these was probably Dr Fagan, mentioned by Piers, of the Waterford clerical family. Among the Irish clerics resident in Rome in 1595, several were natives of Tyrone's lordship in Ulster, and may be identified with those promoting the confederates' cause: Arthur MacGuckin was ordained that summer, and Arthur O'Donnelly on 3 December.[48]

Shortly after his appearance in Rome, presumably under questioning from Irish clerics eager to have news of their homeland from one newly arrived, Piers let his political views be known; reflecting the loyalism of his background in Ireland, he challenged the interpretation presented by some Irish émigrés (Piers gave no names), that the conflict was a Catholic crusade against a heretical government. He may have offered an alternative analysis, along the lines that the revolt was a regional conflict, a reaction by some traditionalist lords against the power of the crown. However, Piers's motivation for visiting Rome was spiritual, not political; in his 'Discourse' he focuses on the merits of Catholicism, and seeks to refute the arguments of Protestant reformers against different aspects of Catholic life. His interests were apologetical; writing in 1604–1605 just after the end of the war, he is largely silent regarding the recent revolt of the Ulster lords, save to note the devastation of his own estates, and the difficulties of Irish merchants in Spain.

---

[47] 'Discourse', 68; Girolamo Mattei (1547–1603), created cardinal 1586. Miranda, *The Cardinals of the Holy Roman Church* http://www2.fiu.edu/~mirandas/bios1586.htm, accessed 29 Jan. 2018. It has not been possible to locate this church with certainty; the Mattei family had a cluster of palaces in the Rione Angelo, and there, in the early 17th century, the cardinal's brother constructed the building known as Palazzo Mattei del Giove; the informal hospice probably formed part of the prelate's extended household, for the average size of a cardinal's household was about 150 people (significantly more in the case of cardinals from richer families), see chapter on 16th-century Rome in Girouard, *Cities and People*, 115–136.

[48] Both of Armagh diocese; these two are the only Irish ordinations listed for 1595; fourteen Irishmen were ordained at Rome between 1572 and 1595, Hugh Fenning, 'Irishmen ordained at Rome, 1572–1697', *Archivium Hibernicum* 59 (2005), 7–8.

This stance quickly created difficulty for the newly arrived layman. Within days, some already-established Irishmen (probably the two Ulster clerics already noted) denounced him to the Roman Inquisition; the political activities of Piers's father, a crown agent for over forty years initially in north-east Ulster, and subsequently on the marches of the Pale, were well known, as was the aggressive Protestantism of Henry's father-in-law, Bishop Thomas Jones. In the case of the cleric Arthur O'Donnelly, antipathy towards Henry Piers was doubtless sharpened by the memory of William Piers's role in dishonouring the Gaelic Ulster warlord Shane O'Neill (d.1567); as a boy Shane had been fostered with the O'Donnellys (a clan subservient to the princely O'Neills), thus creating an intimate and lifelong bond between them; it was Piers senior who had the head of Shane O'Neill sent to Dublin Castle.[49] Thus Henry's initial difficulties in Rome were increased by his father's involvement in Ulster politics over several decades. The Ulstermen's suspicions regarding Henry's background were heightened by his utterances on the contemporary Irish conflict.

Irish political sensitivities were reinforced by Roman practice. From the mid sixteenth century, an appearance before the Inquisition was normal for a foreigner resident in Rome of whom there was a suspicion that he was not an adherent of the Catholic Church. The city's institutions were charged with probing the religious identity of aliens, so as to preserve the religious purity of the population; this concern was accentuated by the large numbers from northern Europe coming into Italy in the last decade of the century.[50] Delation to the Inquisition of aliens suspected of heresy was expected. Thus by the early 1580s it was habitual for those arriving in Rome from England and Scotland to be examined for heresy by the Inquisition.[51]

[49] As constable of Carrickfergus castle, William Piers sent the head of Shane O'Neill (c.1530–1567), the turbulent Gaelic leader, to the crown authorities in Dublin; later, from his base in Tristernagh, William participated in parleys with the Ulster confederates in autumn 1594, *Cal. S.P. Ire., 1592–1596*, 280, William Piers (d.1603), *DIB*; Shane O'Neill (c.1530–1567), *DIB*.

[50] On aliens' experience of the Roman Inquisition at the turn of the 16th century, see Irene Fosi, 'Conversion and autobiography: Telling tales before the Roman Inquisition', *Journal of Early Modern History*, 17 (2013), 437–456; on Irishmen before the Spanish Inquisition, see Thomas O'Connor, *Irish Voices from the Spanish Inquisition: Migrants, Converts and Brokers in Early Modern Iberia* (Basingstoke, 2016); in Aug. 1600, some forty 'English, Scotch, Genevese and Germans' were brought in procession to St Peter's and publicly recanted their heresy, Victor von Klarwill (ed.), *The Fugger News-Letters, Second Series (1568–1605)* (London, 1926), 326.

[51] There is no mention of Henry Piers in the records of the Roman Inquisition which are conserved in Trinity College Dublin (MSS 1224–1230). Sentences and abjurations arising from appearances there, including cases of heresy ('proposizioni eretiche'), have survived

However, there was also a specifically Irish dimension to how Piers was brought to the Inquisition's attention. Those making the denunciation doubtless highlighted the English and Protestant background of his family, and their wide-ranging involvement in government and ecclesiastical service; these considerations would raise the suspicion that Piers, in addition to being a heretic, may also have been a spy in the service of England, liable on his return to damage Catholic networks in Ireland and England. Presumably those Irish people in Rome who were desirous of papal support for the northern revolt were keen to enlist the voice of one just recently arrived from the distant isle, and were commensurately angry at his open challenging of their interpretation. Piers's position in Rome was thus precarious.

In this threatening situation he turned to the man who was fast becoming his mentor, the Englishman Richard Haddock (c.1552–1605). By the mid 1590s Haddock (or Haydock) was one of the leading figures in the small English clerical community in Rome. Born in about 1551 or 1552 near Preston, Lancashire, his uncle was William Allen, founder of the English colleges in Douai and Rome, who was created cardinal in 1587. Haddock was among the first generation of recusant refugees in Douai, arriving there in 1573. Ordained four years later, in 1578 he moved to Rome to help in establishing the English College there and was among its first students.[52] He was deeply involved in the early disturbances between the Welsh rector and the largely English student body, as a result of which the direction of the nascent college was entrusted to the Jesuits.[53] Returning to England in 1580 he spent the following decade as a missionary priest there, with periodic visits to households in Ireland. In 1584 his younger brother George, likewise a priest, was executed, and his sister Aloysia Haydock was imprisoned for recusancy.[54] In summer 1596, in a memorandum to the Spanish authorities, the Jesuit Robert Persons described Haddock as an English priest then resident in Rome, who had 'lived in Ireland many

---

from 1564 to 1582. References to Englishmen and Scotsmen begin in 1582. Entries covering the years 1583 to 1602 are not extant. There are volumes for 1603, 1607, and 1615, each of which contain references to English and Scottish examinees. See T.K. Abbott, *Catalogue of the Manuscripts in the Library of Trinity College Dublin* (Dublin and London, 1900), 243 et seq.

[52] For a short biography of Haddock, see Foley, *Records*, VI, 130–131; his will (undated, but written shortly before his death in Rome in 1605), Archivum Venerabilis Collegii Anglorum de Urbe (AVCAU), Chronologia Monumentorum ab ann. 1589 ad 1605, vol. vi, 341; he became doctor of divinity from the Roman university (Sapienza).

[53] For Haddock's account of these events, see Haddock to Dr William Allen, from Rome, 9 Mar. 1579, printed in M.A. Tierney, *Dodd's Church History of England*, II (London, 1839), cccl–ccclxi.

[54] 'Richard Haydock DD', in Gillow, *A Literary and Biographical History*, III, 221–226.

years and has many gentlemen relatives and acquaintances there, and in Lancashire, his native province'.

In 1590 Cardinal Allen summoned him to Rome as his domestic chaplain, where he lived in the prelate's house close to the English College. A friend and supporter of Robert Persons, he worked to sustain the pro-Jesuit students in the college disturbance of the mid 1590s. Haddock's acquaintance with Ireland led Persons to suggest him as a possible candidate for archbishop of Dublin, in the case of a Spanish invasion of Ireland. According to Persons, Haddock was 'well known to the [Spanish] ambassador in Rome as being a firm adherent of his majesty'.[55] In this regard Haddock received a titular appointment as dean of Dublin some time before 1602. Resuming his earlier engagement with Catholics in Lancashire and Ireland, in October 1602 he travelled there via Douai, and returned to Rome in August the following year. Owing to this intermittent pastoral contact, Haddock was one of those English priests who from about the early 1580s found temporary refuge among the gentry of the Irish Pale, a milieu familiar to Henry Piers. A further service to the English Catholic community was his translation of Cardinal Bellarmine's large catechism from Italian into English, published in 1604.[56] The English cleric died in Rome in 1605.

Thus Haddock's involvement with Piers from September 1595 until October 1597, when Piers was in Rome, formed part of the Englishman's ongoing interest in Catholic life in English-speaking Ireland. Fluent in Italian, with long experience of Rome, Haddock was ideally placed to guide and befriend the young man recently arrived from Ireland. In Haddock, Piers had a confidant who was familiar with Ireland, with considerable personal experience of the older colonial community, Catholic and loyalist, based on extended visits there. Faced with the Roman partisans of the Ulster insurgents against the crown, Piers had found an ally in distancing himself from their ultra-Catholic interpretation of the conflict, thereby supporting him in eschewing political activism while in Rome, and leaving him free to pursue his spiritual development. In recognition of Haddock's pivotal role in supporting him during his Roman sojourn, Piers dedicated the 'Discourse' to the English priest.

[55] Both quotations, Persons to Martin De Idiaquez, [summer] 1596, *Cal. S.P. Spanish, 1587–1603*, 628–633.
[56] On his travels in 1602–1603, see Godfrey Anstruther, *The Seminary Priests: A Dictionary of the Secular Clergy of England and Wales 1558–1850*, 4 vols (Ware, 1969–), I, 159–160; the translation of the Bellarmine catechism is entitled, *An ample declaration of the Christian doctrine: Composed in Italian by the renowned cardinal: Card. Bellarmin etc. Translated into English by Richard Hadock, Doctor of Divinitie* (Douai, 1604); several other editions of the translation were published up to 1624.

Faced with a delation to the Inquisition by the Irish of the confederate line, Haddock advised Piers to present himself voluntarily to the tribunal. This counsel reflected Inquisition practice. Those who of their own initiative presented themselves (a category known as the *sponte comparentes*) were subject to a briefer and milder legal procedure (the *processo sommario*) than the fuller and more formal process.[57] Piers had journeyed to Rome in order to embrace the Catholic faith, a consequence of which was abjuring his previous upbringing in the established church. The Inquisition was a mechanism by which conversions from heresy were given official validation. The overwhelming majority of those appearing before the Inquisition for the purpose of conversion took the initiative themselves; among these were a number of English and Scottish residents, and Piers may be accounted in this category.

The procedure was doubtless similar to that of a certain John Scot, a 21-year old from Tweeddale in Scotland who appeared on 17 May 1607, and whose sentence and signed abjuration have survived.[58] In the sentence it was noted that the young man had presented himself to the Inquisition of his own accord. He deposed that he was born of Calvinist parents and brought up in that denomination, and had hitherto held various heresies. However, his abjuration, attached to the sentence, was wholly written in his own hand, and the usual penances were imposed. As a rule, the proceedings followed a rigid and formulaic course, led by the inquisitor, and recorded by the notary. The convert took an oath before the notary; he made a review of his life and sentiments, indicating his father's name, his country, and the religion of his family; he gave information on his education and instruction in heresy; and he recounted how and why he converted to the Catholic Church. The notary ensured that this formal abjuration was properly documented and certified. When facing interrogation by the authorities in Seville in 1598, Piers was able to present testimonials acquired in Rome vouching for his religious orthodoxy; among these may have been a certificate from the Inquisition.

As a result of this process, the Roman Inquisition exonerated Piers from any charge of heresy. He made a positive impression on the inquisitors; his relatively elevated social background, together with an ability to present his strong spiritual quest, doubtless distinguished him from the majority of aliens appearing before the

---

[57] On the summary procedure arising from a spontaneous appearance before the Inquisition at this time, see Fosi, 'Conversion and autobiography'; Christopher Black, *The Italian Inquisition* (New Haven, CT, and London, 2009), 60–63.
[58] Trinity College Dublin, MS 1229, fos 198r–200v.

tribunal. As a result of these contacts the leading inquisitor, Cardinal Domenico Pinelli,[59] invited Piers for a private conversation. The prelate rejoiced at his coming to Rome in order to convert; on reading the lives of the English saints (perhaps in order to deepen his understanding of the religious situation of northern Europe), Pinelli related that he was saddened by the contrast with the current state of religion there.[60] Piers formed a cordial relationship with the cardinal: on the layman's departure from Rome in October 1597, he carried letters from Pinelli for his brother in Genoa. Piers's dependence on Haddock for advice in negotiating the Roman scene points to the role of clerics long-established in Catholic centres in assisting more recently arrived laity, when these faced possible threats from the authorities. The almost immediate delation of Piers to the Inquisition on arrival in Rome underlines how political and ethnic divisions in war-torn Ireland were replicated in a continental setting.

Admittance to the English College, Rome, October 1595

At the end of these eight days as a pilgrim, it became clear that Piers was willing and able to study, and to avail himself of the opportunity of furthering his grasp of Catholicism which the English College afforded. Richard Haddock made representations on behalf of the two arrivals (Piers, and Philip Draycott) to Cardinal Enrico Caetani, cardinal protector of the English, who had a supervisory role in relation to the college; following the normal procedure, Draycott was accepted as a scholar (or seminarian).[61]

The case for admitting Piers was more problematic. While the mission of the college was to prepare priests for the English mission, exceptionally some laymen were accepted to facilitate their conversion to Catholicism. Although the category of *convictor* (or resident lay student) was provided for in the college's statutes, and apparently designed for those like Piers who were seeking conversion, single men were doubtless intended; Piers was after all a married man.[62]

---

[59] Cardinal Domenico Pinelli (1541–1611); he was involved in the process against Giordano Bruno in 1600, *Dizionario Biografico degli Italiani*, http://www.treccani.it/enciclopedia/domenico-pinelli_(Dizionario-Biografico)/, accessed 20 Jan. 2018.

[60] 'Discourse', 31–32; Pinelli was referring to the lives of the medieval English saints.

[61] 'Discourse', 32; Cardinal Enrico Caetani (1550–1599), *Dizionario Biografico degli Italiani*, http://www.treccani.it/enciclopedia/enrico-caetani_%28Dizionario-Biografico%29/, accessed 20 Jan. 2018.

[62] Examples of men admitted as *convictor*: John Jackson, admitted for one year, from July 1603, Foley, *Records*, VI, 577; William Alabaster, arrived 23 Jan. 1609, ibid. 585; four

A further peculiarity of Piers's presence in the college was his Irish background. Admission was reserved for Englishmen; Piers was one of a small number of those accepted up to 1641 who, though born in Ireland, were designated 'of English parents'.[63] In favour of admission, however, it was advanced that he had sheltered many English Catholics at his own expense, presumably on his estates in Ireland, and that he had given up his lands to become a Catholic.[64] His high social standing, his support of the English recusant network in Ireland together with a demonstrably fervent desire to make progress in absorbing Catholicism all favoured his case. Thus with the knowledge and approval of the cardinal protector, and through the intercession of Richard Haddock, Piers was admitted to the college as a *convictor*. After the probationary period, on 12 October 1595 Henry Piers and Philip Draycott formally entered the college, and donned its uniform.[65] Once his status changed from pilgrim to student, as for all students, his accommodation costs (which included clothing from the college tailor) were met by the college.

Student in the English College, Rome

Piers was to spend two full years (October 1595 to October 1597) in the English College in Rome. By autumn 1595, the college (located in the premises of the English Hospice, standing on the same location in via di Montserrato since its foundation in 1362) comprised 47 students, 8 Jesuit priests, 2 prefects, and 19 domestic staff. The student programme normally lasted seven years, the initial years spent on philosophy before proceeding to divinity. However, due to the student unrest in the college since October 1594, studies had been greatly disrupted.[66] For the duration of his stay, Piers followed the courses offered in logic and physic. The first year was generally devoted to logic. Just prior to Piers's arrival, pleading the disruption, the students had sought and been granted an extension of the logic course from one to two years; in an indictment of the prevailing

noblemen admitted 'for sake of conversion', *c.* Jan. 1630, ibid. 606; Francis Slingsby and Mr Sprewley, his friend, 2 Feb. 1639, ibid. 618.
    [63] In Nov. 1628, Gerard Birmingham stayed several days; one Mr Morris was given alms in Oct. 1629; both were born in Ireland of English parents, Foley, *Records*, VI, 604–605.
    [64] Foley, *Records*, VI, 45.
    [65] Foley, *Records*, VI, 567; Draycott subsequently left the English College and entered the Jesuit novitiate in Rome on 12 Apr. 1598, and died there on 14 Aug. of the same year, Archivum Romanum Societatis Iesu, Rom. 172, fo.25r; Historia Societatis, vol. 42, fo.11r.
    [66] Report (in English translation) on the English College in Rome, by Cardinal Philip Sega, Mar. 1596, in Foley, *Records*, VI, 1–66, at 48, 62–63, 65.

disorder, Cardinal Sega, the official visitor, insisted that this concession be reversed immediately, 'as if instead of punishment, encouragement should be awarded to their indolence'.[67]

By his own account Piers took a full part in the life of the college. He gives an overview of the regime prevailing in the various national colleges, including the English College.[68] The students used to rise at 4.30 a.m. Every week the English students enjoyed a recreation day spent at their college's vineyard on the Palatine hill;[69] athletic pursuits were followed by an extra-fine meal. In the case of a few of the more exceptional students, at the conclusion of their studies a public disputation was held, to which externs including some cardinals were invited; there was one such event yearly for philosophy, and one for theology; the proceedings ended with a festive meal.[70]

The academic year was punctuated by a series of cultural and social events. During carnival (the days preceding the start of the Lenten season) it was habitual to present a dramatic event prepared by the students, to which friends of the college were invited as guests.[71] Tragedies were also staged. The college marked two particular feasts, recalling the patrons of the earlier hospice. External musicians, paid by the college, animated these gatherings, and in the mid 1590s, in addition to the English residing in Rome, other local people were invited, giving a total of over two hundred guests.[72] In early summer, the liturgical feast of Trinity Sunday was the occasion of a college celebration. The Christmas season included several days with particular resonance for the English collegians: the feast of the college's patron, St Thomas of Canterbury (otherwise known as Thomas à Beckett) on 29 December had a special place, and, reflecting the contemporary association of the English Catholics with martyrdom, on St Stephen's Day (26 December) a seminarian of the English College habitually preached in Latin before the pontiff and his cardinals.[73]

As noted, on his arrival in Rome a section of the Irish clerical group denounced Piers to the Inquisition as one of suspect background in Ireland. Simultaneously, Piers also faced opposition from within the English College. In addition to the conventional antipathy between

---

[67] 'Discourse', 116; Sega report, Foley, *Records*, VI, 63.

[68] 'The Rulles of the Colleadges', in 'Discourse', 111–118; for an English Catholic account of life in the college in *c*.1579, see Martin, *Roma Sancta*, 109–114.

[69] 'Discourse', 133.

[70] Foley, *Records*, VI, 46.

[71] Foley, *Records*, VI, 41–42; during carnival 1596 the college guests included Richard Haddock and Gabriel Allen (brother of the late cardinal).

[72] Foley, *Records*, VI, 65.

[73] 'Discourse', 117.

Irish and English, Piers's experience arose in part from the college's troubled recent history. While still a candidate for admission, he became yet one more focus of contention by the anti-Jesuit faction among the students in their campaign to have the fathers removed from the college administration. Thus his first months coincided with another of the internal disturbances which had convulsed the student body at intervals since even prior to the college's formal foundation. In Lent 1579 tensions had erupted between the rector, the Welshman Morys Clennog, and the largely English student body. Shortly thereafter Gregory XIII acceded to the requests of the English students, and in April 1579 the college was established by papal decree.[74] Owen Lewis and Morys Clennog, both Welsh, and both instrumental in starting the seminary, left Rome. Thereafter it was entrusted to the Italian Jesuits. A further dispute necessitated the intervention of Cardinal Philip Sega as visitor in 1585; there followed several years when an English Jesuit was in charge.

On the death of Cardinal Allen, cardinal protector for England and college patron, in October 1594, friction between English and Welsh students threatened to flare up once again. The occasion was an attempt to gain the college's support in favour of Owen Lewis's nomination as protector. The Jesuit rector summoned the respective leaders and effected a reconciliation.[75] A short time later, however, a faction emerged, comprising some secular priests and seminarians, focused on the allegedly too severe regime of the Jesuits within the college, and on a belief that the Society was trying to dominate the nascent English mission. In August 1595 the students sought an audience with Clement VIII, which was not granted. However, Clement responded by ordering an official visitation. This intervention had little effect, and the students continued to petition the pope. In November 1595 four students were expelled, but Clement quickly revoked the decision, and the men returned. The then cardinal protector of the English, Enrico Caetani (Caietan), who was responsible for the college, had been entrusted with a papal diplomatic mission in Poland. In his place the pope appointed Cardinal Philip Sega[76] as vice protector of the English, and asked him to conduct an official visitation of the college once again, and to

---

[74] On the Welsh use of early medieval historic claims in this late 16th-century dispute with the English in Rome, see Jason Nice, 'Being "British" in Rome: The Welsh at the English College, 1578–1584', *The Catholic Historical Review*, 92 (2006), 1–24.

[75] Foley, *Records*, VI, 11, 36; for a defence of Owen Lewis against the critical assessment contained in Cardinal Sega's visitation report from 1596, see Godfrey Anstruther, 'Owen Lewis', in 'The English Hospice in Rome', 272–294.

[76] Cardinal Filippo Sega (1537–1596), Miranda, *The Cardinals of the Holy Roman Church* http://www2.fiu.edu/~mirandas/bios1591-ii.htm, accessed 19 Jan. 2018.

report on the disturbance; this visitation took place in the winter of 1595–1596.[77] In this time the cardinal administered the sacrament of confirmation in the chapel to a number of students, including Henry Piers.[78]

By the end of September 1595 (when Piers and Draycott arrived) the college had been in severe internal disruption for almost a year, and instability continued for much of their first year there.[79] Sega's report enables us to survey the acrimonious relationships that characterized the college community at that time. The students were bitterly divided between the majority who opposed the Jesuits, and the minority who sided with the administration; among the latter were Piers and Philip Draycott.[80] There was universal agreement that an academic year had been 'wasted in strife and contention'; as a result students were demanding that an extra year be added at the end of their course to make good the time lost.[81] Discipline had collapsed; faced with the insubordination of a majority of the student body, the fathers had discontinued the normal practice of imposing penances for infringements of rules.[82] Student homilies in the refectory had to be abandoned, as these had become occasions for the opposing factions to trade invective and ridicule.[83] From the beginning of his sojourn, it was inevitable that Piers (like other new students arriving for the academic year 1595–1596) would be drawn into this conflict, and compelled to declare allegiance between the competing parties.

In this acrimonious situation, Piers's national identity became an issue in the struggle between the disruptive students and the college administration. Despite his English parentage, the anti-Jesuit

---

[77] Sega listened to the students' complaints and requests; he received individual signed written statements of grievance ('lengthy and rambling memorials') from the 37 who formed the opposition (Foley, *Records*, VI, 18–19); he summarized their complaints, and received written replies to these from the college's Jesuits; he also received written observations from those loyal to the administration; his report, addressed to Clement VIII, was concluded on 15 Mar. 1596, Foley, *Records*, VI, 1–66; this report provides contemporary details on college life during Piers's sojourn.

[78] 'Discourse', 34.

[79] For a detailed account of the 1594–1597 dispute in the English College in Rome, see Thomas McCoog, *The Society of Jesus in Ireland, Scotland, and England, 1589–1597* (Farnham, Surrey, and Rome, 2012), 259–272; the role of Edmund Harewood SJ, the college's minister, in relation to the students, features in Arnold Pritchard, *Catholic Loyalism in Elizabethan England* (London, 1979), 102–119.

[80] Cardinal Sega named ten students 'who have remained dutiful', and thirty-seven who opposed the administration, Foley, *Records*, VI, 3.

[81] Foley, *Records*, VI, 28.

[82] Sega referred to 'a wholescale neglect of discipline and subversion of order', Foley, *Records*, VI, 30.

[83] Foley, *Records*, VI, 44.

grouping focused on his birth in Ireland, and dismissed the new-comer as an 'ignorant Irishman'; the fact that he was not born in England, in their view, disqualified him from admission, which was restricted to Englishmen. They protested to the college authorities, alleging that the students were unanimous on his exclusion; the fact that he was married was for them further grounds for rejection.[84] Their opposition endured, for at the time of the visitation they demanded that no Irishman be admitted to the college.[85] The authorities, however, defended his admission, asserting that English parentage (not birth in England) was the relevant criterion; accepted as a *convictor* (as distinct from a scholar, or seminarian), Piers was not obliged to take the missionary oath to be ordained for service on the English mission.

Instability was increased by the rapid turnover of interim protec-tors: Sega died in May 1596; he was replaced by Cardinal Francisco Toledo ('Tollett') (although a Jesuit, he was inimical to Acquaviva's leadership as general of the order, but was reconciled with the Society shortly before he died) who in turn died in September 1596; Piers attended this cardinal's obsequies in the Jesuit Chiesa del Gesù. Cardinal Camillo Borghese succeeded as vice protector.

While not formally a member of the college administration, Richard Haddock interacted incessantly with the students, urging an end to the turbulence and support for the authorities. Haddock was one of those intended by the dutiful minority, who acknowledged 'the authority of certain men of piety, learning, and practical good sense, who, when present, by private counsel, or when at a distance, by letters, sought to warn students, and to deter them by many sound reasons, from taking part in these disturbances and quarrels'; in an indication of his persistence and ability in diffusing the stirs, the recal-citrant party demanded that he be banned from contact with the college.[86]

In the student revolt, Piers's loyalty to the administration was never in doubt. While he may have been isolated as one of the minority within the student body, he enjoyed warm relations with some key figures in the college. Bonds of loyalty and gratitude – for his admis-sion as a *convictor*, and for advice leading to the successful outcome of his recent encounter with the Inquisition – made Piers susceptible to

---

[84] Sega summarized their objection to Piers's admission: 'Despite the objections of all the students, an ignorant Irishman, who moreover has been married, was admitted in vio-lation of the College statutes', Foley, *Records*, VI, 23.

[85] 'No Irishman whatever should be received into the College', Foley, *Records*, VI, 27.

[86] Foley, *Records*, VI, 29–30.

Richard Haddock's prompting, and similarly his erstwhile travelling companion Philip Draycott was loyal to Piers, on the basis of their long and eventful journey together. Another student, Reginald Bates, a young priest, was also of the minority group; with Bates, too, Piers forged an enduring friendship; in October 1597, Piers travelled as far as Milan with the party setting out from the college, which included Bates, 'a man of great virtue and my special frende'.[87] More generally he was deeply appreciative of the support and spiritual counsel he received from the English Jesuits in Rome, and was a firm admirer of the Society of Jesus.[88]

While he noted Richard Haddock's efforts to bolster support for the administration among the students, Piers acknowledged the decisive role of Robert Persons SJ in bringing the unrest to a conclusion. From early 1596 there had been a rumour that an English Jesuit would be sent to Rome to help settle the disturbance. Robert Persons was selected. Despite pressing commitments in Spain, he travelled to Rome, arriving at the end of March 1597. On Easter Saturday (2 April 1597) Persons spoke to the assembled students at the college, outlining his view of the disturbances, and indicating his proposed solutions. To facilitate engagement with the recalcitrants, at the pope's request Persons went to live in the college. There followed a period of intense negotiations between Persons and the disaffected seminarians. An amicable outcome ensued. A settlement was reached between the student representatives and the Jesuit negotiator. The vice protector approved of the articles of agreement. On Ascension Day (15 May 1597), Cardinal Camillo Borghese as vice protector attended celebrations in the college to mark the conclusion of the disturbance and the reconciliation of the parties.[89]

Piers enjoyed a cordial relationship with Persons, and they conversed during the time both were residing in the college, from the Jesuit's arrival in early April 1597 until the Irishman's departure in mid October of the same year. Piers noted the controversy which erupted at that time between secular clergy and the Jesuits within the wider English Catholic community, of which the disturbance in the college in Rome was a part, and in which Persons was a central figure; without entering into discussion of the issues at stake, Piers

[87] 'Discourse', 193.

[88] 'Discourse', 32.

[89] This summary of Persons's involvement in the resolution of the disturbance draws on the account given in McCoog, *The Society of Jesus*, 356–65; the articles of agreement, dated 15 May 1597, are given in Thomas Graves Law (ed.), *The Archpriest Controversy: Documents relating to the Dissensions of the Roman Catholic Clergy, 1597–1602*, Camden Society, NS, 2 vols, 56, 58 (London, 1896, 1898), I, 16–17.

merely remarked that the ensuing series of publications against the Jesuits was damaging to the cause of the English Catholics.[90] In his account of the tumultuous period which he lived through in the college, Piers emerges as an uncritical supporter and admirer of Robert Persons. Prompted by conversations with the celebrated founder of the Valladolid and Seville colleges, Piers decided to visit those establishments after leaving Rome. Showing that he had learned from his encounter with the Roman Inquisition, before departing Piers took care to procure written testimonials to his Catholic orthodoxy. Further, that he had acquired letters of introduction from Rome (most likely from Persons) was implicit in the range of Jesuit contacts on which he could draw while on his travels in Spain.

Henry Piers in Spain, 1597–1598

On 15 October 1597 he set off from the English College in Rome, together with a number of English priests who, having finished their studies, were returning to the mission in England. Among these was Reginald Bates ('Batty'), ordained in 1594, whose friendship Piers particularly valued.[91] The group spent three days at the sanctuary of the holy house of Nazareth at Loreto, near Macerata, at that time the most important Marian shrine in the Catholic world: pilgrims to Rome (including those from Ireland) first visited Loreto. The layman noted the ministry of the international group of Jesuit confessors established at the sanctuary. He parted from his English travelling companions at Milan.[92] Arriving at Genoa, Piers encountered a group of English seminarians whom Robert Persons was sending from Rome to Spain, in the wake of the Jesuit's campaign to restore stability to the college in Rome.

The former Roman student's destination was the English College in Valladolid; during the year he spent in Spain, Piers moved within the English Jesuit network established there by Persons from the late 1580s. On 22 November Piers set sail from Genoa, arriving at Alicante, in the kingdom of Valentia, on 11 December 1597; Cardinal Penelle (his Roman inquisitor) paid for his passage, because Piers had carried letters from Rome to the cardinal's brother in

---

[90] 'Discourse', 35–36; on the conflict between the Appellants and the Jesuits, see McCoog, *The Society of Jesus*.
[91] On Reginald Bates, see footnote, 'Discourse', 193.
[92] 'Discourse', 163, 193.

Genoa. The convert's fellow-travellers on this voyage were of varied nationalities: English, French, Spanish, Italian, Dutch, Irish ('some of or own contrie men'), two Turks, and some Jews in disguise.[93] From Valentia he travelled to Madrid. While there he was received graciously at the Jesuit college and met the English exile, Thomas Fitzherbert, then living as a royal pensioner of the Spanish court, who, together with Joseph Creswell SJ, was acting as lobbyist for the English community with the authorities in Spain.[94]

After the Christmas festivities Piers proceeded to the English College in Valladolid. Founded by Robert Persons in 1589 to prepare priests for service on the mission in England and Wales, by the time of Piers's visit St Alban's College contained approximately sixty to seventy seminarians.[95] He stayed there from 7 to 21 January 1598 as guest of the English Jesuits.

While in Valladolid he chanced to meet an Irish cleric, a native of Piers's home region in Ireland. There were about twenty Irish students at the university in the years 1588–1596.[96] Brian McFergus O'Farrell had been there since about 1590, studying humanities and theology; his academic renown was such that in 1601 Hugh O'Neill, earl of Tyrone, sought to have him nominated to the Irish diocese of Meath. Piers wrote of the scholar's 'great learninge gravetie and good liffe, whose untymely deseace hathe bene an infinitt losse unto his native contrie'.[97] The Gaelic lordship of the O'Farrells was located just a few miles west of the Piers estate at Tristernagh, Co. Westmeath. As a boy, Piers had been fostered with Garret O'Farrell and his wife Elizabeth Tankard; for some years prior to his departure from Ireland Piers had been serving as seneschal in a territory contiguous

---

[93] 'and as it was thought certaine Jewes wch because they were passing into Spayne went disguised for that they are prohibited to resort thither', 'Discourse', 195.

[94] A Jesuit college was established in Madrid in 1560, L. Koch, *Jesuiten-Lexikon* (Paderborn, 1934), 1139; for the career of Joseph Creswell (1556–1623) in Spain, see A.J. Loomie, *The Spanish Elizabethans: The English Exiles at the Court of Philip II* (New York, 1963), 182–229; Thomas Fitzherbert (1552–1640), *ODNB*.

[95] For brief information on students admitted 1589–1598, see Edwin Henson (ed.), *Registers of the English College at Valladolid 1589–1862*, Catholic Record Society, 30 (1930), 1–49; on the college in the 1590s, see M.E. Williams, *St Alban's College, Valladolid: Four Centuries of English Catholic Presence in Spain* (London and New York, 1986), 9–22.

[96] See appendix, 'Irish students in Valladolid (1588–1661)', in Karin Schüller, *Die Beziehungen zwischen Spanien und Irland im 16. und 17. Jahrhundert: Diplomatie, Handel und die soziale Integration katholischer Exulanten* (Münster, 1999), 244–245.

[97] 'Discourse', 199; 'Bernard O Ferail' was described as *sacerdotem theologum* at Valladolid in 1601 for 'seven continuous years'; he studied letters at the University of Valladolid where he spent a further four years studying theology, Benjamin Hazard, *Faith and Patronage: The Political Career of Flaithrí Ó Maolchonaire, 1560–1629* (Dublin, 2010), 172–173; from the details above O'Farrell died *c.*1602–1604.

to the O'Farrell lordship.[98] Thus he was familiar with the priest's wider kin, and may indeed have known Brian McFergus before he left for studies in Spain; they were of a broadly similar age. The warmth of Piers's appreciation is suggestive of earlier acquaintance, and the encounter points to the Gaelic world in which Piers was partly raised.

The traveller visited the royal palace at Escorial on his return journey from Valladolid to Madrid. While in the city he was in contact with Joseph Creswell SJ. Leaving the new capital on 9 April 1598 after a stay of over two months, and with some travel money provided by Creswell, Piers arrived in Seville on 18 April, with the intention of joining the English College there, and continuing the philosophy studies begun in Rome. There is no explicit reference as to why Piers became a student at Seville, as opposed to Valladolid. Candidates were allocated to one or other of the various English colleges according to the places available at the time; presumably this was also the case when Piers requested admission. There were complaints of overcrowding in the college in Valladolid: between 1592–1598, forty seminarians were sent from St Alban's to the recently founded establishment in Seville.[99] In the 1590s those arriving at Valladolid generally had already started their ecclesiastical studies elsewhere; for those needing to study philosophy, the southern college was deemed more suitable. St Gregory's in Seville accommodated lay students of various ages, which does not appear to have been the case in Valladolid. Thus academically, and in terms of the student body, the Seville college was probably more appropriate for a man of Piers's background.

The English College in Seville (St Gregory's), was founded by Robert Persons in 1592. While established to prepare priests to serve on the English mission, lay youths and young men were also admitted, ranging in age from twelve to the late twenties.[100] In April 1598 Father Richard Walpole SJ admitted Piers as a boarder (*'convictor'*), after which he wore the student uniform; having studied logic and physic in Rome, in Seville he proceeded to the metaphysics course until he left the college after five months, about mid September 1598.[101]

By 1598 there were just under sixty students at St Gregory's. The Jesuit staff comprised the Andalusian rector, Francisco de Peralta,

---

[98] Elizabeth Hickey, 'Some notes on Kilbixy, Tristernagh and Templecross, and the family of Piers', 62.

[99] Williams, *St Alban's College Valladolid*, 21, 26.

[100] On the early history of the Seville college, see Martin Murphy, *St Gregory's College, Seville, 1592–1767*, Catholic Record Society, 73 (1992), 1–25, and Martin Murphy, *Ingleses de Sevilla: El Colegio de San Gregorio, 1592–1767* (Sevilla, 2012), 5–46.

[101] 'Discourse', 205; for a short biography of Richard Walpole SJ (1564–1607), see Henry Foley, *Records of the English Province of the Society of Jesus* (London, 1883), VII, 809–810; in 1597–1598 he was serving as prefect of studies at the English College in Seville.

and several English fathers. In that year, the chapel was completed; it was paid for by Dona Ana de Espinosa, widow of Alvaro de Flores, who had been commander of the Fleet of the Indies.[102] The college was housed in a fine building, constructed in 1595, in a central location beside the palace of the duke of Medina Sidonia. The new premises were adjacent to St Hermenegild's, the house of studies of the Andalusian Jesuits founded in 1584, where the collegians attended courses in philosophy and theology. There were four theology professors, three professors of philosophy, and teachers of scripture, moral theology, Hebrew, and Greek; St Hermenegild's enjoyed a fine reputation for its modern teaching, and the curriculum ranged from grammar and rhetoric through to theology.[103] At St Gregory's drama was also cultivated; in 1598 three performances were given of a certain 'tragicomedia', and among those attending were the archbishop of Seville,[104] the Marques de Tarifa and the duke of Alcala.[105]

While in Seville, Piers was part of the vibrant Elizabethan exile community in the city and its environs. Seville was then the largest city in Spain, the gateway to the riches of the New World, and traditionally enjoyed strong trading contacts with England and Ireland. Piers has left no particular testimony to the spiritual impact his time in Seville may have made on him, by contrast to the sojourn in the college in Rome. He enjoyed a number of contacts with merchants (both Irish and English) and other English-speakers while in Seville. Several encounters point to his range of acquaintances. At San Lucar de Barrameda, a town lying downriver from Seville which had served as the city's seaport until the mid sixteenth century, control of the property of the English merchant confraternity of St George (a church and residence) had been transferred in 1591 to a newly formed college or corporate body of English secular clergy. Henceforth the premises served as a hospice for students and priests departing for or arriving from England.[106] Piers visited the San Lucar residence as he was preparing for the return journey to Ireland. At Puerto de Santa Maria,

---

[102] Murphy, *St Gregory's College, Seville*, 8.

[103] Murphy, *St Gregory's College, Seville*, 15; for an internal Jesuit view on the college's foundation and early years to 1595, see McCoog, *The Society of Jesus*, 113–116, 213–215.

[104] Rodrigo de Castro Osorio (1523–1600) became archbishop of Seville in 1581, and was created cardinal in 1583; supporter of Robert Persons SJ in establishing the English College in Seville. Miranda, *The Cardinals of the Holy Roman Church* http://www2.fiu.edu/~mirandas/bios1583.htm#Castro, accessed 20 Nov. 2017.

[105] Jesuit annual letter, Provincia Baetica, for 1598, extract given in Murphy, *St Gregory's College, Seville*, 124.

[106] The Confraternity of St George, comprising English merchants trading in Seville, had been established in 1517; for an account of this residence in the 16th century, see Williams, *St Alban's College Valladolid*, 269–270.

just prior to departing from Cadiz for Ireland, Piers met an Englishman who had served in the Spanish army and navy for many years, Captain Cripes; Cripes gave Piers a gift of a precious stone, suggestive of a friendship between them.[107] At about the same time, needing accommodation in Jerez, he stayed with an English wine merchant long established in that city, John Fletcher,[108] member of the Confraternity of St George.

More regular contacts arose during his time at the English College. At St Gregory's the staff and students engaged in various ways with the numerous Englishmen who were living in Seville, for a shorter or a longer period: merchants, sailors, prisoners of war. The fathers participated as interpreters when the Inquisition was examining Englishmen. Disputations with visiting Protestants took place in the college; the students regularly frequented the gaols to converse with English inmates, who were generally prisoners of war, and to seek their conversion to Catholicism.[109] In visiting and interceding for Irish prisoners, Piers was following the practice of the staff and students of St Gregory's.

The Irishman's contacts with fellow-countrymen in the Seville area may best be understood in the context of trading between Ireland and south-west Spain at the time of the Anglo-Spanish war (1585–1604), a boom time for Irish merchants. The Andalucian ports received about twenty-three per cent of Irish trade with the Iberian peninsula. Traders from Waterford predominated, followed by those from Dublin and Drogheda.[110] As a result Seville hosted a significant network of Irish residents. A few prominent merchant families – including the Comerfords of Waterford, and the Blakes of Galway – had been active in this trade for several generations. Wine was the major commodity transported from Andalucia to the Irish ports.

The presence of English-speakers in sixteenth-century Seville was complicated by the religious issue. There had been a purge of native Lutherans in Seville in 1559–1560, when a number were burnt,

---

[107] 'Discourse', 215; this Cripes may be identified with Edward Crisp, a pensioner in Stanley's regiment in 1589, who by 1604 had served in the army and navy, Loomie, *The Spanish Elizabethans*, 164, 247.

[108] On John Fletcher, see note, 'Discourse', 215.

[109] On the 70 English sailors captured in 1590, and lodged in Seville, who converted to Catholicism due to the ministry of Robert Persons SJ, see Albert Loomie, 'Religion and Elizabethan commerce with Spain', repr. in A. Loomie, *Spain and the Early Stuarts, 1585–1655* (Aldershot, 1996), 36.

[110] For a brief overview of the presence of Irish merchants in the Iberian peninsula at the end of the 16th century, see O'Connor, *Irish Voices from the Spanish Inquisition*, 34–38; for a statistical analysis of Irish trade with the Iberian peninsula during the Anglo-Spanish war (1585–1604), see Schüller, *Die Beziehungen zwischen Spanien und Irland*, 75–92.

thereby ending Lutheranism as a phenomenon within indigenous
society. As a result of an informal arrangement made in 1576 (the
Alva-Cobham accord), English merchants in Spain were not to be
prosecuted by the Inquisition merely for being Protestant.[111]
However, official anxiety regarding Protestantism remained, and
English-speakers arriving in the Seville area were viewed as a poten-
tial threat to religious purity.

The Anglo-Spanish war of 1585–1604 formed the political backdrop to Piers's sojourn in Spain; the consequent heightened suspicion
of English-speaking aliens, and the disruption experienced by merchants from the Tudor realms impinged on Piers in various ways.
The plight of some in the city's Irish community touched him; as
a result he was exposed at first hand to the wartime stresses and dep-
rivations experienced by Elizabethan merchant exiles who were generally perceived as enemy aliens and as heretics ('Lutherans'). Arising
from intensive trading contacts involving English and Irish merchants
and the Andalucian ports, an English merchant community had
been established in the Seville area, from the beginning of the sixteenth century. The outbreak of war in 1585 had an immediate
impact on the English merchants: an official trade embargo against
Englishmen was imposed by the Spanish crown in May of that
year. Tensions were increased by Essex's raid on Cadiz in June
1596, just over a year prior to Piers's arrival. However, as Pauline
Croft has indicated, English traders continued to operate covertly.
One strategy was to use the services of foreign factors or commercial
agents resident in Andalucia; these aliens actively protected
Englishmen at times of coercion. One of these was a Frenchman,
William Anors, based in Seville; in 1585 he sheltered an
Englishman in his house for four months. In September 1598, on
leaving St Gregory's, and prior to his departure for Ireland at the
end of November, Henry Piers stayed in the home of a
Frenchman in the city; in this it would appear he was following a
practice well-established among English merchants.[112]

Although the embargo in Spain was limited to English traders, their
Irish counterparts too became the object of suspicion and, on occasion,
of punitive measures. Faced with the prospect of exclusion from the
lucrative Andalusian trade, a further strategy of English merchants
was to pass themselves off as Irish or Scottish. An Irish guise was

[111] On the Inquisition's treatment of English merchants and sailors in the Andalucian
ports during the Anglo-Spanish War, see Albert Loomie, 'Religion and Elizabethan commerce with Spain'; on the religious context in 16th-century Seville, see Murphy, *St Gregory's
College, Seville*, 1–11.
[112] Pauline Croft, 'Trading with the enemy 1585–1604', *Historical Journal*, 32 (1989), 286.

particularly convenient, given that in Spain the Catholicism of the
Irish, and their antipathy to the English, were well known. Arising
from anti-English antagonism by officials, and their frequent inability
to distinguish between English and Irish, difficulties were also experienced by some Irish traders, with bases in Irish towns and
long-established trading links with southern Spanish ports. Ships
and merchandize were confiscated by royal officials, and occasionally
the merchants themselves were incarcerated. The prominent Galway
merchant Valentine Blake was arrested in Seville in 1598 on the presumption that he was an English trader, and was imprisoned; Blake
persistently denied he was English, but the authorities refused to
believe him, since his vessel's artillery was English, and a crew member
was married to a Londoner. Piers used visit Blake in prison; by April
1599 Blake had been released, and thereafter he returned to
Galway.[113] A further effect of war was that Irish merchants were also
under suspicion of being spies for the English enemy.[114]

Piers's association with Irish traders while in Spain derived partly
from his family's networks in late Elizabethan Ireland. He was familiar with mercantile circles in the seaports of Dublin and Drogheda,
not least through the family alliance with Alderman James Jans of
Dublin, who himself had traded in La Coruña and Seville in
1591.[115] While in Seville, it was from a Drogheda merchant
(Sebastian Fleming) operating in Jerez that he received a loan to
pay his college accommodation, and it was with him he arranged
his return passage to Ireland; these contacts exemplify the web of
relationships linking the outer reaches of the Pale, where the Piers
family home was located, with the Drogheda merchant community.

A further point of affinity was that Piers shared the political loyalism characteristic of the leading ports in Ireland. Irish traders in
Spain faced inconveniences from being identified as English on occasion, but also from the extension to Spain of ethnic and political
enmities arising from war in Ireland. Irish refugees from the
Desmond wars of the 1570s and 1580s, already established in
Spain, formed a lobby in support of the Irish confederates during

---

[113] Croft, 'Trading with the enemy', 287; Valentine Blake (1560–c.1634), a merchant trading with Spain and Portugal, was reputed to be the richest man in Galway in 1592, *DIB*; after
his imprisonment Blake left Spain on 21 Apr. 1599, and reached Galway on 10 May of the
same year, Blake to Sir Conyers Clifford, 12 May 1599, TNA, SP 63/205/58; in 1611 he was
elected mayor of Galway, but was deposed that year for refusing to take the oath of suprem-
acy, M.D. O'Sullivan, *Old Galway* (Cambridge, 1942, repr. Galway, 1983), 18.
[114] Karin Schüller, 'Special conditions of the Irish-Iberian trade during the
Spanish-English war (1585–1604)', in Enrique García Hernán et al. (eds), *Irlanda y la
Monarquía Hispánica: Kinsale 1601–2001* (Madrid, 2002), 464–468.
[115] Schüller, *Die Beziehungen zwischen Spanien und Irland*, 231.

the subsequent Nine Years War (1594–1603) against the English
crown. In the 1590s these exiles were wont to condemn Irish merchants as representatives of the loyalist anglophile towns in Ireland
which refused to support the revolt. Exiles lobbying on behalf of
Tyrone and his allies were denouncing these merchants to the
Spanish authorities; Tyrone's supporters accused the urban oligar-
chies of aiding the English forces in the military struggle. As a result
in Spain the traders suffered confiscation of their goods and other
inconveniences.[116]

Piers was predisposed to help the merchants, and to do so was willing to draw on his English Jesuit contacts. After the death of Sir
Francis Englefield in autumn 1596, the role of intermediary with
the Spanish crown for English exiles seeking a royal pension fell to
Father Joseph Creswell SJ, together with Thomas Fitzherbert.[117]
Returning from Valladolid to Madrid in late January 1598, Piers
was in contact with Creswell, an associate of Robert Persons, and
already resident for several years at court and lobbying for royal support for the nascent English colleges. Given Creswell's growing
prominence in court circles, and his exceptional energy as administra-
trator, this role was understood more broadly to include the welfare
of English exiles in Spain.

Thus it was natural that Piers should seek Creswell's intervention
with the royal authorities on behalf of several Irish merchants
whose ships and goods had been confiscated for the king's use.
Creswell's representations were successful, for a ship of Nicholas
Weston, the Dublin entrepreneur and alderman, was released, and
a similar, though unspecified favour was granted to a member of
the prominent Comerford merchant family of Waterford. In
Seville, as earlier in Madrid, Piers continued to prevail on resident
English Jesuits to intercede with the civil authorities for individual
merchants, presumably to verify that they were Irish, and not
English. Among many instances, Piers recounted the case of
Richard Skerrett of Galway; Father Richard Walpole SJ, of the
English College, made representations to the city governor, and as
a result Skerrett's goods were returned to him.[118]

---

[116] 'Discourse', 202; on the various waves of Irish migration to the Iberian peninsula to
the mid 17th century, see Karin Schüller, 'Irish migrant networks and rivalries in Spain,
1575–1659', in T. O'Connor and M.A. Lyons (eds), *Irish Migrants in Europe after Kinsale,
1602–1820* (Dublin, 2003), 88–103.

[117] Loomie, *The Spanish Elizabethans*, 28; on the career of Joseph Creswell SJ (1556–1623)
in Spain from 1592 to 1614, ibid. 182–229.

[118] 'Discourse', 205.

On several occasions Piers experienced this official suspicion at first hand. Towards the end of his stay in Spain, in September–November 1598, Piers himself had several potentially burdensome encounters with the law. Significantly these occurred after he had left St Gregory's; by then he no longer had the status of a collegian, identifiable by his attire, and so was at risk of being taken for an enemy alien. This hazard was increased by his residing with a Frenchman, probably known as one who sheltered English merchants. Piers was arrested in his dwelling place, accused of seeking to pervert an English youth (a page in the service of the city regent, or governor) from Catholicism to Protestantism. Suspected of being a Lutheran, or member of some heretical sect, Piers was brought before the regent; in response to these charges, Piers presented 'my passports, which I brought from Rome', testifying to his Catholic credentials.[119] The regent's attitude was transformed, and he asked for Piers's forgiveness.

A more threatening incident occurred in September 1598, when Piers inadvertently became embroiled in the fallout from the escape of Captain Richard Hawkins,[120] an English seaman then incarcerated in Seville. Hawkins absconded but was shortly afterwards recaptured. In the search for the prisoner, Piers was arrested under suspicion of being an accomplice, based on his regular visits to the prison, and on being found carrying food and wine on the day of the escape. The Irishman was interrogated, and a session on the rack was scheduled for the following morning; only the capture of Hawkins, and the testimony of Father Walpole saved Piers from this fate.

Even when setting sail on his return voyage to Ireland, Piers was still subject to official harassment. From Cadiz he departed for Ireland on 28 November 1598 with Sebastian Fleming, a merchant of Drogheda; reflecting the place of St Malo in the Irish trade with southern Spain, Fleming had freighted a vessel (the 'Little Delphin') from the French port and had laden it with wines. Just as the ship was leaving Cadiz, an official boarded the vessel, and was about to arrest Piers, accusing him of being an Englishman, and a spy, notwithstanding the testimony to his Irish identity of those present; the encounter suggests that Piers may have been under surveillance as an enemy agent for some time before his departure. In conventional fashion Piers dealt with the situation by paying a bribe.[121]

---

[119] 'Discourse', 213.
[120] Richard Hawkins (c.1560–1622), *ODNB*; while in prison in Seville, Hawkins converted to the Catholic Church, thanks to Fr Walpole, who also gave him 200 crowns, 'Discourse', 210.
[121] 'Discourse', 215; in the late 16th century, Seville Inquisition officials regularly boarded ships to search for heretical books, O'Connor, *Irish Voices from the Spanish Inquisition*, 29–31.

The ship experienced a severe storm, and was chased by Dunkirk pirates, circumstances which led the author to reflect, once again, on divine providence. The sailors also had difficulty in recognizing the southern Irish coastline; after more than four weeks at sea, they landed at Howth, a village outside the city of Dublin, on 28 December 1598.

Contents of the 'Discourse'

A chronological account of the author's travels provides the framework of the 'Discourse': from Dublin to Rome; his sojourn in Rome; from Rome via Genoa to Spain, where he visited the English College in Valladolid, prior to travelling to Seville and residing at the English College; his voyage from Cadiz to Ireland, landing at Howth, Co. Dublin.

Within this structure, the first section covers the journey from Dublin to Rome, in which Philip Draycott, the young candidate for the English College in Rome, accompanied him. The middle section is dedicated to his stay in Rome. He devotes just over half of the entire text (pp. 38–155) to a description of Rome under various headings: its churches (he has entries for seventy-three); religious processions; some of the national colleges established from the mid sixteenth century for training clergy, together with an outline of the daily routine and the rules which prevailed; the city's seven hills, thermal springs, gates, highways, bridges, aqueducts, amphitheatres, market places, triumphal arches, palaces, courts, and magistrates. Here, as elsewhere in the 'Discourse', his apologetical intent is evident. In the account of each church, he notes the festive days on which indulgences may be gained by the faithful who visit. In the antiquity of Christian Rome, he sees an argument in favour of the contemporary sixteenth-century Roman Church as the uniquely authentic expression of western Christianity.

When listing the city's hills, he includes an excursus on the battle of Lepanto (October, 1571); here he draws on the just-published book by Richard Knolles, and makes a plea for Christian unity against the Ottoman empire, the latest expression of the Islamic threat to the Christian world. He concludes the Roman section with a laudatory and uncritical account of the pontificate of Clement VIII (1592–1605); prior to his departure from Rome in October 1597, Piers had an audience with the pontiff, who gave him the 'viaticum', the travel money normally granted by the Holy See to seminarians from Protestant countries who were returning to minister in their homelands at the end of their studies.

The final section of the 'Discourse' treats of Piers's journey from Rome via Genoa to Spain. In terms of content, next to Rome,

Piers devotes most attention to the Marian sanctuary of Loreto, near Ancona, on the Adriatic coast, north-east of Rome. He devotes over ten per cent of his text (a total of twenty-seven pages) to Loreto, reflecting the enormous popularity of the devotion to the Holy House of Nazareth within contemporary piety, and its attraction as a pilgrim destination. Here Piers includes another excursus, giving a summary history of the sanctuary by offering an abridgment of the work by the Italian Jesuit Orazio Torsellino first published in 1598. To the account culled from Torsellino, Piers adds much detail from his own observation. Together with his travelling companions from the English College in Rome, he spent several days (20–23 October 1597) at this shrine.[122]

Leaving Loreto, they proceeded to Milan; there Piers parted with the English travellers, and he continued to Genoa, where he took ship for Alicante in Spain. His destination was the English College at Valladolid (St Alban's College), where he stayed for two weeks as a guest of the English Jesuits. On the return journey to Madrid, he visited El Escorial, the palace recently built by Philip II, and he gives a description in the 'Discourse'. He remained in Madrid from late January to April 1598. Thereafter he travelled to Seville, where he lived as a student in the English College there (St Gregory's College), from mid April to early September 1598. He devotes ten pages (pp. 205–215) to his time in Seville, in which encounters with the Irish community and the Spanish authorities feature prominently. The 'Discourse' concludes with his account of the sea voyage from Cadiz to Ireland. As an appendix he attaches a table giving the distances in miles between the various towns and cities through which he travelled.

Outline of the Contents of the 'Discourse'

Here follows an outline of the contents of the 'Discourse', giving the author's marginal headings; editorial headings are inserted within square brackets; page references are those given in the manuscript:

'The Dedicatorie Epistle' [to Richard Haddock], p. 1

'The preamble to the followinge Discourse', pp. 2–3

---

[122] Travelling from Donegal, Hugh O'Neill, earl of Tyrone, together with other exiled Ulster lords, arrived in Rome in Apr. 1608, and visited Loreto; for an outline of Tadhg Ó Cianáin's account (in Irish) of their journey, see N. Ó Muraíle, 'An insider's view: Tadhg Ó Cianáin as eyewitness to the exile of Ulster's lords, 1607–8', R. Gillespie and R. Ó hUiginn (eds), *Irish Europe, 1600–1650: Writing and Learning* (Dublin, 2013), 44–62.

[Account of journey from Dublin to Rome, 9 June 1595–25 September 1595], pp. 4–30:

> Dublin–Emden, pp. 1–8
> Emden–Trent, pp. 8–20
> Trent–Rome, pp. 20–30

[Arrival in English College in Rome], pp. 30–38

'A Breefe description of the best churches in Rome' [73 churches], pp. 38–76

'A Description of certaine processions wch I sawe when I was in Rome', pp. 76–100

'A description of the chifest Colleadges in Rome', pp. 100–120

> 'Spiritual exercise', pp. 102–104
> 'The Rulles of the Colleadges', pp. 111–118

'A description of the seaven hills whereupon Rome is builte', pp. 120–135

> 'The battell of Lepanto', pp. 121–133

'The description of other antiquities in Rome and first of the thearms and bathinge houses', pp. 135–136

> 'The principall gates of Rome', pp. 136–138
> 'The highe ways of Rome', pp. 138–139
> 'The Bridges of Rome', pp. 139–141
> 'The Aquaeductes of Rome', pp. 141–142
> 'The Amphitheators and other theators of Rome', pp. 142–143
> 'The markett places of Rome', pp. 143–144
> 'The triumphant Arkes of Rome', pp. 144–145
> 'The pallaces of Rome', pp. 145–148
> 'The Courtes and Senackles of Rome', pp. 148–149
> 'The maiestratts of Rome', pp. 149–151
> 'The Antiquitie of Rome', pp. 151–155

'The virtuose life and worthie acctions of Pope Clement the eyght', pp. 155–160

'My Jornie from Rome hom[e]wads', pp. 163–220 [He left Rome, 15 October 1597.]

> 'An abridgement of the holy house of Laurettas historie', pp. 164–178
> [His observations on his visit to Loreto], pp. 178–190
> [Ancona–Milan–Genoa], pp. 190–195
> [Genoa to Alicante, Spain], pp. 195–196

Sources used in the 'Discourse'

It is clear from internal evidence that Piers had several printed books (or extracts made from these) at his disposal while compiling his 'Discourse'. He made frequent quotations from the Vulgate Latin version of the Bible, approved for Catholic use, a revised version of which was published in 1592. He quotes mainly from the psalms, with a few stray references to other parts of the Old Testament (Genesis, the prophet Jeremiah), and the gospels. In each instance the Latin quotation is followed by an English translation. Given that in the period 1595–1598 Piers lived for two years in the English College in Rome and for five months in the English College in Seville, it was likely that he attended the regular daily worship that formed part of seminary life. In this setting he would have become familiar with the recitation of the psalms in Latin. While a student, he may have copied out those passages which he deemed relevant to his spiritual journey, and in this way was able to use these verses in composing the 'Discourse'. At that time, there was no English translation of the entire bible authorized for use by Catholics.[123] The accuracy of the Latin quotations, together with the biblical references, indicate that Piers had access to the text of the Vulgate Bible, either as a student, or later, on his return to Ireland, when he was writing the 'Discourse'. He may have possessed a breviary, or a Latin psalter, in book form. Ownership of a printed Latin breviary (a prayer book containing the psalms and other prayers) was normal for seminarians in the continental colleges at that time.[124]

---

[123] An English Catholic translation of the New Testament was published in Reims in 1582, in 1 vol. with extensive commentary and notes; the Old Testament in English was published in 2 vols in Douai, 1609–1610; the translations were from the Latin Vulgate, F.L. Cross and E.A. Livingstone (eds), *The Oxford Dictionary of the Christian Church* (Oxford, 1997), 504.

[124] For example, of two students accepted into the Irish College, Salamanca in 1606, one brought four books (unspecified) while the other brought a breviary, Karin Schüller, *Die Beziehungen zwischen Spanien und Irland*, 154.

He mentions three printed works by name. At the conclusion to his description of the various categories of buildings in Rome, he refers the reader to the book by 'Hierom Francis', entitled *The antiquities and marvellous things of Rome*.[125] This is Piers's English version of author and title referring to the volume in Italian by Girolamo Francini, *Le Cose Maravigliose dell'Alma Città di Roma* (Venice, 1588). Ten editions in Italian appeared from 1588 to 1595, making it among the most popular guides to Rome in the 1580s and 1590s.[126]

It was for the descriptive section on the churches and antiquities of Rome ('Discourse', pp. 38–76, 120–155) that Piers drew most extensively and consistently on published material. About one-third of the text of the 'Discourse' (73 pages) was based chiefly on Francini, *Le Cose Maravigliose,* together with the description of the battle of Lepanto (1571) from the book by Richard Knolles (to be discussed). Piers drew on Francini's guidebook in several ways. This publication (Francini, pp. 106–127) incorporated a work by the renowned architect M. Andrea Palladio (1508–1580) on Roman antiquities entitled *L'Antichità di Roma*.[127] From the range of themes offered by Palladio, Piers selected several for inclusion in his 'Discourse': the seven hills, 'thearmes and bathinge houses', the principal gates, highways, bridges, aqueducts, amphitheatres and theatres, marketplaces, triumphal arches, palaces, courts and magistrates, and some remarks on the antiquity and population size of the city. Piers followed Palladio closely in structure and content, giving summary lists, and shortening Palladio's entries. Occasionally Piers updates Palladio by inserting contemporary details: regarding the hills, Piers adds a description of statues on the Capitoline; on aqueducts, he appends a note on the reconstruction by Sixtus V; for the marketplaces, he includes the Piazza Navona, the custom of placing scurrilous texts at the Pasqui monument, and the burnings of heretics at Campo de'Fiori; to the section on palaces, Piers adjoins Castel Sant'Angelo, and the residences of various recent cardinals.

A second major use of Francini was in regard to the churches in Rome. Piers listed seventy-three[128] in which he gives information on saints, relics, Lenten station days, and other festive days on which

[125] 'Discourse', 162.

[126] Sergio Rossetti, *Rome: A Bibliography from the Invention of Printing through 1899*, I: *The Guide Books* (Florence, 2000), 49–51; I was able to consult the 1588 copy of Francini conserved in Special Collections, Christ Church Library, Oxford; for an early 17th-century Irish account of Rome in the context of contemporary publications, see M. Mac Craith, 'An Irishman's diary: Aspects of Tadhg Ó Cianáin's Rome', in Gillespie and Ó hUiginn, *Irish Europe, 1600–1650*, 63–84.

[127] Originally published in Venice in 1554.

[128] 'Discourse', 38–73.

indulgences may be gained by visiting the church in question; further, on revising the later entries[129] he subsequently inserted details regarding indulgences, omitted in the first draft. The focus on saints, their relics, and indulgences highlights the convert's attention to features of Catholic piety which were vehemently contested by the reformers. This editorial emphasis conforms to the author's overarching polemical concern to present the distinctiveness of contemporary Catholicism, in opposition to the objections of its Protestant adversaries. For these notes Piers closely followed the section on Roman churches given in Francini.[130] From the 141 churches presented by Francini, Piers selected 66; in drafting his own entries Piers normally summarized those of Francini.

In several cases Piers supplements Francini's account, drawing on his own observations or what he had heard while in Rome regarding the church in question. For St Peter's Basilica, the visitor described a papal mass, and added remarks on the papal residence and garden, and the Vatican Library. Touching the complex at Santo Spirito, Piers noted the attached hospital or orphanage, and a procession of children there. Regarding the basilica of St John Lateran, Piers recounted that in it one of the church councils was held, which issued decrees on heresy; the author proceeded to decry contemporary church disunity, and comment approvingly on procedures against heretics. When listing the church of S. Maria Maddalena ('Delle convertite'), he included remarks on contemporary measures against courtesans in the city. In describing the Gesù church, drawing on his contact with English Jesuits in Rome he offered a sketch of the global reach of the Society of Jesus in the 1590s, and some of its governing procedures. For his entry on S. Maria sopra Minerva, the Dominican headquarters, Piers introduced an excursus on the Roman Inquisition, relating some recent celebrated cases against heretics.

Piers included a small number of churches (up to six) which do not appear in the 1588 edition of Francini. The Irish dimension featured in several: regarding S. Lucia he noted the adjacent commodious residence for Irish students, under the patronage of Girolamo Mattei, cardinal protector of the Irish; he also included S. Bonaventura, the Capuchin church, where he went to meet his fellow-countryman, Francis Nugent, recently arrived in Rome. For S. Maria della Pace, to Francini's account Piers added that St Patrick, the Irish apostle, stayed there while in Rome, presumably an assertion current among the Irish community in the city.

---

[129] 'Discourse', 67–73.
[130] *Le Cose Maravigliose*, 5–71.

The publication dates of Francini's Roman volume suggest that the visitor acquired a copy while in Rome; he took detailed notes, though with occasional errors;[131] he may have done so while in Rome, or he may have brought the book back with him to Ireland; at any rate Francini's guidebook became his major resource in compiling the Roman section of the 'Discourse'. To the account of churches and antiquities, Piers appends the story of the conversion of Emperor Constantine.

Complementing this treatment of Rome drawn from Francini, Piers adjoins several themes derived from his own sojourn in the mid 1590s: an extensive description of processions he witnessed, an account of the rule of Pope Clement VIII, and remarks on the regulation of the Jewish community. Given that most national seminaries in Rome at this time were entrusted to the Jesuits, his survey of these colleges[132] may have been based in part on conversations with English Jesuits resident in the city.

The naval battle of Lepanto (7 October 1571), in which the Catholic confederates (Venice, Spain, and the pope) defeated the forces of the Ottoman emperor, Sulemein II, was of particular fascination for Piers. Living in Rome in the mid 1590s, Piers absorbed the contemporary Christian European preoccupation with the territorial expansion of the Ottoman Turks. The victory at Lepanto was still fresh in popular memory, and the prominence of the princely Colonna family in Rome – Marcantonio Colonna was the papal admiral at the battle – added to the continued interest in the event. The author interrupts his description of the hills of Rome to make an excursus on the encounter, decisive in halting the Ottoman advance in the Mediterranean. At some time in 1604 or early in 1605, he consulted the section on Lepanto contained in a massive volume on the centuries-long struggle with the Turks, published in London towards the end of 1603. Entitled *The generall historie of the Turkes, from the first beginning of that nation to the rising of the Othoman familie: with all the notable expeditions of the Christian princes against them ... digested into one continuat historie until this present yeare 1603*, it was by the Englishman Richard Knolles.[133] The account of Lepanto is to be

---

[131] Regarding the basilica of St John Lateran ('San Giovanni Laterano'), in one sentence Francini refers to 'heretics', and in the next he notes that Pope Nicholas IV refurbished the building (*Le Cose Maravigliose*, 5). Piers conflates these details, and refers to 'the nicholayetane heretickes', 'Discourse', 38.

[132] 'Discourse', 100–120.

[133] The author's introduction was dated 30 Sept. 1603; the book comprises 1152 pages, plus appendices; there were six editions in the course of the 17th century; Richard Knolles (late 1540s–1610), *ODNB*.

found in the section entitled 'The life of Selymus, the second of that name, fift emperor of the Turkes' (reigned 1566–1574).[134]

In his presentation of the battle, Piers summarizes this published history, but focusing on action, and omitting speeches, and discussions on strategy, given by Knolles. While broadly an accurate summary, occasionally Piers misspells names, and in some details, through errors in transcription, inadvertently distorts Knolles's text.[135] Just after this excursus, Piers links the description of the battle to his central theme of the unity incorporated in the Roman church, with a reflection on the need for a united political stance against the Ottoman threat, and decrying once again the religious divisions arising from the Reformation. In this digression, he refers to two fifteenth-century Christian military figures who fought against the Turks, indicating that in addition to the section on Lepanto, he had perused other parts of Knolles's compendious volume.[136] Henry Piers emerges as one of the earliest readers of this influential work.

For his extensive treatment of the pilgrimage sanctuary of Loreto, near Ancona in Italy ('Discourse', pp. 164–190), the traveller offered a brief synopsis of the history by the Roman Jesuit Orazio Torsellino,[137] *Lauretanae Historiae Libri Quinque*, a Latin work first published in Rome giving the year 1597, but with an approbation from Clement VIII dated January 1598. Thus the volume appeared after Piers's departure from the papal city. In drawing on Torsellino, he focused on giving an outline of the story of the Holy House of Nazareth in the medieval period, and on the privileges and favours bestowed by various popes, omitting Torsellino's accounts of miracles and donations by individual nobles.

The publication dates for the works by Knolles and Torsellino indicate that Piers consulted these in Ireland while composing his 'Discourse', in the period from late 1603 to summer 1605, during the years of the initial recovery after the destruction wrought by the Nine Years War (1594–1603). By early 1603 the military threat was over, those loyalists expelled from their properties during the war had returned, and the process of reconstruction was underway, suggesting that by then (if not earlier) Piers had come back to his father's house, the former abbey of Tristernagh, Co. Westmeath.

---

[134] This section comprises pp. 827–916 of the book; Lepanto is treated on pp. 870–884.

[135] Notable deviations from Knolles's publication will be indicated in the footnotes of the 'Discourse' text.

[136] Piers refers ('Discourse', 131) to Scanderbeg (1405–1468), and 'Captain Huniades', otherwise Janos Hunyadi (*c*.1387–1456): both names receive extensive entries in the index of the Knolles volume.

[137] Orazio Torsellino (Torsellini) (1544–1599), *Diccionario Histórico de la Compañía de Jésus*.

These bibliographical details throw some light on the circulation of English and continental books among the landed gentry in Ireland in the early years of the seventeenth century.

The detailed itinerary given for various stages of his journeys, indicating places and dates, suggests that in composing the 'Discourse' Piers could draw on notes – now lost – made while travelling.

The 'Discourse' was completed in 1605, as indicated on the title page. A date in the summer of that year may be posited, for in the text the election of Pope Paul V (which occurred on 16 May 1605) was noted; Piers dedicated his work to Richard Haddock, who died in Rome on 13 July 1605,[138] and typically it took several weeks for any news from Rome to arrive in Ireland; hence the text was probably concluded some time between June and August 1605. The author's aim in writing, as he indicated in the preamble, was for his own enjoyment, and for the benefit of others, 'travellers or others, which shall peruse the same'.[139]

Description of the Manuscript

Only one manuscript of the text is extant (Oxford, Bodleian Library, Rawlinson D. 83). The parchment cover is possibly original. It dates to at least 1648, and is probably earlier. On the spine 'Vol 24 Hi[st]' has been written, corresponding with the entry in the catalogue of books belonging to the Irish antiquarian Sir James Ware in 1648;[140] Ware ordered his books under five headings, one of which was history. The pages measure 29.5 cm by 18.5 cm (11.6 inches by 7.3 inches). The watermark – in the centre of the page, clearly visible on the blank pages at the end of the manuscript – is uniform throughout. There is continuous pagination on the top right-hand corner, from 1–221, probably contemporary with the manuscript. Page 18 is blank. There is no p. 220, merely a blank page. For the table of distances between towns (at the end of the manuscript) there is a foliation numbering 222, 223, and 224, and there follow five blank folios. There is a line drawn under the final line of text on pp. 133, 137, 141, 151, 159, 163, 169, 175, 210.

An insert, measuring 17 cm by 14 cm (6.7 inches by 5.5 inches), has been placed between pp. 100 and 101. This paper has been pasted into the spine at the upper part of p. 101. It was attached by a pin, which remains on the insert, and was originally pinned to the

[138] Anstruther, *The Seminary Priests*, I, 159–160.
[139] 'Discourse', 3.
[140] Sir James Ware (1594–1666), antiquarian and collector of MSS, *DIB*.

lower left-hand margin of p. 101, where the marks or holes left by the
pin are visible. Thus this paper was probably pasted onto p. 101 at
the final stage of preparing the codex, prior to binding. It contains
14½ lines of text. In content it is an addition by the author, as he
explains, in which he underlines the antiquity of practices of piety
and mortification, against the 'Lutherans Calvenistes and other
suche sectories [who] did by there vaine and pernitious inventions
hinder the laudable continuance of the same'. It exemplifies Piers's
concern to defend Catholic practices against the challenges of the
Protestants, a leitmotiv in his memoir. The insert indicates that the
author re-read the manuscript and made changes, corrections, and
insertions. A Protestant reader wrote an acerbic comment on p. 16
(where Piers indicated his intention to become a Catholic) which
was subsequently struck through.

Several hands may be identified in the body of the text, signifying
that a number of scribes were involved; these were presumably working from notes or drafts of individual sections provided by the author.
From the frontispiece to the heading on p. 4, inclusive, was written in
an italic hand. The main body of the text (pp. 4–221) is in a secretary
hand. In the appendix giving the table of distances between towns
(pp. 222–224) an italic hand re-appears, similar to that of the initial
few pages.

Of all the sections, that on the Roman churches (pp. 38–74) shows
evidence of the most intensive revision, arising from the pilgrim's
especial interest in churches, saints, and relics. Often the emendations are minimal; occasionally, however, the author decided to
add more information to the entries, generally on the indulgences
associated with visiting particular churches. Several insertions may
be noted on p. 54: there is an addition to the entry on
S. Pancrazio's church, giving details on the saint, and the stations
(or special devotions); to the standard entry for the church of
S. Onofrio, he added a note on the recent papal prohibition against
removing relics of the martyrs; for S. Spirito, he gave more details on
relics and reliquaries (most likely recalled from his visit there)
together with indulgences. For entries in the latter part of the section
on the churches (pp. 67–74), details on feast days and the associated
indulgences were systematically inserted, possibly by Piers himself.[141]
In this way the author may have been correcting the draft prepared
for him by a copyist.

Another phase of revision may be posited for the marginal material, comprising headings and scriptural references. These are in

---

[141] Confirming this authorial procedure, at the conclusion of the section, with reference
to indulgences Piers inserts the observation 'as in particular hath beene mentioned' (p. 74).

several italic hands, different from the body of the text. One is continuous throughout the manuscript: the sub-headings on pp. 76, 100, 120, 135–163 are also in this hand. In addition, further hands made a smaller number of entries throughout, but especially on pp. 154–174, and on a few pages towards the end (208, 213, 215). For the psalm quotations in Latin on pp. 217–218, an italic hand was used.

Inside the front cover there is written 'Vol. XXIV', referring to the Ware catalogue of 1648; the catalogue reference '(12901)' is to the Bodleian Summary Catalogue, prepared in the nineteenth century. Adhering to the inside of the cover there is also an insert (in the form of a bookplate).[142] Underneath this insert appears 'Rawl. Mss D.83'.

Provenance of the Manuscript

A key moment in the survival of the manuscript was its acquisition by the Irish antiquarian Sir James Ware (1594–1666). Given the close marriage alliances between the Ware and the Piers families, it is not surprising that Sir James acquired the text.[143] The Piers memoir does not appear in the list of Ware's manuscripts dating from about the late 1620s. In 1648, however, Ware entered it in the catalogue of his books which was published in Dublin in that year.[144] Thus it came into Ware's possession after the author's death, probably at some stage from about 1630; in the maelstrom of Irish revolt in the winter of 1641–1642, planter dwellings (including the Piers household in Tristernagh) were attacked and the contents destroyed; books and written materials were a particular target.[145] Thus the Piers memoir probably passed to Sir James Ware some time between c.1630 and

[142] 'Sigillum Univ. Oxon. Diplomati Ric: Rawlinson Pro gradu Doctoris Legum Appensum' [Woodcut of seal].

[143] The antiquarian's brother John Ware married Elizabeth Piers, daughter of Henry Piers; his sister Martha Ware married Sir William Piers (d.1638), son and heir of Henry, TCD MS 1216, fo.29r–v; see also National Library Ireland, Genealogical Office, MS 68, fo.56; the antiquarian's younger son Robert married Elizabeth, daughter of Sir William Piers and his wife Martha Ware, 'Memoirs of family of Sir Henry Piers of Tristernagh' [1748], National Library of Ireland, MS 2563.

[144] In this catalogue the Piers memoir is indicated thus: 'XXIV. Itinerarium Henrici Peirs nuper de Tristernagh Armigeri, inceptum anno Dom. 1595. in fol.', given in William O'Sullivan, 'A finding list of Sir James Ware's manuscripts', *Proceedings Royal Irish Academy*, 97, Section C (1997), 90.

[145] For the destruction of the Tristernagh properties, see deposition of Dame Martha Peirce, 22 Dec. 1642, Trinity College Dublin, MS 817, fo.26; on the burning of books and papers in 1641, see B. Mac Cuarta, 'Religious violence against settlers in south Ulster, 1641–2', in D. Edwards, P. Lenihan, and C. Tait (eds), *Age of Atrocity: Violence and Political Conflict in Early Modern Ireland* (Dublin, 2007), 154–75.

1641; the note on the title page, giving the death of Henry Piers in December 1623, is in his hand.

Another manuscript associated with Henry Piers has also survived by the same route. Owing to his interest in the previous history of the dissolved monastery of Augustinian canons at Tristernagh, the properties of which formed the estate acquired in 1562 by his father, in 1618 Henry commissioned a neighbour, Christopher Fitzgerald of Laragh, to transcribe the chartulary of the medieval foundation. This transcript too was acquired by Sir James Ware.[146]

The antiquarian's son Robert sold the Ware manuscripts to Henry Hyde, second earl of Clarendon, when the latter was serving in Dublin as Irish viceroy in 1685–1687. Thereafter the Ware collection was brought by Clarendon to England. At the sale of the Clarendon collection in 1709, James Brydges, subsequently first duke of Chandos, purchased the library, including the Ware materials. The duke died in 1744, and his library was auctioned in 1747. Richard Rawlinson bought the Piers memoir, along with other Ware materials, and in 1755 presented it, as part of his manuscript collection, to the Bodleian Library, Oxford.[147]

The Dublin antiquarian Sir John Gilbert (1829–1898) was responsible for a partial transcription of Henry Piers's memoir which was undertaken in spring 1891; this transcript (preserved in the Gilbert Collection, Dublin City Library) covers merely the first fifty-six pages of the original manuscript (a quarter of the total).[148] Gilbert had intended to edit the entire text, but this project probably fell

---

[146] Entitled 'A coppie of the register of the lands tythes and other commodities belonging to the priorie of Tristernagh taken out of the original and written in the yeare 1618', this text is located in Oxford, Bodleian, MS Rawl. B 504; it was listed by Ware in his 1648 catalogue, O'Sullivan, 'A Finding List', 88; on the provenance of the medieval register, see M.V. Clarke (ed.), *Register of the Priory of the Blessed Virgin Mary at Tristernagh* (Dublin, 1941), vii–xxiii.

[147] For the provenance of the Ware MSS in the 17th century (including the present text), see O'Sullivan, 'A finding list'; Rawlinson paid 5 shillings for the Piers travel memoir: see Rawlinson's copy (with prices for items purchased) of the auction catalogue, Mar. 1747; for the sale of the Chandos library, see Oxford, Bodleian, Mus Bibl. III 80, 44; the Piers memoir is listed in Gulielmus Macray, *Catalogi Codicum Manuscriptorum Bibliothecae Bodleianae Partis Quintae Fasciculus Tertius … Ricardi Rawlinson* (Oxford, 1893), column 45; Macray identifies Ware's handwriting in the note on the MS's title page.

[148] The transcript, handwritten in ink, consists of 75 loose leaves, and ends abruptly in mid-sentence; on the reverse of p. 72 there is an address and postage stamp, bearing postal frank 'Oxford MY 20 91', with address as follows 'J.T. Gilbert Esq Villa Nova, Blackrock, Dublin'; the transcript has as reference, Dublin City Library, Pearse Street, Gilbert MSS, MS 177 (Box 11); there is no reference to Henry Piers in Douglas Hyde and D.J. O'Donoghue (eds), *Catalogue*.

victim to his propensity to undertake several academic projects simultaneously.[149]

The only previous edition of the full manuscript was undertaken by Thomas Frank (1925–1990) in the early 1950s, and issued in his unpublished BLitt thesis at St Catherine's College, Oxford.[150] One extensive excerpt from Piers's account has been published. This refers to his time in Seville in 1598 (pp. 205–215 of the 'Discourse') and was reproduced as an appendix in Martin Murphy (ed.), *St Gregory's College, Seville 1592–1767* (Catholic Record Society, 73, 1992), 135–141.

Note on this Edition

In the present edition, the original pagination is given by a number set within round brackets. Marginal material on the manuscript is reproduced here in italic within square brackets, placed in the body of the text where the insertion can best aid comprehension. Erasures, insertions, and emendations have been indicated in footnotes; where a hand different from that of the body of the text can be identified in the insertions, this is noted in the relevant footnote. Regarding place names, and names of rivers, the modern version (where this can be identified) has been given within square brackets. Spelling, capitals, and abbreviations are as in the original. In general, in the discursive sections of the manuscript, breaks or paragraphs are infrequent; to facilitate reading, paragraphing (denoted by indentation of the first line) has been inserted throughout the text.

---

[149] Gilbert declared this intention in the course of his short entry on Henry Piers, in Leslie Stephen and Sidney Lee (eds), *The Dictionary of National Biography from the Earliest Times to 1900*, Vol. XV (London, 1885–1900); on Gilbert's habit of engaging with many contemporaneous projects, see Rosa Mulholland Gilbert, *Life of Sir John T. Gilbert* (London, 1905), 36; on Gilbert's contribution to Irish historical studies, see Toby Barnard, 'Sir John Gilbert and Irish historiography', in Mary Clark et al. (eds), *Sir John T. Gilbert 1829–1898: Historian, Archivist and Librarian* (Dublin, 1999), 92–110.

[150] Thomas Frank (ed.), 'An edition of A discourse of HP his travelles (MS Rawlinson D. 83), with an introduction on English travellers in Rome during the age of Elizabeth', unpublished BLitt thesis, University of Oxford, 1954; for an obituary of Thomas Frank (including list of publications), see E.F.K. Koerner, 'Thomas Frank: Obituary', in D. Stein and R. Sornicola (eds), *The Virtues of Language: History in Language, Linguistics and Tests: Papers in Memory of Thomas Frank* (Amsterdam, 1998), 3–10.

BODLEIAN LIBRARY, OXFORD, RAWLINSON, MS D. 83
*****

+

A
DISCOURSE OF HP[1] HIS
TRAVELLES WRITTEN
BY HIM SELFE

Psalme 88

Misericordias Domini in
aeternum cantabo.

I will singe the mercies of god for ever[2]

+

Anno   IHS   1605

---

[1] Note inserted, sign 'a', new hand: 'a Henry Piers Esqr He deceased in December 1623'.
[2] Psalm 88 (89):1.

(1) **The Dedicatorie Epistle**

To the Right Reverend Father Richard Haddocke[3] preiste Doctor of Divinitie

It is evidently seene (Reverend Father) as well in the holy Scriptures, as also in many other bookes written by dyvers learned men in former adges, howe exceedinge hatefull ingratitude hathe bene unto the divine maiestie of god in soe muche as he reiected his owne people, the Jewes for that hai[ ]nous[4] offence, and gave the Greeke churche as a praye unto the Turcke, for that they did ungratefully Seperatt themselves by there Scisme and heresie from the unitie of oure holy mother the Catholicke Churche and therefore if he did cast out his elect people the Jewes, and suffer the Gretians to be over runn by the Turcks, for there ungratefullnes, much more will he extend his iustice againste any particular parson[5] which shalbe founde giltie of that detestable cryme, for the eschewinge of the wch Synn I will (by his gratious assistance) use my beste diligence, and for[6] the better manifestation of my intent therein, I have written this followinge discourse of my travells, and have made choyse to dedicate the same unto your Fatherhoode, one reason movinge me thereunto, was to shewe my thanckfull mynde towards you, for that as an immediat instrument under god of my happines, you did place me in the Englishe Colledge in Rome where I gayned great store of Spirituall treasure, another reason embouldninge me thereunto, was for that I knowe your accustomed affection to be suche towards me, as you will take these my poore endevors in good parte, they beinge intended by me for the good of ye churche of god, Thus hartely wishinge unto yor Fatherhoode all comforts temporall and eternall, I ende

Yor thanckfull godsonn,

HP

---

[3] Richard Haddock (1552–1605), priest. For an overview of his life, see above pp. 17–18.
[4] 'hai[ ]nous' inserted.
[5] *Recte* 'person'.
[6] 'for' inserted.

(2) **The preamble to the followinge Discourse**

Havinge made due consideration wt my self of the manifolde benefitts wch god of his infinitt goodnes hathe from my infancie hetherto bestowed upon me, I doe finde tribulation to be one of the greatest of them, wt the wch I have bene exercised in one degree or other, Since the tyme[7] I was of discretion to conceave of troubles, untill now that[8] I am seaven and thirtie yeares of adge, and I have proved by experience, that those crosses wch seemed moste greevous unto me, have afterwards bene converted unto my greatest comforte for my many troubles (not necessarie here to be rehearsed, beinge diligently considered of) have holpen me to knowe my self and to diserne the dangerouse estate where in my Soule was a longe tyme nurished and insnared,

And I must confess that I was greatly furthered herein by perce-vinge[9] at my beinge in England divers religions and hearinge of there preachers contradict one another in matter of faithe, about wch tyme I was at a great contention wt my self to what parte I should incline, for my parentts, my wife and hir frends beinge protestants and of great account in this Comon welthe did incurradge me to houlde wt them, On the other the accquaintance wch I gatt, with divers Catholicks, by reason of my Sisters marriadge wt a Catholicke gentle-man [*Mary Piers Thomas Jans*] joyned wt the above named respects, did drawe me to the better inclynation, the wch brede dillicke[10] in my greatest frends of me, and then did[11] occurr unto me, as it weare in a mathimaticall pointe, divers occations of discontent the wch[12] weare as Conditions necessarie for the generatinge of a forme of true Religion in me, and Coruptinge of the Contrarie,

But as stately buildings doe require to have there stones well heaved and Squared, fyne Clothe the wooll well Spunn and Carded, soe it is requisitt that the children of god doe suffer adversi-tie before they be made fitt members for his kingdom, for it houldeth noe good proportion that man beinge borne weepinge and dyinge[13] sighinge, shoulde lyve continually in pleasure and (3) laghinge and althoughe that my afflictions have not as yett bene correspondent unto my diserts, yett woulde they farr have exceeded my patience had not god of his unspeakable mercy assisted me wt his grace,

---

[7] 'that' deleted.
[8] 'that' inserted.
[9] Phrase emended; originally 'be seeing'.
[10] Probably 'dislicke': dislike, meaning disapproval, *OED*.
[11] 'did' inserted.
[12] 'which' inserted.
[13] 'dyinge' inserted.

and[14] directed me to the Scoole of his truthe, where all kinde of vertues are to be learned, in the wch place (by his Fatherly assistance) I
endevored to[15] gett som Smale portion of knowledge, accordinge the
tenuitie of my witt and capacitie as hereafter shall more at lardge
appeere in the discourse of my travells, of ye wch god himself was
ye efficent cause and ye finall cause ye obtaininge of true Religion,
wch is the gate of Salvation and for myne owne parte I may well
rejoyce at my passed tribulations and I looke for noe other, but
that I shall have more of them hereafter inflicted upon me, ye wch
I hope shall serve for a parte of my purgatorie, and beinge taken
patiently shall I doubt not advance my Soule towards ye heavens
as ye great waters did the Arke of Noe,[16] But because that all actions
must begine in tyme and that in tyme opportunitie must be sought
for, I made use of my outward Sences whoe havinge found her
posted messengers unto ye inward Sences and imaginations whoe
presented her unto my understandinge will and memorie, wch are
ye po[w]ers of ye Soule; ye wch eternall Substance beinge then in
desperatt estate, and meetinge soe necessarie a guide, was right
glade to be carried unto ye place in ye wch ye Shipp wherein shee
Sayled might be newly trymmed and rigged, and hir pilate well
instructed to direct hir unto ye haven of everlastinge happines,

Nowe for as muche as noe motion can be wtout a place from ye
wch and to ye wch it should be lymitted, I made choise of Dublin
to be ye one and Rome ye other, beinge assisted therin by an
Alderman at Dublin[17] [*James Jans*] whoe for that cause Sustayned
after my departure a longe imprisonment to his great hinderance,
and soe not wtout many difficulties then occurringe leavinge behinde
me, my parents, wife and children, lands, and an office of creditt, I
undertooke my jornye, of the whiche I have in my rude manner here
followinge sett downe a true declaration partely for my owne
Satisfaction, and partely for ye good of those either travellers or others wch shall peruse the Same.

---

[14] 'and' inserted.

[15] Word is located at end of line; 'to' repeated at start of following line.

[16] The story of how Noah survived the flood is recounted in Genesis:6–8.

[17] 'to be the one ... at Dublin' inserted; 'James Jans' in margin; on Alderman James Jans
(d.1610), of Dublin, brother of Thomas Jans who married Mary Piers, Henry's sister, see
prosopography of Dublin aldermen, Colm Lennon, *The Lords of Dublin in the Age of
Reformation* (Dublin, 1989), 258.

(4) A true Reporte of my travells begune on whitson Monday whiche was on the ixth of June and in the yeere of oure lo: god 1595.

Wee[18] weare embarcked nighe Dublin about fowre of the clocke in the afternoone in the day and yeere above named, and weare greatly indangered in strickinge upon the barr, wch happened by reason that wee stayed untill the tyde was almoste spente, for poste letters wch weare sente into England by the nowe lo: Rusell[19] then lo: deputie of Ireland, and havinge by the omnipotente power of the holy ghoste (whose feast then was celebrated) passed that brunt wee Sayled forward, landinge at Hilbrie the xith of the same monthe, From thence the xiith day to the Cittie of Chester, The xiiith wee tooke oure journie to Nantwiche; the xiiiith to Seds[a]lle[20] where I was kindely intertained by Mr Draycott Father unto Phillip Draycott,[21] whoe before that tyme was my servant, and from thence did undertake this travell with me, The xviiith we travelled from thence to Darby, The xixth to Lester, The xxth to Narthampton, The xxiith to Ouborne [Woburn], The xxiith to the Famous Cittie of London, wch is soe well knowen to oure contrimen, wth the rest of[22] the citties of England which I passed throughe, that I neede not make any discription of them,

The xxviiith we wente in a tilt[23] boate from London to Graves ende [Gravesend], wheare beinge in oure Inn there happened som gent. to be present, wch toulde us that the lo: Burrogh[24] was at Margatt [Margate] expectinge a wynde for to Saile into the Lowe Contries, whereupon we hired horsses wch in all haste weare prepared for us

[18] Change of hand.

[19] Sir William Russell (c.1553–1613), 1st Baron Russell, lord deputy of Ireland, 1594–1597, *DIB*.

[20] Sedsall, Derbyshire; it lies on the River Dove, on the border with Staffordshire, about a mile south of Rocester.

[21] Philip Draycott (1573/75–1598), of Lichfield diocese; entered English College, Rome, 4 Oct. 1595; took college oath, 10 Aug. 1596; took minor orders, 25 Aug. 1596, Wilfrid Kelly (ed.), *Liber Ruber Venerabilis Collegii Anglorum de Urbe; I Annales Collegii Pars Prima. Nomina Alumnorum (1579–1630)* (London, 1940), 100; of Derby, Archivum Venerabilis Collegii Anglorum de Urbe, Liber 282, 33; entered Society of Jesus 12 Apr. 1598 in novitiate, S. Andrea, Rome, and died there 14 Aug. 1598, Archivum Romanum Societatis Iesu, Rom. 172, fo. 25r, and Rom. 162 I, fo. 168v.

[22] Word located at end of line; 'of' repeated at start of succeeding line.

[23] 'tilt' inserted; 'litle' deleted; 'a large rowing boat having a tilt or awning, formerly used on the Thames, especially as a passenger boat between London and Gravesend', *OED*.

[24] Spelling amended; Thomas Burgh (c.1558–1597), 3rd Lord Burgh, succeeded to title in 1584; governor of Den Briel (Brielle or Brill) in the Netherlands, 1586/7 to 1597; lord deputy of Ireland 18 Apr. 1597, and died 14 Oct. 1597 in Newry, Ireland, G.E. Cokayne, *The Complete Peerage of England, Scotland, Ireland, Great Britain, and the United Kingdom*, 8 vols (London, 1887–1898), II, 424.

and that day we ridd throughe Rochester and Canterburie, and soe that night to Margatt, there (findinge noe Shippinge but the vessell which was to carrie himselfe and his attendance)[25] wee (5) weare dryven into an uncertaine determination whether we shoulde goe backe to London, travell[26] forward to Dover or speake wth my lo: Burgh[27] wth whom we had noe acquaintance, after we had continued som two dayes in this demurre, we might perceave a Shipp bearinge in towards the lande, which sente hir cockeboate a shoare to take in breade and water, and seeinge they weare dutche men we desired[28] oure hoaste to tell them that we weare to passe[29] for the lowe contries, and did wish[30] muche to be embarked wth them, the wch they did willinglie performe, soe as it shoulde seeme that god did of purpose sende them to transporte us over the Seas, and therefore I doe nowe knowe this his omniptencie did here my praiers, [*A conditionall petition*] for before my departure from this lande I did often make humble petition unto his heavenly Ma[jes]tie that seeinge my intent was knowen unto him, it woulde please him to prosper[e] my jornye, soe as it weare for the good of my Soule, otherwyse to give me som suche crosse as shoulde staye me from that travell by me intended.

on the first daye of July we tooke Shippinge from thence with the said Dutchmen named Cornelius Peeterson, a man of warr whose Shipp was called the Hope of Raterdam, who used us verie kindely; [*A Dutche myle is 3 Englishe myle*] but we did hardly escape in oure passadge from the Dunkirks wch did hotely pursue oure Shippe, and soe we Sayled throughe the Sounde of Mai[t]e, and aryved the thirde daye of the same at Brill [Brielle], the wch Towne is verie well skonsed and fortified The lo: Boorgh was then lo: Governour ther, and had five companies of Englishe men for the defence of the same, [*Holland*] the iiiith we went by water to Roterdam and passed by Delphe haven [Delfshaven] Sukerdam [Schiedam?] and other townes [*Calvenisticall government*] At Roterdam, is the portrature of Erasmus carved in Stone it standethe alofte upon a Bridge in the marckett place gravely readinge upon a booke right under him are ingraven these words, Erasmus natus Roterdamiae Octobris 28 Anno Salutis 1477 obiit Basiliae xii July Anno domini 1536, In Ratherdam we sawe the (6) corpes of a man a woman and a childe founde by a dutche man in a parte of Tartaria, whiche by computation hathe bene wthout inhabitants this three hundred and odd yeeres, the corpes as it is constantly affirmed, weare founde in a hallowe cave and

---

[25] 'and his attendance' inserted.
[26] 'or to goe' deleted.
[27] Name erased; 'Burgh' inserted.
[28] 'willed' deleted; 'desired' inserted.
[29] 'goe' deleted; 'passe' inserted.
[30] 'desire' deleted; 'wish' inserted.

weare brought into Spaine and from thence[31] thether, there bodies weare
as then unconsumed, there teethe standinge in there heades, all there
joynts perfecte, their flesh[e] shruncke from betwene the skine and the
bone, and that wch was strangeste of all, the heare of the boyes heade,
was as faste as if he had bene leevinge,

[*Zeland*] The same daie we toke hoye for Midlboroughe [Middelburg]
and landed there the vi of the same month[32] in oure waye we passed by
[S]tembargau[33] Champheere [Campvere, Veere] and Arumse
[Arnemuiden]; upon the coste of Zelande there hathe bene drowned
twentie myles in leinth divers townes; the steeples and churches whereof
are yett to be seene in the water. at this towne the Englishe marchants
had then there marte The eight day we tooke waggon for Flushinge
[Dutch: Vlissingen] wch towne is mightily well fortified, and had for garrison eleven companies of Englishmen, Sir Robt Sidny[34] nowe lo: Sidny
beinge then lord governoure there, The same day we tooke hoye for
Roterdam, and passed by the Ramykins [Ramekins][35] wch is a castle
verie stronge wherein lay a garrison of Englishe and soe coasted by
Portelane and Lurdane,[36] arryvinge the xth daie of the same monthe
at Roterdam, the 14 daie we wente from thence to Delphe [Delft] we
sawe there a great peece of Ordinance being eight footte aboute the
breeche, five footte aboute the nose, twelve footte in lenithe, and of ix
thousande three hundred[37] weight; we toke oure jorney the same daye
to Haye [The Hague] where the states doe keepe there courte, there
we sawe a Giants bone from the shoulder to the elboe anell[38] longe at
leaste, it is reported that he made a mightie moate wch is adjoyninge
to the courte, one of the goodgins[39] of the wheele barrowe wth the
wch he wrought is there to be sene, beinge five footte longe, and (7)
twoo footte about: this to[wn]e standethe verie plesantly and hathe
many fayre walks of the wch one is in lenithe eight hundred paces,

The xvth day we returned to Roterdam, The xvith[40] we went to see
Dorte [Dordrecht] and came backe againe to Roterdam, This cittie

---

[31] 'Spaine' erased; 'thence' inserted.

[32] 'month' inserted.

[33] Possibly 'Sandenburgh': a castle on outskirts of Veere.

[34] Robert Sidney (1563–1626), 1st earl of Leicester, soldier; was named governor of
Flushing (Dutch: Vlissingen) in 1589, and served there until 1603, *ODNB*.

[35] Lies on the coast just east of Flushing.

[36] Place names uncertain; as given here by Piers, these words have the echo respectively
of 'portolan': 'a book of sailing directions, describing harbours, sea-coasts etc. and illus-
trated with charts', *OED*; and 'lurdan': 'a dull, idle, fellow', *OED*.

[37] 'pounde' deleted.

[38] Ell: 'a measure of length varying in different countries', *OED*.

[39] Gudgeon: 'a pivot, usually of metal, fixed on or let into the end of a beam, spindle,
axle etc, and on which a wheel turns', *OED*.

[40] 'daie' deleted.

of Dort[41] is an Iland of it selfe, where the states have there store howse of there best artillerie the inhabitants there have recovered out of the Sea wth greate paines cost and industrie[42] as good as twelve thousand acres of lande, The xviith daie we journyed to the cittie of Layden [Leiden] where there is an universitie of Calvenists;[43] there they have noe colledges for the Schollers are boorded amonge the burgers amonge other thinges of noate there is there to be harde a very sweete and [tune]able chyme of bells[44] The 18[th][45] to Harlum [Haarlem] wch cittie is the moste antient in that contrie, it hathe the greateste liberties and the faireste churche, in this cittie, and in many other citties and townes in Hollande are a multitude of ana-baptistes whose heresie is moste absurd and wicked[46] the same daye we went from thence to Amsterdam, wch is the greateste and ritcheste cittie in all Holland, there trade is soe great that there belongethe unto them at least a thowsand Shipps beside a wonderfull number of smale vessells, there we sawe a camylian wch livethe by the ayre, and changethe himselfe unto all cullors, exceptinge whyte, in the same place we sawe barbary ratts wth graye cullor and blacke spotts, This contrie in generall is exceedinge ritche full of Shippinge and trafficke, there houses all of Bryke, there churches verie fayre, with many sweete cheems,[47] The Sea and dyvers other waters are farr higher then the land, yett are kept out wth mayne force, all religions in that contrie are[48] tollerated;

[*A pounde Flemishe is xii s str*] at Norden [Naarden] (not farr from Amsterdam) weare then dwellinge divers brownings[49] and Barrones[50] wch weare fledd out of England for there conscience, And (as it was toulde us there) they had brought over with them two ministers one of the wch gatt a mayde of thers wth child and for that cause was banished from there congregation (8) the other beinge of a whueringe disposition forsooke them and became an

---

[41] 'of Dort' inserted.
[42] 'with great paines cost and industrie' inserted.
[43] 'of Calvenists' inserted; 'an excellent chime of bells' deleted.
[44] 'amonge other thinges … of bells' inserted.
[45] 'daie' deleted.
[46] 'whose … wicked' inserted.
[47] Probably 'chimes'.
[48] 'are' inserted.
[49] A reference to the followers of Robert Browne (1550?–1633), religious separatist; in May–Aug. 1582, official coercion impelled Browne's congregation to emigrate from England to Middelburg, in the Netherlands, *ODNB*.
[50] Barrowist: 'one who followed, or held the tenets of, Henry Barrowe, one of the founders of Independency or Congregationalism, executed along with John Greenwood, in 1593, for nonconformity to the Church of England', *OED*; Henry Barrow (*c*.1550–1593), *ODNB*; contemporaries linked the followers of Browne and of Barrow, 'Brownist', *OED*.

anabaptiste the wch mutabillitie and inconstancie in matter of faithe must of necessitie be founde in them, [*The cawse of inconstancie in matter of faithe*] for they will have the Scriptures to be understoode, accordinge the conceite of their privatte spiritts, in the wch there is possibillitie and licklihoode of erroure, and doe not submitt themselves unto the censure of the Catholicke Churche, whose disfinitie judgment in expoundinge the Booke of god, is infallible for that it is guided by the holy ghoste, whoe is the teacher of all truethe

The 23 day wee departed from Amsterdam in a hoye and passed by Edam horne [Hoorn] Arusum [Enkhuizen] and Memlicke [Medemblik] beinge in hollande, and soe passed over the Sowre Sea [Zuider Zee], by [W]arckline [Workum] and Maukline [Makkum] in Frizlande [Friesland], leavinge the Flye [Vlieland, island] and the Tes[f]ell [Texel, island] on the lifte hande, nighe unto the wch (as it was reported unto us) the Dunkirks[51] doe manie roberies, [*Frizlande*] and landed the 24[th][52] at Harlyne [Harlingen], From thence the same daye we tooke waggin throughe Fray[ne] [Franeker] to Lewerd[in] [Leeuwarden], this is the cheefe cittie of Frizlande

The 25th daye we went to Groyninge [Groningen] wch is the principall[53] cittie of that contrie, it was at that tyme twelve monthe, or there abouts wone by grave Morishe from ye Spainards,[54] [*Groyninge lande*] the inhabitants of that contrie maye not buy[55] or sell wth any stranger not havinge the lysence of the Cittie. From thence we tooke Skeeffe the same daye and landed the 26th day at Dellsfill[ge] [Delfzijl] and passed throughe a place called dames from thence we tooke hoye and landed at Emden. [*At Emden, westfalia beginethe one myle there is vi Englishe myles*] the cittizens there have lately befor that bene at Mutinie against there Earle, for that he would have reformed them unto the Catholicke religion; [*The Earldom of Emden*] this Cittie is verie well fortified, the Jewes there have[56] Synagoges allowed them, The Churches of Holland Zeland Frizland Groyninge land, and Emden weare at that time governed by Calvenists, the Catholicks in those contries have libertie of coscience, and soe have all religions whatsoever; the same daye we tooke waggin and passed by a fayer house of the Earle of Emdens called (9) Stickhousen wch is verie well fortified, [*A pounde Ouldenbourge is xiis ixd str*] and travelled all that night to

---

[51] Privateers in the service of the Spanish monarchy during the Dutch revolt (1568–1648).
[52] 'daie' deleted.
[53] 'chieffe' deleted; 'principall' inserted.
[54] In May–June 1594, Prince Maurice of Orange successfully besieged Groningen, held by the Spanish.
[55] 'buy' inserted.
[56] 'there' deleted.

Ouldenbourge [Oldenburg] wch is the cheeffe cittie of all[57] that contrie, [*the Earldum of Oulderbourge*] and is governed by an Earle this Soille is full of woode and heathe; [*Lutheran Government*] here the government of the Calvenists dothe ende, and here beginneth the Lutherane Government

[*Bremer Lande*] The 27th daye we went to the Cittie of Breme [Bremen], and passed by a fayre and well fortified house, of the grave of Ouldenbourges Brother named Dalmanhurste; Bream hathe nyne bridges to be passed[58] over befor you inter the towne, it is governed by the Duke vanhoulte [Von Holstein] wch was elected there Bisshope. there is a great house covered wth Copper and there Steeple [ ]peares wth the licke. The 28[th59] wee Jornyed to Tremule; The 29th daye we came to Stode [Stade] there the Englishe merchants have a marte by there means that towne is growen to good welthe, wch before was but of smale account, [*At Hamboorge doe begine Loe Saxonie a Germayne myle is v Englishe myle*] The 30[th60] we tooke hoye for Hamboorge [Hamburg] and landed there that[61] same daye, leaving Bremer lande on the right hande, and the lande of hoults [Holstein] on the lifte, the Boorgers there dothe governe bothe the Cittie and the Contrie, in ye wch it is deathe for a boore to kill a hare, the reason moveinge them for the makinge of this lawe, was to preserve game for the recreation of the better sorte, The last[62] daye we toke waggine to Lubicke [Lübeck] wch is a Cittie of great antiquitie, and a free state, beinge exceedinglie well fortified, the Ryver Elve [Elbe] runninge thrise aboute the same, it hathe divers fayre and Sumpteuous Churches, [*A rare clocke*] amongste the wch in Oure Ladies church is a notable rare Clocke having a fyne and melodious[63] chyme; In the tope of it is the picture of Christe, wth an angelle on bothe syds, wch sounde trumpetts by arte, at wch tyme[64] an artificiall man dothe open a doore, wheare out doe issue in order the twelve apostles, doinge loelye[65] reverence unto Christe, as they passe by; whoe to everie of them dothe beacken with his (10) head, next, beneathe is a globe of the whole worlde in the wch all the planetts have bothe there naturall, and violent motions,

---

[57] 'all' inserted.
[58] 'to be passed' inserted.
[59] 'daye' deleted.
[60] 'daye' deleted.
[61] 'that' inserted.
[62] 'xxxith' deleted; 'last' inserted.
[63] 'and melodious' inserted.
[64] 'tyme' inserted.
[65] Change from 'loe' to 'loely'.

The second of August we departed from thence throughe Mullum [Mölln] a towne belonginge unto Lubicke and environes[66] wth the s[am]e ryver to Orsumboorge, The thirde daye we travelled to Allneboorge a house of the Duke of Saxonie and passethe wth oure Cotche and horsses over eleve [Elbe] in a boate to Artlamboorge [Artlenburg] from thence over the Ryver Neats [Neetze]. one of the boats of the wch river will carrye ten carts laden at once; [*The Dukedum of Lunaboorge*] and soe to L[u]naboorge [Lüneburg] wch is a verie antient Cittie, there is a hill upon wch in tymes paste the moone hathe bene worshipped wch was because why that cittie was soe caled[67] wheare nowe standethe a stronge Castle, there they have there cheefest provition of artillerie, and have divers Conveyances under grownde a farr waye into the Contrie, with wonderfull Stratagems for warr, it is p[res]ent deathe for any man to inter the Castle of that hill, wthout lysence of the Roders, wch be the cheeffe officers of that Cittie;

we wente into the Rode house wch is a place of great account there, firste we came into a fayre Chamber wch is there Councell place whearein the Couldest daye of winter they are warmed wth a device under there feete, neither fyre nor smoake being in any sorte perceaved; we sawe in Cuppurds ii C ii xx peeces of plate, at leaste whereof halfe weare mightie Cupes broade boules and Salt [s], moste of them double gilte and curiouslye wrought also three lyons of silver an Elephants tooth of an ell longe, and two spaunes[68] about the mouthe, one Cupp a yeard highe a peece halfe yeard broade, soe passed we into a lardge Chamber of fiftie paces longe; rounde about the wch are the pictures of soe manie as have bene Duks of there Cittie tyme out mynde, and a recorde of the houses wch they have matched in, under that is agreat armorie furnished wth muche and costlie armoure;

then went we into a Chamber wheare there Causes of greatest secrecie and state are handled this roome is decked wth rare and Costlye workmanshipp, (11) over one of the doores is moste lively and artificially carved in woode the daye of iudgment, this is soe rarely compacted and soe Cunninglye carved as it is thought it cannot be mended by any man livinge, next is moste curiouslye drawen Allexanders Conqueste, then a Shipp of great wonder, at the Sterne of wch[69] sittethe god the Father upon a gloabe of the worlde deliveringe a goulden bale resemblinge the world unto his Sonn, next unto

---

[66] 'and environes' inserted.
[67] 'wch was because why that cittie was soe caled' interlined.
[68] Perhaps 'spannes'.
[69] 'of wch' inserted.

them in order doe stande (soe there named) Duo confirmator[es],
Saint Peeter and Saint Paule, then pax and Concordia, embrasinge
the mayne maste betwixt them, and kissinge eache other, over whose
heads on the tope maste sittethe the holye ghoste. Upon the prove
the Prophett David firste wth his harpe, Moses next wth the table
of the Lawe, then Janus receavinge a sworde from Noe whoe sittethe
on the spiritte maste, the Roers of this Shippe are the fowre mon-
arches wth there wives, nighe unto them in the Sea are Swyminge
Covetuosnes, hatred, wrathe and Pryde, pullinge and haelinge
moste lively at the Shipp, endevoringe to drowne it before, in another
pte of the chamḅer oure Savioure is pictured sittinge upon the
worlde, and under his feete written give place to none, over him is
peace spreddinge of hir hands abroad, above hir is wysdom strock-
inge of hir head at the right hande of peace in degrees upward sitt
honnor, Pietie truethe, and fortitude, on the lifte hande in oppositte
sorte s[a]te glorie, honestie, chastetie, and Consta[n]tie, next unto
them on[e] the Right hande faithe hope and Charitie, and one the
lifte hande Justice temperance and ma[jes]tie, wth many other
worcks of marvaile and wonderfull rare conceite, wch by reason of
the brevitie of the tyme we coulde not have leasure to peruse,

[*A sumptuous altar*] moreover we sawe there in Sainte Michaell his
Churche a gordgious and a Costlye alter, in the mideste of wch is
placed a puer goulden table in lenithe one yeard iii qz in breadthe
one yeard (12) halfe quarter, therein is the picture of Christe and the
twelve apostles moste curiouslye framed, it is sett wth diamonds
Rubyes Sapheers and other pretious ston[e]s to the number of three
hundred at leaste, the thicknes I could not[70] learne the value is exceedinge greate, and in a manner unestymable, it was gyven unto that
Churche by Othoe Emperour of Rome wch[71] was Duke of
Brumswicke and Lunaboorge; there are divers crosses in that alter
moste Ritchlie sett wth stone; in that Cittie there is whyte Salte
made wch doth serve agreate parte of Germany and other Contries
besyde there are fiftie foure houses that makethe Salte and in[72] everie
one of them are foure pann[er]s, this Cittie is full of Springs invironed
double wth water, and stronge fortfied wales, they are governed by
twoe Roders Certaine Judges and foure [B]oo[rg]ers, The fifte daye
we wente to Ensye wch is within the Dukedom of Lunaboorge,

The vi[73] we passed throughe Gistearne [Gifhorn] wheare the Duke
of Lunaboorge hath a fayer dwellinge house, [*The Dukedum of*

---

[70] 'not' inserted in margin.
[71] 'wch' inserted.
[72] 'in' inserted.
[73] 'daye' deleted.

Brumswicke] and came that day to Brumswicke [Brunswick, German: Braunschweig], this is a cittie of exceedinge streinght, it hathe a great moate thrice about it a[74] woode wale and a stone wale, wth three gates at everie entrance. over eache gate is[75] a towre planted wth iii tyers of[76] ordinance, and betwixte everie twoe gates a drawe Brydge, The viith we went to Wollsfumbeetle [Wolfenbüttel] wheare then the Duke of Brumswicke laye, this hathe a moate five tymes about it, and is wonderfull stronge, that night we returned to Brumswicke. moste of the Citties and villadges wch we passed throughe in Germany, before we came thither, have the doores of there houses soe great that we might easilye passe in wth oure Coatches and horsses. there I bought a cople of nagges[77] to carrye us onwarde in oure Jornye, The viiith we tooke horsse to Wolfumbeetle wheare we weare kindely intertayned by certaine Englishmen wch then served the Duke, The ixth daye to Alverstate [Halberstadt] Cittie passinge through Esume wheare the olde Dutches of Brumswicke dwelleth; the Duke of Brumswicke was[78] ther there[79] Bisshope; wheareby we maye plainely perceave the fruite of Luther his doctryne, by the wch the laitie are warranted to enioye spirituall promotions,

[*The Dukedum of Turingae*] The 10th daye wee passed throughe Mansfielde [Mansfeld], where grave Mansfielde[80] dwellethe in the wch towne theare is great store of leade made, and came that night to the Cittie of Islevyn [Eisleben], ther (13) Martine Luther was borne and there he died whose levine was soe corrupted as it hathe putrified the stomacks of all those wch hitherto have tasted thereof, [*Luther a supposed apostle*] And trulye if his fellowes woulde wth indifferencie consider of the comminge of there supposed apostle unto them, they shoulde easilie perceave howe muche theye are deceaved in him; for in the Newe Testament it is manifestlye seene that the true apostles had there Commission (for the Convertinge of Contries) from Christe himselfe that they wrought great miracles and weare men of moste Chaste life and verteous Carriadge. After whose departure it is well knowen to men of readinge and understan-dinge that all the regions brought unto the knowledge of the Christian faithe, weare instructed by suche holye and pure men of

---

[74] 'a' inserted.
[75] 'is' inserted.
[76] 'iii tyers of' inserted.
[77] 'a cople of nagges' inserted; 'horses' deleted.
[78] 'is' deleted.
[79] 'there' inserted.
[80] There were several military figures in this family, including Peter-Ernst von Mansfeld (1517–1604), governor of Spanish Netherlands, 1592–1594.

life as weare sente for that purpose from tyme to tyme by the severall Popes of Rome, as for example Sainte Dennis sente by Pope Clemente the firste for the Convertinge of France; Sainte Austine by Pope Gregorie the great for same end to Englande,[81] Saint Pathricke by Pope Caelestinus for drawinge of this Realme of Eirland [Ireland] unto the Catholicke faithe; this aucthoritie the Busshoppes of Rome have allwayes exercised as legatts constituted by oure Savioure, havinge receaved there Commission as successors to Sainte Peeter[82] in these words Pasce oves meas, [*Joan. 21*] feede my sheepe,[83] but that Luther was not sente by extraordinarie mission from Christe it is evident, for firste he did noe Myrackles, unlesse it weare in sendinge of thowsands of people headlonge unto the bottomlesse pitt of hell, Secondlye he was not Chaste for he beinge a fryer Comitted spirituall inceste and used a Nunn called Katherin boer, as his wife, not regardinge the admonition of the Princlye Prophett David, where he saithe, Redde altissimo vota tua, paie thy vowes unto the moste highe,[84] [*Psal 49*] the wch includethe that he was of noe verteous behavioure And that he was not sente by ordinarie means It moste manifestlye appeerethe, seeing that he had not his letters Pattents from the Sea apostolicke. This beinge thus proved (14) it cannott be but that he came directly from the Divell, for the augmentinge of the kingdom of Satan, and hathe brought with him suche a pestiferous desease as hathe wounded the Soules of an numerable companie of Christians with an uncurable plague

About the tyme of my beinge in Germanye there was agreat overthrowe gyven upon the Turks by the Christians, at the wynninge of Strigonia [Esztergom, Hungary], Grave Mansfield beinge then generall of oure Christian[85] forces

The xith daie we miste oure waye by reason of great thunder lightninge and rayne wch then befell, and happened upon a dorpe or villadge called Musticke, [*An escape from emynent danger:*] wheare by the myraculous worcke of god we weare delivered from emynent murder, for they of the house whearein we lodged called a companie of uglie fellowes in after Supper wch woulde have forced us to drincke more beere then was convenient for us, and woulde have perswaded us to

---

[81] 'convertinge of' deleted.
[82] 'Peeter' inserted.
[83] John 21:17.
[84] Psalm 49 (50):14.
[85] 'Christian' inserted; Karl von Mansfeld (1543–1595), general who participated in siege of Esztergom, and died shortly afterwards, 24 Aug. 1595. On the renewed military conflict (1593–1606) between Ottoman and Imperial forces in Hungary, see Fernand Braudel, *The Mediterranean and the Mediterranean World in the Age of Philip II*, 2 vols (London, 1973), II, 1196–1204.

lye in the roome whearein they weare[86] drinckinge, wheare by all
probable coniecture they did meane to murder us, but we perceavinge there drifte, with muche adoe gatte forthe and laye in the stable
wheare oure horsses stoode, and least they shoulde have brocken in
upon us in the night, we putt oure Saddles to the doore, and used
them in steede of pillowes, and after this restlesse night was passed
over, we rose and did endevoure to oppen the doore but they made
it faste by settinge a hanginge locke in the out syde of it, at lenithe
after many Callings the good wife of the house unlocked the doore,
and woulde have had us to goe into the roome wheare we weare over-
night to drincke buttered beere with those villanous Companions, The
wch we refused to doe, and craved of hir a reckninge wheareupon shee
called forthe hir husbande and others, and demaunded a som of mony
farr exceedinge the worthe of any thinge which we had receaved of
them, affirminge that we had golde the wch they woulde gladlye
have changed. the goodman of the house lookinge verie earnestlye
at oure cloakebagg and Portemantewe and tossinge them wth his
feete, wherein it shoulde seeme (15) he supposed there was some boutie
fitt for his purpose, The Circumstances considered, I desired him to
sende for the Priste of the towne whoe might make up the —[87] accompt
betwixt us, wch he promised to doe, and after longe expectation we
might see a[88] couple of great illfavored fellowes come in wth terrible
countenance havinge axes in there hands, and we demaundinge wheare
was the Prieste, he answeared pointinge unto them this is the Prieste;
and I doe not doubt but they came to here oure last confession, as
might well appeere by there whisperinge and compassinge us aboute,
soe as by all licklyhoode they had knocked us downe wth there[89]
hatch[tt]s had we not bene upon oure keepinge, wth oure pistolls
ready chardged, when they sawe themselves soe prevented, they
tooke whate mony they pleased of us for oure homely dyett, and
asked of us wch waye we woulde travell, I toulde them to Islevin
[Eisleben]. wheareupon we perceaved som of them goinge that waye
wth there hattchetts upon there shoulders, but we made frustratte
there intention in takinge of a contrarie[90] course; in the greateste of
this extremitie I did make my humble petition unto god that I
might not dye untill I had seene Rome, the wch I obtained at his gratious hands, greatly to my comforte. and therefor I maye well saye wth

<hr>

[86] 'weare' inserted.
[87] Two letters deleted.
[88] 'a' inserted.
[89] 'there' inserted.
[90] 'waye' deleted.

the Prophett David, ad dominum cum tribularer clamavi exudivitt me, [*Psall: 58*] I cryed unto god in my trouble and he[91] heard my voyce,

The xiith daye we passed throughe Hechesperia, wheare the Duke of Turingae hathe a house and that night we came to Ihena [Jena], here is an universitie havinge only one colledge, it is a cittie belonginge to the Duke of Turinga whoe then was protector of the yonge Duke of Saxonie, my oaste wheare we laye in this towne beinge a Lutheran suspected that I was a Prieste, and lately com from Rome, and therefor by reason of his blinde zeale did refuse to lodge us, but after understandinge that we came from Englande he changed his opinion, and affirmed that we weare Calvenists wheareupon I demaunded what opinion he held of (16) Calvenists wheareupon he aunsweared that he loved Calvenists as little as he did[92] Papists, but because he was noe magistratte we refused to answeare directly to any of his questions, and therefor had not ye[93] Schollers which then weare by intreated him for us, we had bene without lodginge there that night; heare havinge considered the wante of unitie which I perceaved to be betwixt the Lutherans, Calvenistes,[94] Anabaptists, and other newe sects, and[95] the difference which is amongste them in essentiall points of Faithe, I did fullye resolve to forsake the religion which I was brought up in, and to be a Catholicke which afterwards by the assistance of the holie ghoste I performed [*An absolute Resolution – well grounded upon ye [opinion] of an Inkeeper It seems ye religion you were bred in lost a syncere professor yt left it on so sleight an occasion.*][96]

The xiiith day to Cala [Kahla], The xiiiith throughe Ulstate [Uhlstadt] and Rudlestate [Rudolstadt], wheare Grave harlott dwellethe to Sallvelte and that night to Gravatoll [Gratenthal], wch townes[97] stande seated in a vallewe wth mightie Mountaines one eache syde The Ryver Zola [Saale] runninge by them. Gravatolly is situated[98] verie stranglye in a bottom inclosed wth hudge hills growinge full of ewe,[99] [*the [king]dom[100] of Franconya*] The xvth to the cittie of Nesta[b]le [Neustadt bei Coburg] there I founde an oulde booke of armes, [*the Armes of Christe*] in the beginninge of wch was verie fayrlie sett down the armes of Christe, whearin his five wounds and the

---

[91] 'he' inserted; *recte* Psalm 119 (120):1.
[92] 'did' inserted.
[93] 'ye' inserted.
[94] 'Protestants' deleted.
[95] 'and' inserted; 'for' deleted.
[96] 'well grounded … an occasion' different hand; this material deleted.
[97] 'townes' inserted.
[98] 'is situated' inserted; 'standethe' deleted.
[99] 'ewe': a form of 'yew', *OED*.
[100] Word emended.

instrumts of his deathe weare quartered, [*the Armes of Ireland*] and in another pte of the booke the armes of Ireland, wch there was sett downe to be halfe a spred Eagle, in a Scuttchion parted by pale, and a hande houldinge a speare in the other syde thereof, The xvith to the Cittie of Cowbroocke [Coburg] nighe unto the wch upon a great hill standethe a stately house of Duke Cassimere, and from thence the same daye unto the Cittie of Pambrocke wheare the saide Duke hathe another house builded[101] in licke sorte +

[+ *In oure way towards Nerumboorge we mett wth the Earle of Sussex*[102] *whoe then was returninge homewards from Italy*][103]

The xviith throughe[104] Fortin[u]m unto Noremboorge [Nuremberg] wch is a free Cittie all builte verie fayre of Stone and walled foure times about wth the same theye maie bringe the Ryver Pengres [Pegnitz] wch runnethe throughe it, Rounde about the cittie in the middste of the fowre wales when they will[105] there is a sumpteous crosse, and a curious condacte;[106] In the cheefe markett place of the same, in Sainte Lawrence his churche within that city[107] is an exceedinge curious and rare worcke of Stone wch continued three mens lyves[108] in makinge, viz: the grande Father the Father and the Sonn, it is (17) from the bottom of the Churche to the tope in leinthe and all of one Stone, as it is reported; at the nether[109] part wheareof there are three cupords, whearein is kept there Sacrament, in all the other worckmanshippe upwards is cuningly ingraved[110] the birthe, liffe and passion of Christe moste lyvely and artificially[111] sett forthe, in the same churche there is a well adorned[112] altar under the wch is buried a servante of one of the cheefe[113] cittizens wch was[114] by his mr wrongfuly[115] accused for stealthe, and executed for the same accordinge to the lawe of Germany: wch is that malefactors shoulde

---

[101] 'builded' inserted; 'situated' deleted.

[102] Robert Radcliffe (1573–1629), 10th earl of Sussex; succeeded to title in 1593; colonel of foot regiment in the Cadiz expedition, 1596. Cokayne *The Complete Peerage*, XI, 526–528.

[103] Marginal material in different hand.

[104] 'the cittie of' deleted.

[105] Phrase inserted, and then deleted.

[106] 'condacte': probably variant of 'conduct', 'an artificial channel for the conveyance of water or other liquid', *OED*.

[107] 'within that city' inserted.

[108] 'lyves' inserted.

[109] 'nether' inserted; 'bottome' deleted.

[110] 'ingraved' inserted.

[111] 'and artificially' inserted; different hand.

[112] 'well adorned' inserted; different hand.

[113] 'cheefe' inserted; different hand.

[114] 'wch was' inserted; different hand.

[115] 'wrongfuly' inserted; different hand.

hange on the gallowes untill one member doe rotte from the other; but his mr beinge penitent for the doing of soe greate an injury[116] caused his body to be taken downe and three of his bones to be tipte wth goulde and sett in the backe of that altar, under the wch the reste of his body liethe, the wch coste he bestowed, that it might remaine as a testimonye of his penance don for that cause; at Nerumboorge I soulde my horsses and toke waggin,

The xxiith daye we departed from thence throughe Ronude to the cittie Wissringboorge [Weissenburg in Bavaria], The xxiiith we passed throughe Cesuria [Kaisheim],[117] wheare there is a monestarie of Benardine moncks wch was exceedinge ritchlye furnished wth many devoute [wr]itings.[118] this was the firste churche of Catholicke government wch we sawe in those contries, here wee might well per-ceave the fruits of true religion for[119] the moncks there[120] intertayned us verie charitably and[121] kindely; [*Catholicke and Lutheran Government myngled*] in this dukedom the Catholicks have there monestaries and profession[122] publickely used[123] in Churches, and the Lutherans have the licke libertie, From thence the same daye we travelled to the cittie of Donaverte [Donauwörth], wch is fortified after the manner of Norenboorge, and is a free State, the river of Danubias [Danube] run-nethe harde by it, the heade wheareof is ten myles from thence, at the gate of a castle called Donsingana, not farr from Donaverte, on the lifte hande liethe Novenboorge where dwellethe the Pallatine of the Ryne, Englestode [Ingolstadt][124] in Bavaria standethe som three myles from Donaverte, wheare there is a famous colledge of Jesuitts,

From thence to Ousboorge [Augsburg], otherwyse called Augusta wch is an imperiall cittie, and agreat free state, it is fortified in sutche sorte as Nerumboorge is, and hathe the ryver Leighe [Lech] runni-nge by it, there are dyvers of the cittizens created Earles and barrons for there abundance of[125] welthe, three of theise ritche merchants havinge layde asyde a hudge[126] som of mony for the buinge of a

---

[116] 'for the doing ... injury' inserted; different hand.

[117] Latin 'Caesarea': the imperial abbey of Kaisersheim (now Kaisheim).

[118] 'furnished ... writings' inserted; different hand.

[119] 'wee ... for' inserted; different hand.

[120] 'there' inserted; different hand.

[121] 'charitably and' inserted; different hand.

[122] 'profession' inserted; 'there religion' deleted.

[123] 'used' inserted; different hand.

[124] Ingolstadt: a Jesuit college was founded there in 1556, Ludwig Koch, *Jesuiten-Lexikon* (Paderborn, 1934), 870.

[125] 'abundance of' inserted; 'great' deleted.

[126] 'a hudge' inserted; 'a great' deleted.

mightie proportion of merchandise,[127] (of wch one was a Lutheran, and the other two Catholicks) and they not well agreeinge upon that commoditie theye shoulde bestowe that mony, the matter was putt to moste voyces, [*A religious policie*] but the Catholickes did enforce the Lutheran, by that meanes to contribute to the buildinge of a fayre and[128] (18 Blank) (19) + lardge colleadge for the Jesuits wch there is nowe to be seene;[129] here wee mete the poste of Venis[130] wch horste us and bare our chardges[131] thether for five poundes 17s str the wch iorney contayned of myles, some three hundred of Italian mesure or thereabouts;[132] in this cittie the Catholickes and Lutherans dwell verie peaceably together but there are noe Calvenistes suffred to remaine amongest them.

At my beinge here I hard it verie constantlye reported that there was then in the cittie of Dreasonn [Dresden] to be seene, a cheerie[133] stone havinge one hundred seaventie five faces, pictured upon it, allso an artificiall shippe whose mayne maste beinge oppenede, ther was to be seene the picture of the blessede trinitie, and dyvers other portratrures verie ritchly sett forthe; moreover I have bene crediblye enformede that there was[134] a Peacocke made by arte wch did bothe walke and crye; Furthermore it was toulde me that there was an armorye in Dreasonn wch containede furniture sufficiente to sett forthe fowre score thowesande men, and a vessell of woode in Lipsicke [Leipzig] wch maye containe one hundred Tonnes of wyne;

[*The dukedum of Bavaria*] From Augusta we wente the xxiiiith daye by Hollenboorge, Caveringe and Leyghinboorge beinge Grawemidlemans[135] houses and soe to Lanceboorge [Landsberg] all standinge by the River Leighe [Lech]. The xxvth[136] by Swainge wch is at the footte of the Alpes to Amboorge by the River Amber [Ammer]. The xxvith[137] by the monasterye of Etolle [Ettal] wch is at the heade of the River Sticxs [Styx] wch River runnethe downe

---

[127] 'a mightie proportion of merchandise' inserted.
[128] 'lardge college for the Jesuitts' deleted.
[129] Augsburg: a Jesuit college was established there in 1582, Koch, *Jesuiten-Lexikon*, 134; change of hand from page 19 onwards.
[130] 'poste' denotes 'men with horses stationed or appointed in places at suitable distances along the post-roads'; also, 'one of a series of stations where post-horses are kept for relays', *OED*.
[131] 'horste us': 'to provide with a horse or horses', 'our chardges': form of 'charge', 'a load, burden, weight', here, presumably referring to luggage, *OED*.
[132] 'the wch iorney ... or thereabouts' inserted.
[133] 'cheerie': a form of 'cherry', *OED*.
[134] 'was' inserted.
[135] Presumably Graf Midleman.
[136] 'daye' deleted.
[137] 'daye' deleted.

wth great roaringe betwixt two mightie montaines, and soe over the floode accorone [Acheron], to [M]itavell [Mittenwald] throughe wch runnethe the River Fleggitan [Phlegethon]. These three rivers are those supposed by Virgill to be the passadge to hell,[138]

[*Catholicke Government*] from thence to Seavelte [Seefeld, north-west of Innsbruck] in Austria, (20) this contrie is all Catholicks and there duke then lyveinge a greate benefactor to the Church, and in him maie be verie well verified, the sainge of the prophett David potens in terra erit semen eius[139] [*plal III*] Generatio rectorum benedicetar, His posteritie shalbe potent in this oure worlde the generation of the iuste shalbe blessed,[140] for god did soe abondantly rewarde him as one of his[141] daughters became Queene of Spaine, and his seconde sonn was advancede to the title of a Cardinall;[142] [*The dukedum of Austria*] In Seavelte is a monestarie in the wch one of the Dukes of Austria is buried; In the which[143] Oswaldus mildsece a noble man for usinge contempt againste the blessed Sacrament inforcinge the preiste to give him agreater hoste then the reste had, wch receaved wth him, for his presumption sancke into the grownde, for the verifyinge of the wch at this daie there is to be seene the prente of his fingeres in[144] an alter of the Churche wch he tooke holde of when he sancke into the earthe, from thence the same daye to Iseboorge [?Innsbruck] wch is a Cittie of great antiquitie, and hathe the river Rie runninge by it. The xxiith by Staine wch standethe by the river Riser to Steetchin [?Sterzing] by the wch passethe the river O[b]riane. [*The dukedum of Tiroll*] The xxviiith by the Cittie Prickes [Brixen], by yt is the floode Trysacke [Eisack]. and soe that might [*recte* night] to Solle. The xxixth throughe the Cittie Bonsone [Bolzano] to Numarde,

[*At the river wch runnethe throwe Trent dothe Germany end and Italy begins*] The last[145] to Trente by it runnethe the riever Titch[146] here wee sawe the seapullket of Snt Symone wch was a childe martered by the Jewes, whose body liethe there as yet uncorrupted; [*Italye*] at oure beinge there wee weare in the place where the laste generall

---

[138] Virgil, in his description of the underworld (*Aeneid*, Book VI) notes the rivers Acheron, Phlegethon, and Styx.

[139] 'potens … eius' interlined.

[140] 'His posteritie … shalbe blessed' interlined; Psalm III (112):2.

[141] 'his' inserted.

[142] Andreas von Austria (1558–1600), son of Archduke Ferdinand of Austria, created cardinal in 1576; succeeded as bishop of Brixen in 1591. Salvador Miranda, *The Cardinals of the Holy Roman Church* http://www2.fiu.edu/~mirandas/bios1576.htm#Austria, accessed 20 Nov. 2017.

[143] 'In the which' inserted.

[144] 'in' inserted.

[145] 'xxxth' deleted.

[146] Trent is located on the river Adige (in German, Etsch).

councell[147] was helde, the wch was a verie faire lardge and bewtifull halle but nowe it is converted unto a stately Churche, The Cardinall Midcouche[148] was then commaunder there, and helde the cittie for (21) the Pope, in the wch he hathe a moste gorgious Pallace. from thence the same daie to Alboorge, where we passede som danger by reason of the Bandettoes,[149] wch doe often make greate roberies ther abouts.

All these dukedoms[150] before named stande in Germany; and are Governed for the more parte by Lutherans, but the Catholicks amongest them have free liberty of conscience, there citties are soe stronge as they will yeelde noe obedience more then pleasethe them, unto there duks, there cheefe vertue is truthe, there greateste vice is droncknes.

[*Lumbardy*] The firste daie of September we passed by Preeso here is[151] one whoe dwellethe in a rock, wch is in the side of a mightie mon-tayne all the people of that house are cariede up som fortie fadoms in a baskett befor they com to there dwellinge; [*The dukedum of Venis begineth at Basania*] and soe to the cittie Basania [Bassano del Grappa] by wch runnethe the river Prente [Brenta], Basania standethe at the fotte of the Alpes. they are of all heights from two myles to xxtie[152] of Englishe measure. The seconde daie throughe the cittie of Castle francke [Castelfranco Veneto] to mestris [Mestre], where dothe begine the Italliane miles wch are skante soe great as the Englishe.

[*Venis the ritche*] The theerde[153] to the famous and renownede cittie of Venis [Venice], wch for the situatione beinge in the sea, The ritches and stately buildinge thereof is the myrror of the whole worlde, The duke his house is four square builded upon four rankes of stone pillers, xxtie in everie rancke. There are there two chambers of great beautye verie lardge (22) and sumptuously[154] ritchly sett forthe wth divers curious (worckes gilte wth golde) right over against it is the mynte hous builte in licke sorte, betwixt them neighe the sea side stande two pillers of one stone apeece, beinge three fadomes aboute everie of them, and of a great height, before the gatte dothe stande a payere of gallowes, upon the wch as wee were informed a duke was hanged wch woulde have made the dukedom his inheritance by murthering of the

---

[147] Council of Trent, 1545–1563.

[148] Lodovico Madruzzo (1532–1600), also listed as 'von Marrutz', 'Madrucci'; created cardinal in 1561; elected prince-bishop of Trent in 1567. Miranda, *The Cardinals of the Holy Roman Church* http://www2.fiu.edu/~mirandas/bios1561.htm#Madruzzo, accessed 20 Nov. 2017.

[149] 'Bandettoes': a form of 'bandits', *OED*.

[150] Word emended.

[151] 'is' inserted; different ink.

[152] 'miles' deleted.

[153] 'daye' deleted.

[154] 'sumptuously' interlined.

Nobillitie, harde by the house is St Marke his churche wch is exceedinge ritchly adorned, under the highe altere of the wch liethe his body; yt hathe five stately gattes at the entrance therof,[155] the rooffe is made in forme licke five half globes of verie strange worckmanshipe. the steeple is framed in suche sorte as a horse maye be[156] riddene to the toppe of it. right against the churche doores stande three tall pillers wch signifie as it was toulde me that theie can kepe warr wth three kinges, [*A Ritche Iueall house*] in the Duks Juell house are said to be[157] two unicornes hornes of ayarde longe, apeece[158] a turkis[159] sett in golde of great bignes, apoynted diamonde of exceedinge muche valewe sevene corsletts of golde sett[160] wth pearle and precious stone wth many other Juells of singular worck-manshipe and unspeakeable worthe, soe as Venis for the inestimable welthe is accounted the ritcheste Cittie in Itallie; There is an exchange called the Rialto verie faire and lardge neighe unto it is a Bridge [*A strange Bridge*] of one arche fortie yards broade, it hathe two courses of shoppes uppon it and is (23) fiftie stepps in the ascendinge on eache side,

[*A worthy armorie*] In the armorye of Venis at the intrance thereof[161] are eight roomes foure score yards longe eache of them full of armour, as pycks swordes and other weapons,[162] there are divers roomes full of oares som for five and som for seaven men to rowe wthall, beside som other furniture for Gallies. Alsoe wee sawe there[163] three hundred gallies lyinge drye under houses, wch doe rowe wth twentie five oares aside,[164] more forteene Galliasses[165] wch doe use thirtee oares on a side;[166] one Galley ritchly gilte wth golde wherein the Duke on St Marckes daie dothe use some sportes upon the water, there are fowre roomes full of Sailes, and fowre roomes full of Cables, alsoe one gallie made in one daie for the receavinge of the kinge of Fraunce, as ther it was toulde us; more over[167] wee viewed[168] five roomes wherein weare contayned[169] twelve

---

[155] 'weste ende' deleted; 'entrance therof' interlined.

[156] 'be' inserted.

[157] 'said to be' interlined.

[158] 'of' erased.

[159] 'turkis': a form of 'turquoise', 'a precious stone', *OED*.

[160] 'sett' interlined.

[161] 'thereof' interlined.

[162] 'furniture' deleted; 'weapons' inserted.

[163] 'there are' deleted; 'alsoe wee saw there' inserted.

[164] 'There' deleted.

[165] 'galliasses': denotes 'a heavy, low-built vessel, larger than a galley, impelled both by sail and oars, chiefly employed in war', *OED*.

[166] 'There -' deleted.

[167] 'over' interlined.

[168] 'sawe' deleted; 'viewed' inserted.

[169] Emendation: from 'are' to 'weare contayned'; insertions in different hand.

hundred caste peeces or more, the greateste peece there was founde in Candie[170] (wch is a kingdom subiecte to the Dukedom of Venis) this wch[171] is eighteene inches broade in the mouthe and soe passing forwards[172] also wee[173] might perceave one roome wch was full of bulletts for great Ordinance, and (as they wch weare there informed us) it had in it noe les[174] then seventeen thowsande soe we went frome thence[175] throughe seaven roomes wch weare full of musketts Callyvers[176] and other furniture, of the wch[177] three of them contained armour sufficient for 70 thowsande soldiors;[178] There is armour there in all sufficiente to furnishe oute three hundred thowsande men, wee tooke note of[179] one maste there wch coste the duke three hundred ducketts,[180] The duke keepethe many men a worcke in that armorie, to his greate cost and chardge[181] he is at peace wth all the worlde, and yet dothe[182] (24) dailie make great provision for warre,

In the Nunerie of Saint Sepullcher is a patterne of[183] the Sepullcher of our Saviour Christe, it was wrought at Jerusalem, as is reportede and brought thether, At Morana [Murano] one myle from Venis is the glasse house, the shippinge of Venis come noe further then Mollomocke [Malamocco] wch is five myle from the Cittie; Venis standethe farr wthin the straights and therefore the sea dothe not wth them ebbe nor flowe, There are in it of parishe churches xxiii and four, and religious howses fortie eight, as allso six Synagoges of Jewes, in the wch they doe use there Ebrue sarvice, and ancient ceremonies,[184] whoe are in number as good as ten thowsande. I did observe at my beinge there that[185] the noble men of Venis[186] doe use to salute one another

---

[170] 'Candie': a form of 'Candia', name of an island in Mediterranean, formerly called Crete, *OED*.

[171] 'peece' deleted; 'wch' inserted.

[172] 'and so … forwards' interlined.

[173] 'sawe' deleted; 'might perceave' inserted.

[174] 'contained'; 'fewere' deleted.

[175] 'passed forwarde' deleted.

[176] 'callyvers': a form of 'caliver', denoting 'a light kind of musket … introduced during the 16th century', *OED*.

[177] 'rooms' erased.

[178] 'men' deleted.

[179] 'sawe' deleted.

[180] 'ducketts': form of 'ducat', 'a gold coin of varying value … Also … a silver coin of Italy', *OED*.

[181] 'to his … chardge' interlined.

[182] 'is at … yet dothe' line through these words.

[183] 'Saint Sepullcher is a patterne of' interlined.

[184] 'in the wch they doe use there Ebrue sarvice, and ancient ceremonies' interlined; different hand and ink.

[185] 'when' deleted.

[186] 'they' deleted.

wth a kisse, but theye doe not accustom (either there or in any parte of Italie) to kisse there wyves or any other women in open presence;

The ixth daye wee wente by water and passed by Lusefesina [Fusina], where our hoye was cariede upp agreat waye uppon a fledge, wth a windeglass,[187] and lett downe againe, and soe came to Padua. [*Padua the Learned*] wch is a verie antiente cittie, builte by Antenor[188] whose tombe is to be sene in the streete, There is the beste universitie in all Itallie,[189] verie faire and publicke Scooles,[190] and agreat number of scollers, in the Churche of St Luke liethe under the highe alter his bodie; we sawe there a monastarie of St Justina, shee is baried under the highe alter of the same, yt containethe one hundrethe and thaetie[191] moncks there revenious come to fiftie (25) thowsande crownes yearly: [*At Padua wee mett two of Lo: Burlie*[192] *his sonns that nowe is*] there is arare quier and manie faiere galleries wth lodginge in eache syde, and everie monkes name written over the dore of his chamber or sell, the monkes of this place intertained us verie kindely: In the great halle of Padua is Tytus livias[193] his heade sett for a monument. five miles from Padua are verie medsenable[194] bathes, there buildinge is suche as one maie walke drye in the streets any daye in the yeere; at my beinge in Padua[195] I listened at a doore where I harde verie sweete musicke, whereuppon I was earnestly desired by one of the house to beare them companie, I was by them verie kindely usede and did singe wth them som two howres;

[*The dukedum of Ferara*] The xith daie wee departed from thence and wente a foot for companie sake of certaine Englishe gent[196] men wch

---

[187] 'windeglass'; probably, form of 'windlass', denoting 'a mechanical contrivance, working on the principle of the wheel and axle', *OED*; an inland waterway (comprising the Naviglio del Brenta and the Piovego canal) linked Fusina on the Venetian lagoon with Padua.

[188] Antenor: in Greek legend, was one of elders of Troy; Virgil, *Aeneid*, I, lines 242–247 mentions that Antenor had escaped from Troy and subsequently founded the city of Patavium (modern Padua).

[189] 'and' deleted.

[190] 'there' deleted; 'and' inserted.

[191] Presumably denotes 'thirtie'.

[192] Thomas Cecil (1542–1623), known as Lord Burghley from 1598–1605, son of William Cecil, 1st Baron Burghley; Thomas's sons Edward Cecil (1572–1638) and Sir Richard Cecil (1570–1633) were granted leave to travel abroad late in 1594; Edward matriculated at Padua University in 1595. Thomas Cecil, *ODNB*; Edward Cecil, *ODNB*; Jonathan Woolfson, *Padua and the Tudors: English Students in Italy, 1485–1603* (Cambridge, 1998), 218.

[193] Titus Livius (known in English as Livy) (*c.*64 BC–*c.* AD 12), Roman historian, born in Patavium (Padua).

[194] 'medsenable': form of 'medicinable', denoting 'having healing or curative properties', *OED*.

[195] 'there' interlined.

[196] 'gent' interlined.

we mett at Venis, and came that night to Ruiga [Rovigo], [*Ferara the stronge*] The xiith[197] to Ferrara wch is accounted the strongeste cittie in Italie, by the walls of the wch[198] runnethe the river Poe. The Duke his house is stately builte wth fowre highe towres, and hathe a stronge mote aboute it; In[199] the monestarie of St Benedicte is Ariostus[200] the famous Poet buried, The Duke hathe two stables wch maie containe three hundred horses; since my beinge there he[201] wch then livede is dead, and hathe lefte no heyre male behinde him, by reason whereof the dukedom is fallen into the Popes hands for it is originally belonginge[202] unto the sea apostolicke, the reveneus of it doe amounte to two hundred[203] thowsande crownes yearly; [*The dukedum of Bolonia*] The xiiith daie wee iornyede to a villadge called Snt George; (26) [*Bolonia the plentyfull*] The xiiiith to Bollonia [Bologna] in this cittie is an universitie, in the wch the Civill and Canone Lawe are beste redd, yt belongeth to the sea of Rome, and is builte after the maner of Padua, there a Cardinall dothe governe for the Pope, the river Reno runnethe by it; The xvth daie to Scargulisanae wch is uppon the alpes[204] Betwixt Bolonia and Florence,

The xvith wee passed by an oulde buildinge called Castle Ougent the Cheefe reason wch moved me to take note of this Castle was, [*The notable virtues of ye Barron of Delvine*][205] for that yt had affinitie in sounde wth the noble familie of the Nugents in Ireland of the wch name at that tyme lyved a lord Barron of great honnor and compleate vertue whoe for zeale in religion, learninge in divinitie philosophie, musicke, and other sciences, true valor, civill conversation, playne dealinge, hospitallitie, and constancie towards his frends, was a patterne for all noble myndes, to Imitate, and as his liffe was examplar good, soe was his deathe an Edification to all suche good Christians as have[206] had notice of the maner thereof; [*The dukedum of Eutruria*] nighe unto Castle Ougent is the division betwixt Tuscany and Lumbardie. from thence wee iornyed to Ferenzola [Firenzuola],

---

[197] 'daye' deleted.
[198] 'cittie' deleted.
[199] Change from 'i' to 'I'.
[200] Ludovico Ariosto (1474–1533), Italian poet; the duke of Ferrara was his patron.
[201] 'the duke' deleted; 'he' inserted.
[202] 'belonginge' interlined.
[203] 'hundred' interlined.
[204] Alps: denotes 'any high, especially snow-capped, mountains', *OED*.
[205] Christopher Nugent (1544–1602), 14th Baron Delvin, succeeded his father in 1559; matriculated at Clare Hall, Cambridge, in 1563; was detained in England, 1582–1586, returning to his estates in Ireland in 1586; in June 1595 was appointed leader of crown forces in Co. Westmeath; died in custody in Dublin Castle, Aug. or Oct. 1602, *DIB*.
[206] 'have' interlined.

wthin one myle of wch as wee hard[207] is aplace in the earthe wch dailye burnethe wth scorchinge flames and soe that night to Scarperia,
[*Florenc ye faire*] The xviith to the faire cittie of Florence, wch standethe in avaleye the Duke hathe there anewe howse and an oulde
betwixt wch is a gallerie of agreat leinthe, builded over[208] the topp
of the Cittie houses, and soe over a bridge wch standethe (27)
upon the River Arna [Arno]. [*At Florence I mett the Lo graye*][209] it is[210]
said for a truthe that all things that belonged to the buildinge of
his newe house viz. Stone morter timber and other[211] necessaries
whatsoever, were[212] carried by one only mule, wch lived fiftie six
yeers, the picture of wch mule standethe in marble wth the subscription contayninge in substanc as[213] above is[214] named, to remaine
there[215] as a monumt to all posterities; at the same Pallace there
are[216] also two Adamante Stones of mightie quantitie, There is a piller of marble in Florence three yards in compasse and 30 footte in
lenithe;[217] also a churche of great devotion called, Anuntiatio, beatae
mariae virginis, where many resorte from farr contries for ther
helthe, as well Popes kinges, and other potentatts, as those of the
meaner sorte, but the faireste churche in the towne is dedicated
unto our Lady; whose outside wth the steeple is builte all wth marble,
there is another litle churche adioyninge unto this made in maner of
Jewes Synagoge, wch was once the temple of Mars in the heathen
tymes, but nowe dedicated unto St John baptiste, where all the
childeren of the towne as was related unto us[218] are baptized, in St
Lawrence his churche all the dukes of Eutruria are buried[219] amonge
the wch I tooke particular note of Cossimus De Medices, who was a
man of great worthe and meryte (28) as maye apeere, [*The memorable
Deeds of Cosmus de medices*] in that he builte an hospitall in Ierusalem, a

---

[207] 'as wee hard' interlined.
[208] 'in' deleted; 'over' inserted.
[209] Thomas Grey (1575–1614), Baron Grey of Wilton; inherited barony in 1593, *ODNB*;
matriculated at Padua in 1594, Woolfson, *Padua and the Tudors*, 240–241; however, 3 lines
were placed through this note, perhaps indicating cancellation.
[210] 'is' interlined.
[211] 'all' deleted; 'other' inserted; new ink.
[212] 'was' emended to 'were'.
[213] 'contayninge in substanc as' interlined; different ink.
[214] 'is' inserted.
[215] 'to remaine there' interlined; different ink.
[216] 'is' deleted 'are' inserted, different hand.
[217] 'there is' deleted.
[218] 'as was related unto us' interlined; different hand.
[219] Five lines of text cancelled: 'vid. Alexander the first duke of that cittie, Sonn unto one
Lawrence duke of Urbin, wch Alexander died wthout issue; whereupon the Contri[e]
assembled together and chose' [Cossimus De Medices].

lybrarie in Venis, two Abbayes in Florence, in Syena afaire Pallace and a colledge called Pater Patriae, besids many other things of great reckning and accounte,²²⁰ in the forsaide churche of St Lawrence, is buried the Father of Pope Leo the tenthe and Pope Clemente the seventhe,²²¹ and²²² one Paulus Jonius a historiographer,²²³ and one Antonious Cuffinus apoette²²⁴

[*A monument of Englishe man*] There is a tombe²²⁵ in our Ladies Churche of an Englishe man, whoe as it is thought came by chance into the contrye, when the gothes and vandales, weare subduinge of them,²²⁶ he beinge agood soldiour helped them to wyn manye battles: whereupon at his deathe that monument was bestowed upon him, there are different opinions held conserninge his righte Sirname, som saie that his name was Hackwoode and that the Italians not knowinge the pronuntiation of Englishe called him accutus, others saide his name was sharpe and therefor termed²²⁷ accutus,

adioyninge unto the Duke of Florence his oulde house there are seaven severall courtes for desciedinge of controversies, The firste is appointed for the preservation of²²⁸ the peace, The seconde is for the administratinge of Justice to the poore, The thirde courte is for monnie matters, The fourthe is for merchants to the ende that they maie deale truly in bueing and selling, The fifte is for phisitions and apotthegaries, The sixt is for artificers, The seventhe (29) is apoynted for the exacte searchinge forthe of truthe and equitie, There are three hospitalles in the same cittie, whereof one is for orphants wch weare in number one thousande eight hundred another of men wheare there is in one roome one hundred and thirtie bedds, in everie of wch²²⁹ were twoo lodged²³⁰ the thirde of women, where there are²³¹ three score bedds, in each²³² of them three women; Here wee mett the poste of Rome wch horste us and

---

²²⁰ 'of great reckoning and accounte' interlined; 3 lines cancelled: 'The wch Cossimus had two sonnes Fraunces and Ferdinando, Fraunces died wthout issue, soe that Ferdinando nowe raig[ne]the'; Cosimo de' Medici (1519–1574), grand duke of Tuscany.

²²¹ Pope Leo X, reigned 1513–1521; Pope Clement VII, reigned 1523–1534, both of the Medici family.

²²² 'and' interlined.

²²³ 'historiographer' inserted; 'writer' deleted.

²²⁴ Line through 'Antonius Cuffinus apoette', but legible.

²²⁵ 'monument' deleted; 'tombe' inserted, different ink.

²²⁶ 'this Englishe man' deleted; 'he' inserted.

²²⁷ 'called' deleted; 'termed' inserted.

²²⁸ 'of' interlined.

²²⁹ 'of wch' interlined; 'bedd' cancelled.

²³⁰ 'lodged' inserted; 'men' deleted.

²³¹ 'is' deleted; 'are' inserted.

²³² 'each' inserted; 'every one' deleted.

bare our chardges thither, being aiorney of some 7 score mils[233] for four double pistoletts,[234]

+ From Florence the xxith by the cittie of Swanoto to Syenna [Siena] where there is a churche of greate devotion and agreat Pillgrimadge daylie frequented[235] to St Katherin of the same[236] in the Colledg[237] thereof weare to the number of three hundred scollers, yt is averie faire cittie standinge on the topp of a hill wch maie easilie be[238] perceaved in twentie miles distance, From thence the xxiith over the river Ardia [Arbia] by Lucimano [Lucignano d'Arbia] and a cittie called Montelchino [Montalcino] to Rhodocaphone [Radicofani], The xxiiith to Monteflesca [Montefiascone] and travelled[239] in our waie throughe Aquapendeance [Acquapendente], [*Churche Lande*] nighe unto the wch wee[240] passed over a Bridge made by Pope Gregorie the thirteenthe wch is the divitione betwixt Tuscanie and the Churche Lande, and by agreat loughe called Aquadebullsana [Lago di Bolsena],

The xxiiiith wee iorneyed[241] by a bathe lyinge upon the northe syde of the antiente cittie Viterbo, wch boylethe naturally two footte heighe, and is of suche heate, that a man cannot well suffer to toutche the water untill it be cooled, there is another bathe of the same nature half a myle more westewarde wch as wee were informed boyllethe amans height above grounde (30) and is of suche an intemperatt heate that it would have[242] scald to deathe any lyvinge creatur that had[243] fallen into yt, this bathe by reasone of the intemperature servethe to noe good[244] use, in Viterbo are two faire condites and many monumts of great antiquitie wch we did not staye to take[245] viewe of. from thence wee passed the same daye by Ron[s]hilliano [Ronciglione] to Backano [Bracciano].

[*Rome the holye*] The xxvth of September to the moste holy cittie of Rome: That daye wee hapned into the companie of certaine Itallian gent. and alighted wth them at aplace wthin the Cittie called Mount

---

[233] 'being aiorney of some 7 score mils' interlined; ink and hand as in immediately previous emendations.

[234] 'pistoletts': denoting certain foreign gold coins, *OED*.

[235] 'daylie frequented' inserted.

[236] 'Syenna' deleted; 'of the same' inserted.

[237] 'in the Colledg' interlined.

[238] 'be' inserted; different ink.

[239] 'travelled' interlined; 'passed' deleted.

[240] 'wee' interlined.

[241] 'iorneyed' inserted; 'travelled' deleted.

[242] 'have' interlined; different ink.

[243] 'had' interlined.

[244] 'good' interlined.

[245] 'not staye to take' interlined.

Jordan [Monte Giordano],[246] From thence on of the gent. verie cor-
teouslye shewed us the waye unto the Englishe Colledge where wee
spake wth one Father Edmonds[247] ane Englishe Jesuite, whoe (after
som ceremonies of curtesie used, tolde us that wee[248] coulde not[249]
be receaved there as pillgrimes or scollers unlesse wee[250] had commendations in writinge from som good Catholicke, or were verie
well knowen to som of the Englishe or Irishe there remaininge;
whereupon he sente one wth us to Doctor Fagan[251] a Waterforde
man, whoe kindelie intertainede us and while wee weare in talke
with him, Doctor Haddocke came in, whoe having very frindly
saluted us[252] was right ioyfull to see me, and was verie inquisitive to
heare of his frends in Ireland, but especiallye for Mr Gerralde
Dillon[253] at whose hands he accknowledgeth to have receaved very
frindly and curteous intertainmt when he was in his company com-
mending him for his true zeale in religion and [much] sufficiency
in managing matters of greate weight[254] and moment[255] (31) From[256]
thence Doctor Haddocke wente wth us to the Englishe Colledge,
whear by his meanes wee weare receaved as pillgrimes for eight
dayes. Provided that wthin that tyme wee shoulde be reconsiled
unto the Catholicke Church,[257] receave the blessed Sacrament and
visett the seaven principall Churches of Rome, wch accordinglie
was performed by us, [*An unspeakeable benefit*] Father Richard
Coolinge beinge our ghostlie Father,[258] whoe hard our confession[259]

[246] Located near Castel Sant'Angelo, in Rome.
[247] Edmund Harewood SJ (1554–1597) was minister in the English College in Rome from 1593. For an outline of his Jesuit life, see 'Edmundus Harvardus', Thomas McCoog SJ (ed.), *Monumenta Angliae: English and Welsh Jesuits*, 3 vols (Rome, 1992), II, 349.
[248] 'wee' inserted; 'none' deleted; different ink.
[249] 'not' inserted.
[250] 'theye' deleted; 'wee' inserted.
[251] Possibly Nicholas Fagan from Waterford ordained at Rome in 1582, Hugh Fenning, 'Irishmen ordained at Rome, 1572–1697', *Archivium Hibernicum*, 59 (2005), 7.
[252] 'whoe having very frindly saluted us' interlined.
[253] In the 1590s there was a Gerald Dillon of Balgoth, Co. Meath, another of Lessonhall, Co. Dublin, and yet another of Harold's Grange, Co. Dublin, J. Ohlmeyer and E. Ó Ciardha (eds), *The Irish Statute Staple Books, 1596–1687* (Dublin, 1998), 206.
[254] Margin: 'The sufficiency of Garrott dillon' erased.
[255] Following 4 lines erased; illegibile.
[256] Previous 1½ lines erased; illegible.
[257] 'be reconsiled unto the Catholicke Church' interlined; 'make our confession' deleted; different hand.
[258] A 'father confessor', *OED*.
[259] 'reconsiled us' deleted; 'hard our confession' interlined'; 'Richard Cowlinus' SJ (1562–1618), born in York, ordained at Rome 1587, entered SJ at Tournai 1588; served as English pentitentiary at St Peter's, Rome, from 1593; in Sept. 1596 received permission to travel to Flanders. McCoog (ed.), *Monumenta Angliae*, II, 277–278.

in St Peter his Churche wch was one of the greateste benefitts that ever was bestowed upon us,[260] as well in respecte of the matter of reconsiliation to god, as also in regarde that in that churche doe lie the bodies of the princes of the apostles and many other glorious saints;

[*A prosecution of Tribulation unexpected*] In that tyme som of the Irishe wch did favor the commotion lately stirred up in Ireland presented matter againste me to the holy[261] house because I did not concurr wth them in reportinge that the warre in Irelande was begune for religion, but in this and in all other matters wch did concerne me, I founde doctor Haddocke, rather a Father then a frend unto me, whoe for preventinge of there malice caused me to make me self knowen unto the Cardinalls and other officers of the inquisition, whoe beinge throwghly informed of me, did reiecte the accusations of my enemies and used me verie gratiously, but especially Cardinall Penelle,[262] whoe talked wth me verie familiarly in his privatte gallerie, and tolde me that he did muche[263] reioyce at my maner of comminge unto that (32) Cittie, and amongeste other speetches he affirmed that in reedinge of the Snts lyves of England, he did often shedd teares, when he did consider howe farre different, there religion then professed in England, was from that of there saints,

At the expiration of those eight dayes wch is the ordinarie allowance of pillgreemes, Doctor Haddocke, perceavinge that I was willinge to study, soe used the matter wth Cardinall Caietan,[264] then protector of the Englishe, that I was receaved as convictor in the Englishe Colledge and Phillip Draycatt wch came wth me thither, as scoller of the same;[265] There I lived for the space of two yeers and odd dayes, obayeinge the rules of the Colledge, and wearinge the garmts wch weare there usede, in the wch tyme[266] I hard my course of lodgicke and phisicke, there I was instructed by Father

---

[260] 'me' deleted: 'us' imposed.

[261] 'holy' interlined; 'inquisition' deleted.

[262] Domenico Pinelli (1541–1611), born in Genoa, of a patrician family; created cardinal 1585. Miranda, *The Cardinals of the Holy Roman Church* http://www2.fiu.edu/~mirandas/bios1585-ii.htm#Pinelli, accessed 4 Dec. 2017. At the beginning of his pontificate (in 1592) Clement VIII appointed him a permanent member of the congregations of the Council, and of the Holy Office (Inquisition).

[263] 'muche' interlined.

[264] Enrico Caetani (1550–1599), Latin 'Henricus Gaetanus', created cardinal, 1585; legate *a latere* in Poland, 3 Apr. 1596–23 June 1597 (Miranda, *The Cardinals of the Holy Roman Church* http://www2.fiu.edu/~mirandas/bios1585-ii.htm#Caetani, accessed 4 Dec. 2017). After the death of Cardinal Allen (16 Oct. 1594), Clement VIII appointed him protector of the English.

[265] Register of English College, 12 Oct. 1595, AVCAU, Liber 282, 33; convictor: 'boarder', *OED*.

[266] 'the wch tyme' interlined; 'that two yeeres' deleted.

Cowlinge Father Warford[267] and other vertu[e]s Fathers to followe the pathe of good liffe and true devotion, and was muche incouradged thereunto by there godly example and saintlicke[268] carriadge;

[*Incredibl profitt reaped in ye English Colledge*] In this Colledge I receaved a suer impression of Catholicke religion, and a iuditiall knowledge of the meere necessitie thereof, wch in this contrye I coulde not have well atained unto, for firste my kinred in all siddes are protestants, and som of them of great account whose displeasures woulde have terrified me, secondly my preferment in this common welthe, beinge by that meanes hindred, woulde have turned my good disposition into a luke warme indifferentie, Thirdly the o[w]n civill[269] and careless (33) livinge of a great parte as well of them of the spirituall callinge as of the Layetie wch profess religion in this land, woulde have soe scandelized me, as I should have[270] rune on[271] wth many others, wch for those respects doe deferr[272] there convertion, and heape to themselves perdition, but god of his infinitt mercye hathe nowe gyven me suche a measure of fortitude as none of these occasions can be any stumblinge blocke unto me, and therefor I maie well saie wth the Prophett David [*Psalm. 39*] Domine direxisti semitas meas, et posuisti supra firmam petram pedes meos, Lord thowe haste directed my foote stepes and haste placed my feete upon a sure rocke, therefor have I cause above thowsandes of others, to give all possible laude and praise unto god, and to render hartie thanckes unto those godlie Fathers, wch (as instrumts of his devine providence instructed me, sainge wth the same kinglie prophett David, [*psal: 85*] misericordia tua[273] domine magna est super me et eruisti animam meam ex inferno inferiori. thy great mercye o lord hathe bene plentifully extended towarde me, and thowe haste delivered my soule from the deepeste[274] hell;

[*A faction in ye Colledg*] About that tyme there was som of the seculer priests and scollers wch thinckinge the gevernmt of the Jesuits to be somwhate too straight and severe, did ioyne themselves in a faction againste theire superiors, and made petition to his holines, that the governmt of the Colledge might be altered, alleadginge many

---

[267] William Warford SJ (*c.*1560–1608), born in Bristol, ordained Dec. 1584 in Rome, entered SJ in Rome 23 May 1594; was in Rome until June 1596; died in Valladolid. McCoog, *Monumenta Angliae*, I, 11; II, 522.

[268] 'saintlicke' inserted; 'goodly' deleted.

[269] 'cold carriadge' deleted; perhaps 'uncivill' intended.

[270] 'have' inserted.

[271] 'on' interlined.

[272] 'deferr' inserted, different hand; 'diferr' deleted.

[273] Letter inserted: possibly 'i'.

[274] 'deepeste' inserted; different hand and ink; the text is Psalm 85 (86):13.

reasons for the same, whereupon the Pope sente Cardinall Segare[275] to examyne the cause of there discontente, wch was (34) by him verie uprightly performed; In this tyme of his resorte thither,[276] he did wth great solemnitie confirme me and divers others of the Englishe scollers;[277] he then beinge vice protector of them,[278] in the absence of Cardinall Caietane,[279] [*The good Service of Cardinall Caietane*] whoe at that tyme was Imployed as legate from the Pope in Polonia [Poland] as well for the suppressinge of the trynitarian heresie wch there is revived, as also for the makinge of agreemt betwyne the kinge of Polonia and the prince of Transilvania,[280] in bothe of wch businesses he did great and good service to the Churche of god,

But befor his returne Cardinall Segare died, and in[281] his place did succeede as vi[ce] protector Cardinall Tollett,[282] whoe bare noe greate favour towards the Jesuitts, and therefor did purpose, as it was thought, to take the government of the Englishe Colledge from them, but his purpose was prevented by sicknes wch cutt of his life; In the wch[283] his infirmity[284] he was reconciled unto the Jesuits, and in token of his unfained[285] affection[286] did leave unto them amonge other things his librarie wch conteined agreat number of moste[287] learned bookes, and by his owne will and appointmt was burried in the Churche of Jesus adioyninge to the professed house of the Jesuits, in the wch I did see the Cardinales in sollemne and

---

[275] Filippo Sega (1537–1596), created cardinal 1591; died 29 May 1596. Miranda, *The Cardinals of the Holy Roman Church* http://www2.fiu.edu/~mirandas/bios1591-ii.htm#Sega, accessed 4 Dec. 2017.

[276] 'thither' inserted; 'to the Englishe Colledge' deleted.

[277] 'scollers' inserted; 'Colledge' deleted.

[278] 'Englishe' deleted.

[279] Enrico Caetani (1550–1599); on Caetani's diplomatic mission in search of an alliance between the emperor, and the rulers of Poland and Transylvania, against the Turks, and on his subsequent involvement in English Catholic affairs, see *Dizionario Biografico degli Italiani,* http://www.treccani.it/enciclopedia/enrico-caetani_(Dizionario-Biografico)/, accessed 16 Jan. 2018. He was appointed legate 'a latere' 3 Apr. 1596, and left Warsaw for Rome in Feb. 1597.

[280] Sigismund III (1566–1632), king of Poland; Sigismund Báthory (1572–1613), prince of Transylvania.

[281] 'in' inserted.

[282] Francisco de Toledo Herrera SJ (1532–1596), created cardinal 1593, died 14 Sept. 1596 (Miranda, *The Cardinals of the Holy Roman Church* http://www2.fiu.edu/~mirandas/bios1593.htm#Toledo, accessed 4 Dec. 2017). A leading theologian, he was among those Jesuits who opposed Claudio Acqauviva as General, *Diccionario Histórico de la Compañía de Jésus,* sub Toledo.

[283] 'wch' inserted.

[284] 'infirmity' inserted; 'sicknes' deleted.

[285] 'unfained' inserted.

[286] 'towards them' deleted.

[287] 'moste' inserted.

dolefull maner singe the office for the deade, his body lyinge then as it were upon a bedd in the midest of the Churche wth his roabes about him, his Cardinales Capp upon his head and his[288] face bare;

Then weare all the matters of the Colledge helde in suspence, untill Cardinall Caietane returned from Polonia, at the wch tyme (35) he made a reexamination of all there controversies, and for the better furtherance of that bussines Father persons[289] came from Spaine to Rome, by whose wysdom and grave providence, ioyned wth the diligent care and travell[290] of Doctor Haddocke, and som others, all things were well composed soe as the Cardinall Caietan beinge by there meanes fully informede of everie particuler matter belonginge unto that cause, [*The faction of ye Colledg suppressed*] procured the Popes derection for the dismissinge of those wch had bred the factione in the Colledge,

But befor Father persons cominge to Rome Doctor Haddocke did labor muche in quiettinge this contention, and thereby gott Creditt and greate reputation wth his holines; he was about that tyme made doctor in the Colledge of sapientia,[291] there he did preache greatly to his comendations in the presence of the learnedeste doctors in Rome; [*The kinde disposition of Doctor Haddock*] He is exceedinge wyse, indued wth great patience, and of[292] averie kynde dispositione towards his frends, of the wch [several words erased],[293] my self, and divers others have made experience, and is exceeding[294] carefull for the good and prosperous[295] estate of this contrie[296] [Ireland] as by his deeds is dalie manifested.

Sythence the tyme that the factions of the[297] Englishe Colledge were dismiste, som of there favoritts in Englande have written certaine invective bookes against the Jesuits,[298] wch might verie well have bene

---

[288] 'his' inserted; funeral took place in Gesù church, Rome.

[289] Robert Persons SJ (1546–1610) entered SJ 1575; while in Spain (1589–1596) founded seminaries for English students in Valladolid and Seville; in early 1597 moved to Rome where he became rector of the English College in Nov. 1598, which post he held until his death in 1610, *ODNB*.

[290] 'travell': travail.

[291] Sapienza: The University of Rome, founded 1303.

[292] 'of' inserted.

[293] Unclear – possibly 'Henry Dillon'.

[294] 'more' deleted; 'exceeding' inserted.

[295] 'and prosperous' inserted.

[296] 'then moste of them be wch are borne and nourished in yt' erased.

[297] 'the' inserted; different ink.

[298] For a list of these books (published 1598–1603), see Peter Milward, *Religious Controversies of the Elizabethan Age: A Survey of Printed Sources* (London, 1977), 'The Appellant controversy', 116–124; on the campaign of the Appellant group within the English secular clergy, see John Bossy, *The English Catholic Community 1570–1850* (London, 1975), 35–48; see

forborne by them, consideringe howe litle profitt yt hathe don to themselves, and howe much yt (36) hathe scandalized men of othere religions,
but this hathe bene wthout doubt, the driste of the divell whoe seekethe
to sett them at variance wch ought to cooperatt together in bringinge in
of gods harveste, never theless this muste be noted, that there controversie was for matter of governmt, and not for matter of faithe,

The Englishe Colledge was at the firste made for an hospitall, and
founded by St Edmond kinge of England,[299] and the livinge thereof,
augmented by divers of his famous and Catholicke successors, But in
the time of kinge Henry the eight[300] by reason of his revoult, from the
Churche, there was but smale resorte of Englishe pillgreemes to
Rome. in soe muche as the hospitall grewe unto decaye, and they
wch had the governmt of it made awaye muche of the livinge therunto[301] belonginge,[302] [*Gregorie the xiiith a great benefactor to the English
nation*] But at leinthe Cardinall Allen[303] aman of great learninge
and vertue made humble petition unto Pope Gregorie the xiiith[304]
cravinge that yt woulde pleas his holines to convert that hospitall
to a seminary whoe verie gratiously yeelded unto his requeste, and
for[305] there further mayntenance gave unto them a pention of two
thowsande crownes a yeare out of his treasurie, and another pention
of four thowsande crownes ayeare out of a monasterie of Benedictane
monckes, in the Cittie of Placentia [Piacenza]. The ritche monasteries of Itallie, wch have the number of there religious men decaied,
doe yeerly by the Popes apointmt, paye som (37) hundred thowsand
crownes, the wch mony is bestowed in pentions, upon suche poore
religious men as for there great learninge good life and vertue are
exalted unto the titles of Cardinales, as also uppon suche
Colledges as have moste nede of the same.

---

also T.G. Law (ed.), *The Archpriest Controversy: Documents Relating to the Dissensions of the Roman
Catholic Clergy 1597–1602*, Camden Society, NS, 2 vols (1896, 1898).

[299] St Edmund (d.869), king of the East Angles, *ODNB*; here Piers is mistaken, for in
1362, when the hospice was founded, Edward III (1312–1377) was king of England; Piers
may have had in mind St Edward, known as Edward the Confessor (c.1003–1066), king
of England, *ODNB*.

[300] Henry VIII (1491–1547), king of England, *ODNB*.

[301] 'therunto' inserted.

[302] 'to yt' deleted.

[303] William Allen (1532–1594), English cardinal; founded Douai College (1568), English
seminary; from late 1585 resided in Rome, and was involved with the English College, living in a simple house next to it; created cardinal, 1587; died in Rome, 16 Oct. 1594. *ODNB*;
Miranda, *The Cardinals of the Holy Roman Church* http://www2.fiu.edu/~mirandas/bios1587.
htm#Allen, accessed 4 Dec. 2017.

[304] Pope Gregory XIII, reigned 1572–1585.

[305] 'for' inserted.

[*The meritoriouse deedes*[306] *and rare partes of father parsons*] Since the deathe of Cardinall Allen, Father Parsons hathe bene the cheefe man wch hathe wroght and travelled for the good of that Colledge, and for the Englishe natione on that side the seas, he hathe bene the meane of erectinge of two semenaries in Spaine the one at Civill [Seville] and the other in Valedelitt [Valledolid], he procured a pention for the Englishe Colledge in Dowey [Douai] helped to the settinge up of a Colledge at St Thomas, and established two Englishe resydences the one at St Lucar [Sanlucar] in Spayne, and the other at Lisbone[307] in Portingall, sheowinge himself in all his actions to be a right religious man whose propertie[308] is[309] to labore for those thinges wch are for the common good of gods Churche and not for his owne privatt commoditie, wch divers tymes hathe bene manifested in him, for that he hathe refused many prefermts unto great dignities, as is well knowen unto dyvers; his deepe iudgmt, great zeale gravetie learninge, and rare witt is soe well knowen to the worlde, by his worckes and writtinges as I neede not make any further reporte of him, I meane (god willinge) after a while to make some rehearsall of the commodities of the Englishe Colledge when I shall descreebe the other colledges of (38) the holy cittie but heere followwinge, I purpose to sett downe,

A Breefe description of the best churches in Rome

[*i St John Laterane*][310] The firste is called Sainte John Lateran his churche, wch was builte by Constantine the greate, and is the Cathedrall Churche of the bishoprick[s][311] of Rome, yt standethe upon mounte Celio, where in tymes paste stoode a stately Pallace of the saide Constantines, whoe indowed that churche wth great reveneus, yt was after the firste buildinge of it, ruinated by the nicholayetane heretickes, and afterward reedfyied by Pope Martine the firste,[312] and ritchly adorned by Pope Sixtus Quintus[313] lately deceased, yt was firste consecrated by St Sylvester uppon the ixth of November and dedicated to our Saviour, St John baptiste, and St John Evangeliste, at the consecration of ye wch churche, [*A wonderfull aparition*] there appeared an Imadge

---

[306] 'good indevours' deleted.
[307] 'in Spayne, and the other at Lisbone' inserted; different ink.
[308] 'peculiar or exclusive attribute'; 'the characteristic quality of a person', *OED*.
[309] 'is' inserted.
[310] 'his church' deleted.
[311] Final 's' possibly deleted.
[312] Pope Martin I, reigned 649–655.
[313] Pope Sixtus V, reigned 1585–1590.

of our saviour wch nowe is to be seene over the highe alter, and not wthstandinge that this churche hathe twyce bene burned since the buildinge of it, yet hathe that Imadge escaped unblemished, There are stations there[314] one the first Sondaye (39) in lente, on Palme Sondaie on the feaste of St John Baptiste, and St John Evangeliste, and at the daie of the deditation of the churche, at ye wch tymes there are great indullgences there to be obtained

There is to be seene the heade of St Zacharie wch was father unto St John baptiste, the challice out of the wch St John Evangeliste by the comanndemt of Domitian The Emperor, did drincke poyson, wch by miracle did never hurte him,[315] also the chaine wch he was lead bounde wthall, from Ephesus to Rome, there are some of the ashes of St John baptiste, and parte of his hayre shurte, parte of the heare of our blessed[316] Lady; the towele wherewth our Saviour wyped his disciples feete, the rodd wherewthall his heade was strooken the garmt wch[317] Pilatt putt upon him, and[318] alitle cruett of his moste pretious blood, over the papall altar are to be seene the moste glorious heads of Sts Peter, and Paule, at the shewinge of the wch there are great indullgences graunted to those wch be presente, under that altere was the oratorie of St John Evangeliste when he was prisoner at Rome, the fowre greate pillers of brasse, wch stande before that alter, weare brought from Ihesuraleme, and are full of the earthe of the holy Land, nighe unto the great gate of the churche is the altar wch St John baptiste had in the deserte, there is the Arke of the Covenante the rodd of Aron, the rodd of Moyses, and the table (40) on the wch our Saviour eate his last supper wch was brought from Ihesuralem by Tytus the Emperor,

[*A place of great resorte*] not farr from the great doore of the churche are apaire of steayres[319] of twentie eight stepps in height, wch were in Pilatt his Pallace at Iherusalem, there is yet to be sene upon one of the stepps a dropp of our Saviour his bloude, inclosed wth a small grate of Iron[320] great indulgences are[321] graunted unto suche as devoutly doe visite those stayres, at the other ende of the churche

---

[314] 'at that churche' deleted; stations: 'a service at which the clergy of the city of Rome assembled at one of a certain number of churches … each of which had its fixed day … for this celebration', *OED*.
[315] 'there is' deleted.
[316] Word underneath 'blessed' erased.
[317] 'wch' inserted.
[318] 'and' inserted.
[319] 'steayres' inserted; word deleted.
[320] 'there is' deleted.
[321] 'are' inserted.

there is a Chappell covered wth leade and borne up wth fayer marble pillers, in the wch is a fonte wherein Constantine the great was Christned by St Silvester then Pope.[322] and not farre from thence is an hospitall wch was builte by the moste noble house of Collumna,[323] and amplified after by divers worthie[324] personadges; manie[325] ritche ornamts of golde and silver were[326] gyven unto it by Constantine the greate, wch were spoyled and carried awaye by those ungodly wretches wch[327] burnte the Churche,

There is a faire Pallace adioyninge to the church[328] lately built by Pope Sixtus Quintus, before the gatte of the wch standethe a fayere pyramedes and not farr from that Pallace is the place where the Councell of Laterane was helde, at the wch there were assembled a thowsande Bishoppes and lerned fathers[329] wch amongst other whol-som lawes did[330] decree that suche as denied the reale presence of the altare shoulde be burnte as heretickes, and yet the sectaries of this tyme[331] doe make litle account of ther difinitive iudgmt herein; But if it were (41) possible that one hundred of them[332] congregated together coulde agree, in defininge of all substantiall pointes of faithe, as this[333] of Laterane and all other Catholick Councells have don, [*The cause of Discorde amonge sectories*].[334] then wthout doubt they will vaunte[335] verie muche thereof the wch cannot be performed by them for[336] that they wante the spirite of unitie wch is the gyfte of the holie ghoste. whose bountifull liberallity they have not iustly deserved to be extended towards them.[337]

---

[322] Pope Silvester I, reigned 314–335.

[323] Probably denotes the Colonna family.

[324] 'noble' delete; 'worthie' inserted; change of ink.

[325] 'There were' deleted.

[326] 'were' inserted.

[327] Word deleted; 'wch' inserted; different ink.

[328] 'to the church' inserted.

[329] 'and lerned fathers' interlined; different hand; the IV Lateran Council (1215) promul-gated the docrine of transubstantiation regarding the real presence of Christ in the Eucharist; regarding heretics, the council merely decreed that those condemned as heretics were to be handed over to the secular authorities for due punishment, Norman Tanner (ed.), *Decrees of the Ecumenical Councils*, 2 vols (London and Washington DC, 1990), I, 230, 233–5.

[330] Word possibly deleted; 'did' inserted.

[331] 'and' deleted.

[332] 'were' deleted.

[333] 'councell' deleted.

[334] Change of ink.

[335] 'u' interlined.

[336] 'for' interlined.

[337] 'whose bountifull … towards them' inserted; different ink.

[*2 St Peeter*][338] The Churche of St Peter in the Vaticano was builded by[339] Constantine the greate, and indowed by hime wth riche[340] lyvinges, yt was consecrated by St Silvester on the ixth daye of November, there are stations helde one twelthe daye,[341] one monday in Easter weeke, on the ascension daye, whitsondaye, Corpus Cristie daye, on all the festivall dayes of St Peeter, one St Andrewe his daye, in the daye[342] of the dedication of the Churche and divers other tymes in the yeere, at wch[343] there are great indullgences to be had at that churche. in the body of the Church[344] doe lye the corpes[345] of St Symon and Sainte Jude, St John Chrisostom St Gregorie the greate and of St Petronilla wch was daughter unto St Peeter, in that Churche is to be sene the heade of St Andrewe, wch was brought to Rome in the tyme of Pope Pius the seconde,[346] by the prince of marka, a ribbe of St Christofer, and many other relickes, as you passe into the Churche on the right hande, [*Relicks of great account*][347] over an altar wch there standethe are kepte the handter[c]here wherewth our Saviour wyped his[348] face, when he swett water and bloude in the garden, the (42) perfect figure of whose hevenly visadge is at this daye to be sene in it, there is also the heade of the speare wch was thruste into his moste glorius syde, thes two relicks were sente by the great Turcke unto Innocent the eight[349] then Pope, and are preserved there wth great veneration. at the shewinge of thes relickes there are great indullgences gayned by suche as are then presente,

[*An incomparabl and statly building*][350] The Channcell of the Churche is newly builte and is made in the forme of a Crosse beinge tenn score yards longe everye waye, the highe altar is sett iuste in the middeste of the Crosse and right over is builte a stately hie towre in the form of a lanterne,[351] and is double wauted[352] from the height of the Churche up

---

[338] 'his church' deleted.

[339] Word deleted; space.

[340] 'great' deleted; 'riche' inserted; different hand.

[341] Presumably the 12th day of Christmas, i.e. feast of Epiphany.

[342] 'in the daye' inserted.

[343] 'dayes' deleted.

[344] 'the body of the Church' interlined.

[345] 'bodies' deleted; 'corpes' inserted; different hand.

[346] Pope Pius II, reigned 1458–1464.

[347] Different ink.

[348] 'his' inserted; different ink.

[349] Pope Innocent VIII, reigned 1484–1492.

[350] Different ink.

[351] Lantern: 'an erection … on the top either of a dome or of an apartment, having the sides pierced, and the apertures glazed, to admit light', *OED*.

[352] Presumably 'vaulted'.

to the tope of the saide towre, in the wch is placed a mightie ba[u]le
of brass, wch will well containe twenty men, and in the middeste of
that boule standethe a crosse of four yards longe, wch hathe many
relickes inclosed wthin yt, This Lanterne is of[353] soe mightie a height
that when a man standethe beneathe upon the grownde, he will
Imagine that the bale is noe bigger then an ordinary brasse pott,
and the crosse dothe seeme to be but one yard longe, [*The sepullcher
of the principall apostles*] under the heighe altar wch standethe in the
middeste of the Channcell doe lie half the bodys of St Peeter and
St Paule buried in a waute underneathe the channcell; and there
also is Imediatly over them another faire altar, at the wch whoesoever
saithe masse hathe greate indullgences for the same,[354] nighe unto
there sepulcher are buried divers holy and vertues Popes, There
(43) may noe woman enter into the vault[355] of St Peeter his churche,
but upon one day in the yeere and on that daye yt is not laufull for
any man to visitt the same,

[*A costly and curous chappell*] on the right hand as you asend unto the
highe altar, is a stately Chappell builte by Pope Gregorie the xiiith
at the four corners whereof towards the tope of the same, are the por-
tratures of the four Latine doctors made all verie ritchely wth moysai-
call worcke,[356] the bottonn of Snt Gregorie his cope as it was toulde
me, is a diamonde valued at two thowsand crownes, in that chappell
is a fayer altar under the wch liethe the body of St Grogorie
Nazensine, and in itt are[357] a faire peare of organs of silver,[358] at
the[359] entrance thereof[360] Gregorie the xiiith himself is buriede,
neighe unto this Chapell standethe apiller wthin a grate of Iron,
againste the wch our Savior was accustomed to leane when he
preached unto the people in Iherusalem [+] At the heade of St
Peeter his Steares is buried the Emperor Otho, the cause whie he
was interred at the entrance[361] of the Churche, doth signifii unto
us[362] that all good Christian Emperors and kinges ought to be defend-
ers of the same.[363]

---

[353] 'of' inserted.
[354] 'there is also' deleted.
[355] 'vault' inserted; word deleted.
[356] Final letter (after 'e') deleted.
[357] 'and in itt are' interlined, different ink and hand; 'there is' deleted.
[358] 'and' deleted.
[359] 'the' inserted.
[360] 'chapell' deleted.
[361] 'cause whie he was interred' inserted, different hand; 'is buried' deleted.
[362] 'doth signifii unto us' inserted, different hand; 'by the which is signified' deleted.
[363] 'same' inserted, different hand; 'Churche' deleted.

[*A magnificent Pallace*] Adioyninge unto this churche the Pope hathe a stately Pallace, and a fayer chapell unto the wch, on all the sondayes in advent, lent and other good tymes, doe resorte, the Cardinalls Imbassedors and greateste noble men in Rome wth great pompe and maiestie, in soe muche as I have seene myself som of the Cardinales atended upon wth (44) at leaste two hundred horss, and a hundred cotches; at there passinge over Ponte Angello, towards the popes Chapell, the great Ordinance of St Michaell his Castle were shott of, and at the dayes of the election and Coronation of the pope, there are many Peales of Ordinance thundred[364] from that castle, and divers rare fyere worckes used. [*A lardge Gallery*] In the Popes house are manye faire roomes and galleries amonge the wch there is one[365] four hundred yards longe, [*An unmatchable Liberary*] in the middeste of wch you maie passe into a doore wch leadethe unto the Popes liberarie wch is verie lardge and costlie in yt are abondance of the only beste bookes in the worlde, all of them for the more parte beinge tyed wth chaines unto the places where they doe lie, Right under this liberarie is his holines[366] Garden in the wch standethe a towre called belvider[367] of great height and bewtie; whosoever stealethe abooke out of this liberarie cannot be obsolved by any man, but by the Pope himself.

Right before St Peeter his steares standethe aguillio or piramides of a mightie heighte wch was sett up there in the tyme of Sixtus Quintus aboute it is a voyde roome where one festivall dayes you shall see at once above a thowsande catches,[368] belonginge unto suche cardinalls noblemen and others wch for devotion sake goe to[369] visitt that holy place.[370] this guilio was founde at St Rocke his churche and is 3 score footte longe and some viii foote brode in the bottome[371] in the tope of itt[372] were Julius Ceasare his ashes kept (45) in a brasen boule, this pira-medes was sett upe wth suche rare cunninge and arte as was wonderfull unto them wch sawe the same, and therefor he wch effected that worcke had a[373] great reward in mony; and for that the erecting[374] thereof, was

---

[364] 'thundred' inserted; 'shott' deleted.
[365] 'gallery' deleted.
[366] 'his holines' inserted, different ink and hand; 'the Popes' deleted.
[367] i.e. Belvedere.
[368] coaches.
[369] 'to' inserted.
[370] 'holy place' inserted, different ink and hand; 'churche' deleted.
[371] 'and some viii foote – in the bottome' interlined; different ink and hand; 'brode' inserted; 'guilio': cf. 'aguglia' (Italian), obelisk.
[372] 'this giulio' deleted.
[373] 'a' inserted.
[374] 'erecting' inserted; 'setting up' deleted; different ink and hand.

wth wonderful and extraordinarie skill performed he was knighted for the same, wch is a degree unto the wch artificers are rarely preferred unto;[375]

[*A moste divine and gloriouse sight*][376] At the feasts of Christemas, Easter Penticoste St Peeter is daye, and all Sts daie the Pope himself dothe use to singe highe masse, at the heighe altar of St Peeters Churche, the cardinales att[377] those dayes doe sitt[378] there[379] as Cannons;[380] the Pope is served at masse wth three deacons, three subdeacones, and three assistances, byside the master of the Ceremonies, accolleties[381] and other officers, one of the deacons, and another of the subdeacons are of the beste cardinalls in Rome, and doe imediatly attende upon his person;[382] two of them are men of[383] great learninge wch[384] doe[385] singe the gospell and Epistle in Greeke, and the other two beinge men of speciall[386] choise doe singe the same[387] in latine one of his assistances is a Pathriarke, and his office is to turne over the leafe as the Pope readethe, the seconde is an archbishoppe[388] whoe with a smale wax candle lighting in his hand, he [epeth]eth his holines [r]ight hand nigh unto the booke, The theerd is a (46) bishoppe whose chardge[389] is, to holde the masse book, upon these great dayes moste commonly som learned religious man doothe preatche, for the hearinge of whom as also for the seeinge of those heavenly ceremonies there doe resorte an infinitt companie unto that churche as well of regular persons[390] as laye people.

[*3 Sainte Paule his church*] Sainte Paule his churche standethe in the waie of Ostia amile without the wales of Rome, it was alsoe builte by Constantine the greate and indowed by him wth ample and large[391]

---

[375] 'unto' possibly deleted – unclear.
[376] Words in margin: change of hand.
[377] Word deleted; 'att' inserted; different ink and hand.
[378] 'in' deleted.
[379] 'Churche' deleted.
[380] Canons: members of cathedral chapter.
[381] Acolytes.
[382] 'other' deleted.
[383] 'of them are men of' inserted; 'are men of' deleted.
[384] 'wch' inserted.
[385] 'doth' emended to 'doe'.
[386] 'great' deleted; 'speciall' inserted.
[387] 'same' inserted; 'gospell and Epistle' deleted.
[388] Line deleted; 'who with a smale wax candle lighting in his hand, he –eth his holines right' inserted.
[389] 'whose chardge' inserted; 'and his office' deleted.
[390] 'regular persons' inserted; 'religious men' deleted.
[391] 'ample and large' inserted; 'greate' deleted.

revenius, in the place where nowe it standethe was miraculously found his blissed[392] heade,[393] it was consecrated by St Silvester on the same daye that St Peters[394] was,[395] yt is averie spacious and wide[396] Churche, and is nowe possessed by Benedictane monckes, there are stations on tuesdaye in Easter weeke, one the sondaye called Septuagesima,[397] on the dayes of the Convertion and Comemoration of St Paule, and at the daye of the dedication of the Churche, at wch times[398] great indullgences are[399] to be had by those wch shalbe presente, + in this churche liethe the body of St Tymothie and many other saints, there is[400] to be seene an arme of St Anne whoe was mother unto our blessed Lady; the chaine where wth St Paule was tied, the heade of the Samaritane a toothe of St Nicholas, and many other relickes; + under the heighe alter wherein[401] liethe half[402] the bodies of Saint Peeter and St Paule, [*A wonderfull miracle*] on the right hand of the same altar is a Crusifix wch spake to St Bridgett (47) Queene of Swetia shee prainge in the same place devoutly befor it, as in the perusing of hir life will more at large apeere[403]

[*4 Sancta Maria Maior*] This great churche of our Ladie is the firste wch was dedicated unto hir wthin Rome yt was builded by one John Pathricke a Romane gent. whoe was a verie ritche man but had noe children, and therefor he and his wife did humblie crave of god, to derecte them in som good course for the bestowinge of there welthe, whereupon there appeared in the night unto them avition, beinge the 5[th] of Auguste, wch did admonishe them, that on the next daie in the morninge they shoulde walke unto the mounte Esquilan, and whe[re]soever theie shoulde fynde the grounde covered wth snowe theie shoulde in the verie same place builde a churche to the honor of our Ladie, the verie[404] same night the licke vition was presented[405] unto him wch then was Pope whereupon,

---

[392] 'blissed' inserted.
[393] 'of St Paule the apostle' deleted.
[394] 'his churche' deleted.
[395] 'consecrated' deleted.
[396] 'spacious and wide' inserted; 'lardge' deleted.
[397] Septuagesima Sunday, 'the third Sunday before Lent', *OED*.
[398] 'there are' deleted.
[399] 'are' inserted.
[400] 'in the churche' deleted.
[401] 'wherein' inserted.
[402] 'half' inserted.
[403] 'as in the perusing of hir life will more at large apeere' inserted.
[404] 'verie' erased, but legible.
[405] 'was presented' inserted; 'apeered' deleted.

the next morninge he wente him self and founde all[406] to be true, and did wth his owne hands begine to take the snowe of the earthe,[407] in the wch place nowe the churche standethe; there are stations everie wenesdaye in imber weeke,[408] on Easter daie, the firste sondaie in advente, on St Iearam [Jerome] his daie, and one the festivale dayes of our Ladie, at wch tymes there are greate indullgences to be obtained there, whatesoever Preiste saithe masse in the Chappell of the persepe[409] wch is in that churche shall deliver a soule out of Purgatorie; under the (48) highe altare of that churche liethe the body of St Mathias the Apostle, in the same churche liethe the body of St Jerame and of St Romulloe, in it is to be seene the linnen clothe wherein our blessed Ladie wraped our Saviour, there is in a cruett som of the bloode of St Thomas of Canterburie, as alsoe his maniple and stoole[410] wch he used in sainge masse, St Mathewe his arme and many other relickes, wch are there shewed after evensonge one Easter Daie; in it[411] there is an altar of Silver wch is of foure hundrethe pounds weight three chaines of silver of fortie pounde weight, and many other ornamts, in the Chappell of the persepe thereof the[412] Pope Sixtus Quintus did build, lyeth his body interred.[413]

[5 *St Lawrence his churche*] Saint Lawrence his Churche standethe one myle wthout Rome in the waye of Tybartine, and was edified[414] by Constantine the great whoe gave unto yt alampe of golde of twentye pounde weight, and many other ritche ornamts, yt is nowe possessed by Cannon regulares, there are stations on wenesdaie in Easter weeke, on tuesdaie in whittson weeke, and on the feasts of St Lawrence and St Steeven, at the wch tymes there are great indullgences there to be gained, whosoever saithe [a][415] masse at an altar wch is there under grownde shall deliver a soule out of purgatorie, under the highe altar of this churche liethe the bodies of St Steeven proto-marter and of St (49) Lawrence, there is to be seene one of the stones

[406] 'all' inserted; 'that vition' deleted.
[407] 'nowe is' deleted.
[408] Ember week: refers to one of four periods of fasting and prayer, in each of the four seasons, following these dates: first Sunday in Lent, Whitsunday, Holy Cross Day (14 Sept.), and St Lucia's Day (13 Dec.), *OED*.
[409] Denotes the crib (Italian 'persepe') of the Infant Jesus, a relic of which was conserved in this basilica.
[410] Maniple and stole: priest's liturgical vestments.
[411] 'this churche' deleted.
[412] 'body of' deleted.
[413] 'did build, lyeth his body interred' interlined; 'the wch was built by himself' deleted.
[414] 'edified' inserted; 'builded' deleted.
[415] 'a' erased, but legible.

wth the wch St Steeven was martired,[416] and the stone uppon wch St Lawrence was layed after he was boyled, the strecks of his blode are yett to be sene, in yt, there is also apeece of the gridiron uppon the wch he was rosted and many other relicks,

[*6 St Sabastin*][417] The Churche of St Sebastean[418] is in the waie Apia amyle and a half from Rome, yt was builte by St Lucina[419] on St Sabastine is daie, and on all the sondayes in maie, there are great indullgences to be obtained, there is aplace under grownde wherein weare found the bodies of St Peeter and St Paule,[420] in the church and[421] churche yard thereof are buried[422] a hundrede seventie four thowsande martires[423] putt to deathe by the weecked Emperors, of the wch there were eightene Popes. in that same[424] are the bodies of St Sabastine and of Saint Lucina[425] the virgine, in it are to be sene verie many relickes, there are Caves under yt in the wch the preistes of the primative Churche were wonte to saie masse, in the time of persecution,

[*7 the churche of the holy crosse in Iherusalem*][426] This Churche of the holy cross in Jerusalem[427] was builded by Constantine – Sonn unto Constantine the greate, and was consecrated by St Silvester. on the xxth daie of marche, there are Stations on the fourthe Sondaie in lente; on holy thursdaie the seconde sondaie in advente all the feasts of the holy Crosse, and upon the day of the deditation of the (50) Churche at wch tymes[428] are great indullgences there to be gained, in itt[429] is to be sene a smale vessell full of our Saviour his moste pretious bloode, the spunge wch was gyven him to drincke full of veniger and gale, twoo of the thornes wch were plotted as a crowne upon his heade, one of the nailes wth the wch he was fastned upon the crosse, the superscription written by Pilatt upon the

[416] 'martired' inserted; 'stoned' deleted.
[417] 'his church' deleted.
[418] 'of St Sebastean' inserted.
[419] Emended from 'Lutisa' to 'Lucina'.
[420] 'there are buried' deleted.
[421] 'church and' inserted.
[422] 'thereof are buried' inserted; 'and the churche' deleted.
[423] 'martires' inserted.
[424] 'same' inserted; 'churche' deleted.
[425] Emended from 'Lutina' to 'Lucina'.
[426] 'the church of the holy .. in Iherusalem' deleted; 'Holy' superimposed; 'crosse' not deleted.
[427] 'of the holy cross in Jerusalem' inserted.
[428] 'there' deleted.
[429] 'in itt' inserted; 'there' deleted.

same,[430] a peece[431] thereof[432] sente thither by St Helina whoe founde the crosse at Iherusalem, wch longe before had beene hidden under grownde; there is also one of the thirtie pence for the wch Judas solde our Savior, and many other relickes, wch are allwayes to be seene uppon good[433] frydaie,[434] in it[435] is agorgious altar dedicated unto ye forsaid[436] St[437] whoe was a woman of noble and kingly parentage descended from the bloode royall of Englande, The seven churches before namede are the moste[438] principall[439] of Rome, in eatche of them are seaven speciall priviledged altars for the visitinge off the wche there are greate indullgences graunted,[440] in them are[441] many more ornaments of golde and silver, and agreat number of relickes, the naminge of the wch in particular for brevetie sake I have omitted,

[*8 the churche of Our Lady Depopulo*] This Churche of our lady de Populo[442] standethe by the porte Flaminia wch is nowe called Porte populo and is possessed by Augustin fryers, in the highe altar there is apicture of our Lady; wherby her intercession (51) there have bene greate miracles wrought. in the place where this altar stands there was in tymes paste growinge a nott tree,[443] under the wch were buriede the ashes of Nero the wicked Emperor, wch were soe well garded wth divells, that noe man coulde passe that waie, but he shoulde be sorely vexed and tormented by them, [*A greate miracle wrought by fastinge and praier*] whereupon the Pope Pascall caused a Sollemn fast and praier to be made by all the people of Rome, by wch meanes our blessed Lady appeered unto him, and willed him to cutt downe that tree, to throwe those ashes into the river, and to make[444] a Churche wch there nowe standethe dedicated unto her; by wch meanes the divells were banished, and the people quieted; this Churche was consecrated by Pope Pascall whoe was asisted

---

[430] 'crosse' deleted; 'same' inserted.
[431] 'of' deleted.
[432] 'of' inserted; 'same' deleted.
[433] 'good' inserted.
[434] 'there is' deleted.
[435] 'it' inserted; 'that churche' deleted; 'is' inserted.
[436] 'ye forsaid' inserted.
[437] 'Helina' deleted.
[438] 'moste' inserted.
[439] 'churches' deleted.
[440] 'there are' deleted.
[441] 'are' inserted.
[442] 'of our lady de Populo' inserted.
[443] 'a nott tree': obsolete form of 'nut-tree', a tree that bears nuts, especially the hazel, *OED*.
[444] 'there' deleted.

in the concecration thereof by ten Cardinalls foure Archbishopes, tenn bishopes, and many other prelatts; on all the feasts of our Lady; and at the daye of the dedication of this Churche there are greate indullgences to be obtained by visitinge of the same, there are to be seene the relickes of St Androwe the apostle of Sainte Marie Magdeline,[445] and of many other saints. this[446] maie be visited in steedd of St Sabastin his Churche as[447] one of the seven before named; right before the greate gatte therof[448] standethe a faire (52) piramedes all of one stone of a great height,

[*9 St John Callavita*][449] This Church of St John Calavita[450] is nowe a nun-erie neighe unto the wch dwellethe a companie of poore people wch[451] are growen unto an order called fatebene fratelli; in Englishe, doe well my good bretherin,[452] the wch wordes theie doe commonly speake in the streetes as theie goe a begginge of there almes, thereby to stirre men up to followe the pathe of good life, the cheefe poynte of there profession is to[453] take care of suche sicke people as are friendlesse

[*10 St Bartlmew*][454] This Church of St Bartolomew by the Iland of Tyber[455] was builded by Pope Gellatious the second,[456] yt is nowe pos-sessed by Franciscan friers, there under the highe altare liethe the body of St Bartlmewe the apostle,[457] in it are[458] many relickes to be sene, on the feasts of St Bartlmewe, and on Palme Sondaie there are greate indullgences to be obtained by visitinge of the same;

[*11 St Cicillia*][459] This Church of St Scicilia[460] was made by Pope Pascall in the place whereof[461] St Scicillia[462] dwelt yt is dedicated unto her, and under the highe altar of that churche shee is buried,

---

[445] Emended from 'Mamdeline'.
[446] 'Churche' deleted.
[447] 'an' deleted.
[448] 'ther' inserted; 'this churche' deleted.
[449] 'his churche' deleted.
[450] 'Church of St John Calavita' inserted.
[451] 'nowe' deleted.
[452] 'bi' deleted; 'the' inserted.
[453] 'look and' deleted.
[454] 'his church in the Iland of Tiber' deleted.
[455] 'of St Bartolomew by the Iland of Tyber' inserted.
[456] Pope Gelasius II, reigned 1118–1119.
[457] 'there are' deleted.
[458] 'are' inserted.
[459] 'hir churche' deleted.
[460] 'Church of St Scicilia' inserted.
[461] 'of' inserted.
[462] Emended from 'Cicillia' to 'Scicillia'.

[*12 St Crisogono*][463] This Church of St Crisogono[464] is a monesterie of Carmelett friers, there are stations on mondaie after the fifte Sondaie in lente, in itt[465] you maie see an arme of St James the greate, a ribe of Snt Androwe, the heade and hande of Snt Crisogono, and divers[466] relickes of other sts,

(53) [*13 of Our Lady beyonde Tyber*].[467] This Church of our Lady beyond Tyber[468] was built, where heretofor in ye tyme of ye Pagan Emperors[469] there was a place in the wch, olde soldiors wch had spente there tyme in the warr were relived, in itt[470] there is a hallowe place covered, wth agrate of Iron, out of the wch at the birthe of our Savior there issuede abondance of oyle, and continued soe for one daie, as by ancient tradition is delyvered unto us[471] there are stations the seconde sondaie in Lent, the Sondaie after Easter, and on the assumtion of our Ladie, under the highe altar are the bodies of St Calisto, and St Cornelio, wth divers other sts;[472] there are to be sene many relickes of St Marie Magdeline[473] and divers other Saints,

[*14 St fraunces*][474] The[475] Church of St Fraunces[476] is a monasterie of franciscan friers ther is a Chappell where there is buried the body of blessed Lodivica, and in this monasterie St Frannces dwelt when he was at Rome,

[*Adioyning therunto is an orchard wherin are certayne orenge trees sett by himself, and in the eyud [epud.?] of every stalke of those orenges at the fastning of that fruite, is as it weare [a cross.?] devided unto five partes. wch should seeme[477] to be an everlasting miracale, as a recorde or register to continue in our minds the remembrance of the five glorious[478] wounds wch he receaved by*

---

[463] 'his churche' deleted.
[464] 'Church of St Crisogono' inserted.
[465] 'in itt' inserted; 'there' deleted.
[466] 'other' deleted.
[467] 'The church' deleted.
[468] 'Church of our Lady beyond Tyber' inserted.
[469] 'in ye tyme of ye Pagan Emperors' inserted.
[470] 'this churche' deleted; 'itt' inserted.
[471] 'as by ancient tradition is delyvered unto us' inserted.
[472] 'sts' inserted.
[473] Emended from 'Mamdeline' to 'Magdeline'.
[474] 'his churche' deleted.
[475] Change from 'This' to 'The'.
[476] 'Church of St Frances' inserted.
[477] 'seeme' inserted.
[478] 'glorious' inserted.

a splendant Caeraphin[479] *frome our Saviour as aremarkable and speciall favour unto him*[480]]

[*15 of St Peeter montorio*]⁴⁸¹ This Church of St Peeter Montorio. standeth uppon ye hill Janicula⁴⁸² is a monasterie of franciscan friers nighe unto it is a Chappell in wch place St Peeter was crucified, wth his heade downewarde; It was his owne desire to be in that maner martyred, for that he would not presume to suffer as our Savior did, at my beinge in Rome there died a fryer of that house, wch in tenn yeeres before his deathe did eate neither fleashe, fishe nor whitemeate, nor dranck any wyne, his strictnes of life and vertuous (54) carriadge was suche as manie men of great accounte and iudgmt, did crave his advice in matters of weight, not doubtinge but that he was illuminated wth an extraordinarie spiritt of divine knowledge,

[*16 St Pancratius*]⁴⁸³ This church of St Pancratius⁴⁸⁴ is a monasterie of the order of St Ambrose,⁴⁸⁵ yt standethe wthout the goulden gate in the waie Aurelia and⁴⁸⁶ was built by Pope Honorius the firste, this hath the tytle of a Cardinall, there are stations ye Sondai after Easter and there doe lye interred the bodyes of S Pancratius Bishop, and of S Pancratio, a valiant soldier and devout gent.⁴⁸⁷

[*17 St onofrio*]⁴⁸⁸ This church of St onofri[u]s⁴⁸⁹ is a monestarie of the order of St Jearame, it standethe upon the mounte Janiculo towards the vaticana, and nighe unto the gate of the holie ghoste, there is verie wholsom ayer upon that hill, it was made the tytle of apresbiterall cardinall⁴⁹⁰ by Pope Sixtus quintus, there are ye relicks of St Onufrio and many other saints, There in it are an innumerable company of martyrs buried but none of there relicks can laufully be taken

---

⁴⁷⁹ Variant of 'seraphim'; referring to type of angel, *OED*.
⁴⁸⁰ Material inserted in right-hand margin, different ink and hand.
⁴⁸¹ 'The churche' deleted.
⁴⁸² 'Church of St Peeter Montorio. standeth uppon ye hill Janicula' inserted.
⁴⁸³ 'his churche' deleted.
⁴⁸⁴ 'Church of St Pancratius' inserted; words following deleted.
⁴⁸⁵ 'his order' deleted.
⁴⁸⁶ 'yt' deleted.
⁴⁸⁷ 'This hath the tytle of a Cardinall … ' inserted, different ink and hand.
⁴⁸⁸ 'his churche' deleted.
⁴⁸⁹ 'church of St onofrius' inserted.
⁴⁹⁰ 'tytle': 'each of the principal or parish churches in Rome, the incumbents of which are cardinal priests; a cardinal church', *OED*.

away by any man wthout the Pope is special licence, under payne of ye greatest excomunication[491]

[*18* [492]*holy ghoste*] This Church of the Holy Ghost[493] is very[494] fairely built[495] (and standeth in Burgo nigh unto ye thriumphant Brige)[496] by the wch is situated[497] the moste famous ritcheste and lardgeste hospitall that is in the whole worlde, yt is of so[498] great, and hudge proporccion for receite[499] as noe man can throwly conceyve thereof, unlesse in parson[500] he dothe vewe the same[501] [*it hath in it parte of the holy cross inclosed in a reliquary of silver gilt wth gould and set out wth pearles and pretious stones, an arme of St Androw inclosed wth silver, and divers other relicks adorned wth greate coste and workmanshipp, there is plenary indullgences to be obtayned uppon whittson Sonday and during ye octaves therof* +][502]

there is agratte of Iron in this hospitall, throughe the wch if any Childe be putt, yt is there receaved nurished and broght up upon the Chardges thereof[503] untill he or shee be sufficiently instructed in some good trade, by the wch they shalbe able to live, or enter into som religious order, I me self did see above five hundred of the children of that hospitall in procession som goinge on there feete, and some in the nurshes armes on St Marks Day[504] (55) I did also observe[505] in one day seaven score maides in procession everie one of them beinge leade by a matrone of Rome, as after a wheele will in more particular apeere[506] wch all receaved there mariadge goods out of that hospitall, there are allwayes in it great numbers of sicke folke, relived and curede as well of gent. as of the meaner Sorte, in itt[507] are divers altars soe conveniently placed[508] that the sicke folkes maye here masse, theie lyinge in there bedds, the

[491] 'There in it are an innumerable company ...' material inserted on right-hand margin, different hand.
[492] 'The churche of the' deleted.
[493] 'Church of the Holy Ghost' inserted.
[494] 'a' deleted'; 'very' inserted.
[495] 'Church' deleted.
[496] Material between brackets interlined.
[497] 'standethe' deleted.
[498] 'suche' deleted; 'so' inserted.
[499] 'and hudge proporcion for receite' inserted; 'capacetie' deleted.
[500] i.e. person.
[501] 'see' deleted; 'vewe the same' inserted.
[502] Material inserted on left-hand margin; different ink and hand.
[503] 'the hospitall' deleted; 'there' inserted before 'of'.
[504] 'on St Marks day' inserted; different ink and hand.
[505] 'see' deleted; 'observe' inserted.
[506] 'as ... will in more particular apeere' inserted.
[507] 'in itt' inserted; 'there' deleted.
[508] 'in yt' deleted.

reveneue ther[509] of[510] amountethe to five hundred thowsande crownes yeerely, the lodgings and howses of office belonging to ye Hos: are soe many lardg and curio[e]d as to be repeated will seeme incredible +[511]

when I was in Rome yt happenede in the yeere 1596 that in the space of two or three monthes (while the fervencie of the heate[512] continued) there died of an hott augewe fifteene thowsande persons, at the leaste[513] in the wch time there comonly departed this life in that house[514] of the holy ghoste betwene twentie and thirtie everie daye, the Sonn in that season did give suche an extraordinarie heate in Rome, as yt did burne to ashes suche drye strawe as did lie in the streets, as I meself can testifie[515]

[19[516] St Lazerus St martha and St marye magdelin] The Churche of St Lazar[o] St Martha e St Mary Magdalen[517] is adioyninge unto the wch an hospitall for curinge of the[518] leaprosie, where there is good government used and much cost be served[519]

[20 St Catherins][520] this Churche of St Caterin is builded nigh unto St Peeters [word unclear] wherin is contayned in av[ei]sall parte of the bloode wch issued from her necke when her heade was cutt of, and of the oyle [de]stilled frome her sepullcher

[21 St James][521] This Churche of St James[522] is in Burgoe [Borgo] and hathe in it the stone upon the wch our Saviour was offred in the Temple, the daie that he was circumsiced (56) and the stone upon the wch Abraham woulde have sacrificed his Sonn Isacke, the wch were sente unto Rome by St Halina ye Empress[523]

---

[509] 'ther' inserted.

[510] 'this hospitall' deleted.

[511] 'the lodgings ... will seeme incredible +' inserted.

[512] 'heate' inserted.

[513] 'at the leaste' inserted.

[514] 'died in the hospitall' deleted; 'departed ... that house' inserted.

[515] 'as I meself ... testifie' inserted; on right-hand margin: 'standeth about St Peeter is gate'.

[516] 'The churche of' deleted.

[517] 'of St Lazaro St Martha e St Mary magdalen' inserted.

[518] 'the' inserted.

[519] 'where there is ... be served' inserted.

[520] 'his churche' deleted.

[521] 'his churche' deleted.

[522] 'of St James' inserted.

[523] 'the wch ... the Empress' inserted.

[*22 our Ladye*][524] The Churche of our ladye beyond Pont Angelo was built be Pope Pius the fowrth belongethe unto the Carmelett friers, in itt[525] are manie relickes, amonge the wch is St Basell his heade, and a piller unto wch St Peeter was tyed, when he was whipte, on the sonday caled quinquagessima[526] there is plenary Indullgence to be obtayned ther[e].

[*23*[527] *the blessed trinitie*] This[528] is in the tope of the hill pincio possessed by the order of St francisco depaul[o] otherwise cale minimes[529] it[530] was founded by ye[531] moste Christian kinge Charles the eight of Fraunce unto whome ye Pope did graunte a priviledge [that] of ye friers there should be governed by a Frenchman of there owne order[532]

[*24 St James*][533] The Church of St James in Augusta, adioyninge unto wch is an hospitall for the Curinge of the moste uncurable deseases on ye Annunciation of our blessed Lady there are plenary Indullgences there to be obtayned.[534]

[*25 St Ambrose*][535] The Churche of St Ambros[536] in the Campidolio[537] was builded by the Cittizens of Millane by the wch theye have builded an hospitall for ther owne Contrie men; Pope Clement ye 7th hath graunted many Indulgences and priviledge therunto.[538]

[*26 St Athanatious*][539] This Churche of St Athenatius[540] is possessed nowe by the gretians, in ye wch[541] theie doe singe and saye masse

---

[524] 'The Churche of' deleted.
[525] 'itt' inserted; 'this Churche' deleted.
[526] Quinquagesima, 'the Sunday immediately preceding Lent', *OED*.
[527] 'the churche of' deleted.
[528] 'churche' deleted; 'of ye' interlined.
[529] 'otherwise cale minimes' inserted.
[530] 'churche' deleted.
[531] 'ye' inserted.
[532] 'unto whom … owne order' inserted.
[533] 'the churche of' deleted.
[534] 'on ye Annunciation … obtayned' inserted.
[535] 'the churche of' deleted.
[536] 'of St Ambros' inserted.
[537] 'm' inserted above 'p'; 'and' deleted.
[538] 'Pope Clement … therunto' inserted.
[539] 'his churche' deleted.
[540] 'of St Athenatius' inserted.
[541] 'ye wch' inserted.

in greeke, It was built by Pope Gregory the xiiith and indowed by him wth ma[nie] [   ] [ead] comodities.[542]

[*27 The churche of*[543] *or Ladye*] This church of Or Lady[544] was builded by Cardinall Barronius,[545] wherein he hathe instituted an order of Regular priestes, this Cardinall hathe verie exactly written the moste parte of ye Eclesiasticall historie, and intendethe (if god spare him life) to finishe the same,

[*28 St Rocke*][546] The churche of St Rocke nighe unto the wch is an hospitall for the nation of the Lumbards and was builded by[547] the Company of St Martine, There is every day their plenary Indulgences to be obtayned graunted by many Popes but specially by Pope Pius ye fourth[548]

(57) [*29 St Jerame his churche*] The Churche of St Jerrame, by the wche is an hospitall for the Slavonians.[549] there are to be seene many relicks, and it is honnored wth the tytle of a Cardinall[550]

[*30 St Lawrence*][551] The churche of St Lawrence[552] in the wch place heretofor was a temple dedicated unto Juno Lucina. but afterward consecrated by Pope Celestino ye third[553] unto ye honour of St Lawrence the Martyre. there are stations on ye Wanesday after the third sonday in lent. In it are contayned the body of St Lurntio and divers other Sts wth many relicks of great account. it is allsoe ye tytle of a Cardinall[554]

[542] 'It was … comodities' inserted.
[543] 'The churche of' deleted.
[544] 'Church of Or Lady' inserted.
[545] Cesare Baronio [Baronius] (1538–1607), church historian, author of *Annales ecclesiastici* (12 vols, published 1588–1607); created cardinal 1596; he succeeded Philip Neri as superior of the Oratorians. Miranda, *The Cardinals of the Holy Roman Church* http://www2.fiu.edu/~mirandas/bios1596.htm#Baronio, accessed 4 Dec. 2017.
[546] 'his churche' deleted.
[547] 'by' inserted; 'for' deleted.
[548] Pope Pius IV, reigned 1559–1565.
[549] 'Slavonians': the Slavs, *OED*.
[550] 'there are to be seene … Cardinall' inserted; change of ink.
[551] 'his churche in Lucina' deleted.
[552] 'in Lucina' deleted.
[553] Pope Celestine III, reigned 1191–1198.
[554] 'Lucina … Cardinall' inserted; change of ink.

[*31 St Silvester*][555] The Churche of St Silvester in wch is the heade of St John baptiste[556] of St Stevene Pope, and of Saint Margett of the house of Collumba, this+ is a monasterie of Franciscan friers, + it is also and is the tytle of a Cardinall.[557]

[*32 St Marie Magdleynes*][558] A Churche dedicated unto St Marie Magdlin in the wch are nunes wch heretofor had bene common women; and therefor they are called convertitts,[559] all the rents wch be receaved out of the houses where light women doe dwell, doe rune to the mayntenance of that monasterie and to other holie uses; if any Curtisane be founde in a Cotche,[560] the horsses and Cotche are confiscate, and solde for the use of the convertitts and the curtisane whipt home throughe the streets, there is plenary Indullgences graunted by Pope Clement ye 7th unto those that shallbe present there on the feast of ye said st[561]

[*33*[562] *ye twelve Apostles*] The Churche of the twelve apostles builded by Constantine the great where liethe the bodies of St Phillip and Jacobe, and of manie other Sts; yt belongethe unto the Franciscan friers there the generall of that order is comonly resident. it contayneth in it many relicks and is intuled by a Cardinall[563]

[*34 St Marcellus*][564] The Churche of St marcellus, wherein is to be seene the heades of St Cosmo and Damiano wth manie other relickes; yt belongethe to the order of the Crucefix,

[*35 our Ladies*[565] *in via lata*] The Churche of oure Ladie in Vialata is builded where heretofor St Paule had his oratorie (58) and in the same place St Luke did write the actes of the apostles, and did drawe a picture of Our Ladie wch is there to be seene,

---

[555] 'his churche' deleted.

[556] 'of St John baptiste' inserted.

[557] '+ it is also … of a Cardinall' inserted; different ink and hand; scratch marks on 'it is allso'.

[558] 'churche' deleted.

[559] Variant of 'convertite': 'a reformed Magdalen', *OED*.

[560] On the lifestyle of Roman courtesans, and on the ineffectual efforts to expel them, see M. Girouard, *Cities and People: Social and Architectural History* (New Haven, CT, and London, 1985), 135; for a contemporary English Catholic discussion, see Gregory Martin, *Roma Sancta (1581)*, ed. G.B. Parks (Rome, 1969), 145–151.

[561] 'there is plenary Indulgences … said st' inserted; different ink and hand.

[562] 'A churche dedicated to' deleted.

[563] 'it contayneth … by a Cardinall' inserted; different ink and hand.

[564] 'his churche' deleted.

[565] 'churche' deleted.

[*36 St Marke*]⁵⁶⁶ The Churche of St Marcke is⁵⁶⁷ builded by blessed marke Pope, nighe to the wch standes a lardge Pallace where the Pope somtyme liethe.

[*37 Our Ladies*⁵⁶⁸ *of Loreta*] The Churche of Our Ladie of Loreta builded nighe unto Traiane his piller, this is aplace of great devotion,

[*38 St Marie de monte*] The churche of St Maria⁵⁶⁹ demonte in wch is a picture of Our Ladie, by prainge before the wch there was a Romaine gentlwoman restored unto hir sight, and since that, manie other miracles have there bene done,

[*39 St Androwe his churche*] A Churche dedicated unto St Androwe, possessed by an order called the theatins, wch doe goe in there attyre as the Jesuits doe, but whereas the Jesuits doe cutt there beardes close, they⁵⁷⁰ do use to weare them longe,

[*40 St Maria de Angelis*] The Churche of St Maria de angelis is a verie lardge and fayer builded churche, wthin the ruines of Diocletian his thearmes or bathinge houses, yt nowe belongethe to the Carthutian monckes,

[*41 Jesus his churche*] The Churche of Jesus was founded by the moste worthy Cardinall Ferneso⁵⁷¹ brother unto the duke of Parma, the buildinge of the wch and of the professed hous adioyninge unto yt, cost the⁵⁷² Cardinall twentie thowsande poundes, it⁵⁷³ is one of the fairest and sompteous Churches in Rome, and belongethe to the fathers of the societie of Jesus, on the right hand (59) of the highe altare is buried the body of Father Ignatious, whoe was the first Jesuit, he begoone⁵⁷⁴ that order about the tyme, that Luther bagane his newe doctrine, wch nowe in Germanie, and many other places is followed, and there is noe doubte but that god did rayse blessed

---

⁵⁶⁶ 'his churche' deleted.
⁵⁶⁷ 'is' inserted; different ink.
⁵⁶⁸ 'churche' deleted.
⁵⁶⁹ 'Maria' inserted.
⁵⁷⁰ 'they' inserted.
⁵⁷¹ Alessandro Farnese (1520–1589), created cardinal in 1534. Miranda, *The Cardinals of the Holy Roman Church* http://www2.fiu.edu/~mirandas/bios1534.htm#Farnes, accessed 5 Dec. 2017.
⁵⁷² 'him' inserted.
⁵⁷³ 'yt' deleted; 'it' inserted.
⁵⁷⁴ 'begoone' inserted; word deleted.

Ignatius to controulle[575] his interprises, as heretofor he hathe done in all other adges, uppon the licke occations, for there was never yett anie newe heresie sprunge up, wch was not Confuted by som newe order of religeous men;

adioyninge unto the[576] Churche is the professed house of the Jesuits, where Father generall himself liethe; [*The extraordinarie good gifts of father general*] he that at my beinge in Rome lived was[577] a Dukes sonn and[578] worthely called Father aqua viva,[579] beinge a man verie well learned moste devout and an excellent good preacher, from whom as from a fontaine dothe runne a melifluous streame of howlsom doctrine, wch refreshethe the hartes of a true beleevinge audience; he hathe four assistantes, wch are as it[580] were Councellours unto hime, eache of them hathe his severall Chardge, the first takethe care of all the houses of that Societie wthin Italy, the seconde of them in Spaine, the thirde in Portugall and Japonia, wch is a mightie region lately Converted by the Jesuits, the fourthe of the Contries on this side of the Alpes, as Germanyia, Fraunce, Englande, Ireland, and (60) Scottland, everie one of these assistances have substituted under them, in everie great Contrie a provinciall, and everie provinciall hathe under hime Rectors of Colledges, and suche others wch doe certifie frome tyme to time the estats[581] of the places wherein they dwell, soe as there is noe matter of Reckninge wch ca[n] happen in all Christendum, but father generall wthin fewe dayes is certified thereof,

there are none admitted into the professed house but suche as be men altogether mortefied, and of extraordinarie virtue and if anie one of the societie doe comitt an offence of importance (in makinge breache of the Rules) before his intrance thereunto, and takinge of his last vowe, then is it laufull for father generall to expulse him from the[re] Companie. [*A severe sentence*] A president whereof I sawe when I was at Rome, of one father Buindoe[582] (an excellent precher) whoe for that he Consented to take the Archebisshopricke of Naples (beinge not constrained thereunto by virtue of sacrede obedience) for his ambition was expelled notwthstandinge that he was then all

[575] 'u' inserted between 'o' and 'll'; different ink.

[576] 'the' inserted.

[577] 'was' inserted.

[578] 'and' inserted; 'was' deleted.

[579] Claudio Acquaviva SJ (1543–1615), father general of the Society of Jesus from 1581 until his death, *Diccionario Histórico de la Compañía de Jésus*, II, 1614–1621.

[580] 'it' inserted; 'yt' deleted.

[581] Estate: 'state or condition in general, whether material or moral, bodily or mental'; 'an account of the state or condition of anything', *OED*.

[582] Bartolomeo Biondi (b. *c.*1548, Rome); became a Jesuit; was dismissed from the Society of Jesus, 27 July 1596, Archivum Romanum Societatis Iesu, Hist. Soc. 54, f.15.

hore, and of great yeers, he beinge at that tyme ghostlie Father unto Cardinall Montalto[583] Lord Channcellor to the Pope and to Cardinall Fernesoe[584] brother to the Duke of Parma, by whose perswation he then yelded to that motion; this is a thinge wch perhapes will seme strange unto men not (61) experienced in those affaires, but theie wch knowe the strict rules of the Jesuits will nothinge wonder at it, for amongste other things, it is accounted an intollerable offence[585] if anie of them should once give consent in his harte to be preferred to anie secular promotion, unlesse he be comaunded as aforsaide. Yt dothe thereof moste evidently appeere that they are voyde of all pride and vaine glorie, and replenished wth humillitie and dutifull obedience, derectinge there courses in the waye of Righteousnes, and clyminge to the topp of absolute perfection. To be brife theie are maligned by the followers of Lucifer, for that they are the true servants of Jesus; from whom there name is derived, and therefor we maie well saie that theie are of those, quos deus elegit in hereditatem sibi, wch god hathe chosen for his inheritance; In this Churche of the professed howse[586] is Cardinall Fernesoe buried;[587]

The cheefe patrone daie therof[588] is the feaste of the circumsition of our Savior, on the wch daie there are great indullgences there to be obtained, the licke are there to be gotten one shrowsondaie, mondaie, and [tue]sdaye, [*A notable institution*] at the wch time the Churche is hanged all wth blacke, and nott[589] soe litle as a thowsande lampes and wax candles burninge in it, but especially upon the highe altar wch then is extraordinarily (62) adorned, duringe these three dayes there is bothe in the fornoone and afternoone great preachinge, and exortation used by the beste learned in Rome, as well Cardinalls and Busshoppes as by the Jesuits themselves and other religious men, the cause whie Father Generall (by the Popes licence) did begine this custum was[590] for that he sawe moste men

---

[583] Alessandro Damasceni Peretti di Montalto (1571–1623), created cardinal in 1585, vice chancellor of Holy Roman Church from 1589 until his death. Miranda, *The Cardinals of the Holy Roman Church* http://www2.fiu.edu/~mirandas/bios1585.htm#Damasceni, accessed 5 Dec. 2017.

[584] Odoardo Farnese (1573–1626), created cardinal in 1591. Miranda, *The Cardinals of the Holy Roman Church* http://www2.fiu.edu/~mirandas/bios1591.htm#Farnese, accessed 5 Dec. 2017.

[585] 'intollerable offence' inserted; 'mortall sinn' deleted; different ink.

[586] 'howse' inserted; quotation from Psalm 32 (33):12.

[587] Line through 'In this churche of the professed howse is Cardinall Fernesoe buriede'; Cardinal Alessandro Farnese died in 1589.

[588] 'of this Churche' deleted; 'thereof' inserted, different ink.

[589] 'nott' inserted; context here is to days before start of Lent.

[590] 'was' inserted.

gyven unto extraordinary pleasures, at that tyme of shrostide as[591] playes, maskes, runinge at the ringe, ridinge upon bu[f]lers, banck-ettinge and suche other sportes, and therefor as well for this respecte, as also for that other orders of religious men doe at that time use extra ordinarie libertie, he instituted this preachinge and Cathekesinge to remember all sortes of men of there dutie towards god, lest that in there mirthe and ioletie they shoulde growe carelesse in matters of devotion and pietie,

[*42 St maria Super Mynervam*].[592] The Churche of St maria Super Mynervam,[593] heretofor was dedicated by the Heathens[594] unto ther false goddas Mynerva,[595] but since Christianitie begane to be publicke in Rome, it[596] hathe bene consecrated to the honnor of our Lady; it[597] is the cheefe monesterie of Dominicane fryers wthin the Cittie. In this Churche doe the Cardinales of the inqui-sitione sitt when they doe arrayne suche heretickes as are produced befor them.

And not longe before my goinge to Rome there was one Marsche[598] an Englisheman (as wee were (63) there informed) arrayned, condemned, and burned for heresie. this Marshe[599] had bene a Scholler for a time in the Englishe Colledge, and seeminge to fale into som sicknes, desired leave for the recoverie of his helthe, to returne into England, the wch was graunted unto him.

But at his Cominge thether the plants of Catholicke Religion (beinge not sufficientlie radicated in him) were easilie supplanted, and in steede thereof did growe weedes and brambles in the grownde worcke of his harte, as by his deeds were manifested, for he thinck-inge to sett a faire vizer[600] on a foule face, came againe to Rome wth afained shewe of holines, but letters were posted after him from England, wch certified the maiestrats of the inquisition, that

---

[591] 'as' inserted; for a contemporary description of carnival in Rome, see Anthony Munday, *The English Roman Life*, ed. Philip Ayres (Oxford, 1980), 95–99.

[592] 'Mynervam' – capital 'M' inserted; changed from small 'm'.

[593] As in previous note.

[594] 'Heathens' – change from small 'h' to capital 'H'.

[595] From small 'm' to capital 'M'.

[596] 'yt' deleted; 'it' inserted.

[597] 'yt' deleted; 'it' inserted.

[598] Walter Marsh (bapt.1560–1595), spy and Protestant martyr; educated at Cambridge University (graduated MA 1585), ordained 1586; by 1590 had vacated his benefices. Entered English College in Douai, 1591; admitted to English College in Rome, Mar. 1593; knocked host from priest's hands in procession, Rome, 15 June 1595; shortly thereafter was burnt as a heretic, *ODNB*.

[599] From small 'm' to capital 'M'.

[600] Variant of 'visor': 'a mask to conceal the face', *OED*.

he wente thether as an intelligencer,[601] where upon he was comitted
to prison, where he confessed that the information was true, and
shewed to the Cardinalls of the holie house the plott laide downe
for his proceedinge in that busines, protestinge wth an impudent spirite that he was exceedinge pensive for his badd act intended, and
thereupon obiured all points of heresie and subscribed therunto,
wth an outwarde apparance of great repentance, whereupon the
Pope sente him to remaine at (64) Doctor Lewes[602] his howse
(whoe was then busshope of Cassana) meaninge wthin a shorte
time to have given him good maintenance but he beinge possessed
wth an outragious spirett walkinge forthe uppon St Agathas daie
and perceavinge that there was agreat procession wch issued out of
that Churche, stoode at the doore thereof, and at the returne
backe of the Companie, [*An execrable fact*] moste wickedlie strocke
the blessed Sacram[en]t out of the priests hande, and thereupon
he had bene torned in peeces by the common people, had not the
Cardinalls wch were there Commaunded the Contrarie; it was suspected then by divers in Rome that he had som p[ar]tners in the
Englishe Colledge, but uppon his examination it fell out otherwise;

I hard it constantly reported by men of good creditt there, that at
his deathe he beinge demaunded whether he helde wth Luther or
Calvin, answered that he[603] was none of bothe there packe horse,
and beinge questioned of the Pope his supremacie in matters spirituall he fully denied the same: then he was interrogated what he
thought of ye Queenes supreamacie in England, he wth earneste
speeches affirmed that the Churche wch had a woman to be head
of it, muste nedes be a monster, lastlie they moved him to tell
them of[604] what religion he was, (65) he told them that he was
directed by the spirit of god, and that there were many of his profession[605] and faithe in[606] the worlde althoughe they were not oppenlie

[601] Intelligencer: 'a spy', *OED*.

[602] Owen Lewis [Lewis Owen] (1533–1594), bishop of Cassano, Naples; born in
Anglesey, Wales; scholar at Winchester College, 1547; fellow, New College, Oxford,
1554, later resigned; matriculated at Louvain, 1563; by 1566 was doctor of law and regius
professor of canon law at Douai University, and rector there, 1568; archdeacon of Hainaut
from 1572; 1574–1580 was agent for Cambrai diocese in Rome; involved in emergence of
English College in Rome; 1580–1584 served as vicar general of Milan; 1588 was named
bishop of Cassano in kingdom of Naples; 1590 was called to Rome and was involved in
church visitations there; was accused of inciting unrest between English and Welsh in
the English College in Rome; died in Rome 14 Oct. 1594, and was buried in the church
of the English College, *ODNB*.

[603] 'he' inserted.

[604] 'of' inserted.

[605] 'religion' deleted.

[606] 'in' inserted.

knowne, [*The burninge of Marshe*] and soe in an exclaiminge fashion (for the wch he was tormented wth hoate Irons, and gaged)[607] he finished his life, the wch (thoughe he woulde have recanted) he coulde not have bene saved;[608] for that he was a formall relappes; by this man his end, we maie take warninge to followe the knowen[609] truthe and not by inconstantie, and Changeablenes in matters perteininge to our soules, run into ungodlie and desperatt courses, to oure utter banishmt. from the ioyes of heaven, where eternall felicitie remainethe;

This wch I have rehersed of Marshe[610] Cannot in reason be offencive to any Christian for althoughe there bi many sectes in the worlde of men baptized, yet I thincke none of them will take wth him, as one of there Congregation, for that in som matter or other of faithe he differed escentially from them, and where there is not unitie and consente in all substantiall pointes there muste needes be deversities of Religion. There weare also after my goinge thether certaine heretickes arrayned and condemned[611] in the foresaide Churche, and beinge in state of relappes coulde not have there lives saved, althoughe they (66) had changed there opinions; but Clement the eight then Pope a man of extraordinarie pietie, by reason that they were florentines and his Contrie men, Comaunded Prayer and fastinge to be made for there Conversion, ye wch was accordinglie performed, and it wrought suche effecte that they were strucke wth compunction of there wicked heresies, and moste humbly craved to be reconsiled, whereupon for the matter of ther[612] soules they were absolved. but the favor gyven them in ther execution was, that where as obstinate heretickes were burned alive, they were firste hanged untill they were deade, and then ther carkasses burned;

In this Churche of our Lady liethe the body of St Katherine of Syinia [Siena], upon the highe altare of that Churche standethe a rare Imadge of our Saviour on the daie of the anuntiation of our blessede Lady; The Pope and all the Cardinalls doe ryde wth great sollemntie unto this Churche, at the wch time one of the Cardinalls dothe singe masse, and then as I partlie touched befor, dothe passe thorowe the Churche the procession of the maides and matrons wch doe com from the hospitall of the holie ghoste and doe everie of them in order kisse the Popes footte [*A charitable bountie*]

[607] 'gaged': gagged.
[608] Semicolon: different ink.
[609] 'the' deleted.
[610] Changed from small 'm' to capital 'M'.
[611] 'a' deleted.
[612] 'ther' inserted.

everie maide receavinge of his purse bearer wch standethe by him, [a] velvett pursse wth a hundred Crownes of golde the wch monie is gyven them towards there perfermt

(67) [*43 St maria Rotonda*][613] This Churche of St maria Rotonda in time of Paganisme was dedicated to Jupiter and[614] all the gods, but in time of Focus the Emperor, yt was Concecrated by Pope Boniface the fourthe,[615] unto the honnor of our blessed Ladie and all the Saints; this Churche is made as rownde as anie bale, and at the intrie thereof doe stande eight faiere marble pillers, the gate[616] is all of Copper verie lardg and Costlie, wthin it there is a verie fayere highe[617] altare wth seven others[618] in eache side[619] wch stand as itt were wthin little chapples in ye thicknes of the walle,[620] it hathe never a windowe but onlie one hole in the tope[621] wch gyvethe light unto all the[622] churche. + theere are Stations on ye friday next after ye octaves of Easter on ye day of invintion of the holy cross, at ye feasts of our lady and all the saints, at the wch tymes greate indullgences, and remissions of sinns are there acquired, in it lieth the body of St Anastasius and divers other sts, and is governed after acollegiall fashion[623]

[*44 the churche of the blessede trinitie and St Thomas of Canterbury*] This Churche of the blessede Trinitie and St Thomas of Canterburie belongethe to the Englishe nation and is adioyninge to there Colledge, it is verie well furnished wth Churche stuffe a great parte whereof was left unto it[624] by Cardinall Allen, and Doctor lewes busshope of Cassana, whoe is buried in the same, there is to be seene an arme of St Thomas of Canterburie som of the heare of St Maria Magdelyn[625] and divers others relickes; on there patrone dayes they use to have verie sollemn service and extraordinarie good musicke, and at those times the singingemen of the Popes Chappell doe assiste them for the setting forthe of the quire wth manie excellent voyces,

[613] 'churche' deleted.
[614] 'Jupiter and' inserted.
[615] Pope Boniface IV, reigned 608–615.
[616] 'of this Churche' deleted.
[617] 'highe' inserted.
[618] 'altares' deleted.
[619] 'of yt' deleted.
[620] 'wch stand … of the walle' inserted.
[621] 'of it' deleted.
[622] 'altars' deleted; 'churche' inserted.
[623] From '+' material inserted.
[624] 'yt' deleted; 'it' inserted.
[625] Changed from 'ma[u]delen' to 'magdelyn'.

on the wch[626] dayes, divers of the best Cardinalls in Rome and other men of great account (68) doe resorte theether gracinge the Colledge wth there honnorable presence,[627]

[45 *St Lucia*][628] The Churche of St Lucia standeth nieghe unto the pallace of Cardinall Mathias wch then was[629] Protector of the Irishe nation, adioyninge unto this Churche there is aplace of residence for the priestes and scollers wch com from Ireland where theie have hansom lodginges and other good commodities,

[46 *St Lewes his*][630] The Churche of Saint lewes was builte by the frenche natione, wch have bestowed great coste uppon it, and uppon festivall daies it is verie ritchly adorned, att ye wch tymes manie indulgences are to be gayned.[631]

[47 *St Augustin*][632] The Churche of Saint Augustin is a monestarie of Augustin fryers, in it dowelt martine Luther while he did remaine in Rome, whose wicked life and false doctrine were verie s[ut]able. in this Churche liethe the body of St Monica mother unto St Augustin and devers other sts. on ther daies of yt [that] happie mother and blessed sonn manie pardons are there receaved[633]

[48 *St apollinarios churche*] The Churche of St Apollinarius[634] nowe partainethe to the Germaine Colledge where in ould tyme the temple of Apollo stood[635] and is ecceedingly well served by them as well wth excellente musicke as wth Costlie Churche stufe, it is a Cardinall is tytle, and hath stations on ye monday after ye fift Sonday in lent.[636]

[49 *St James*[637] *the greate*] The Churche of Saint James the greate[638] standethe in a place called Piatsanavona wch is the lardgest marckett

---

[626] 'those' deleted; 'the wch' inserted.

[627] 'the patrons dayes thereof indullgences are there to be obtayned' inserted, and overlaid on top of material erased.

[628] 'hir churche' deleted; 'c' in Lucia was originally 't'.

[629] 'was' inserted; Girolamo Mattei (1547–1603), created cardinal 1585. Miranda, *The Cardinals of the Holy Roman Church* http://www2.fiu.edu/~mirandas/bios1586.htm#Mattei, accessed 20 Nov. 2017.

[630] 'churche' deleted.

[631] 'att ye wch tymes … gayned' inserted.

[632] 'his churche' deleted.

[633] 'on ther daies … receaved' inserted.

[634] 'A' inserted before 'Pollinarius'.

[635] 'where in old tyme … stood' inserted.

[636] 'it is acardinall … in lent' inserted.

[637] 'his churche' deleted.

[638] 'the greate' inserted.

place in all Rome, and hathe in it two fayere Conditts, as more at lardge shall appeere, in the discours of the pressessions wch were used at my beinge in Rome; This churche was built by Don Alphonsoe Sonn unto (69) kinge Alphonsoe of Spaine; There are divers hospitalls adioyninge unto it, built by the Spanishe nation for the use of there Contrie men on the said Apostles Dai greate indullgences are thereunto graunted by Pope Inocent ye eight[639]

[*50 Or Ladyes*[640] *of peace*] The Churche of Or Ladie of peace perteinethe to the Cannon Regulers, here Saint Pathricke lived while he dwelled at Rome, and was one of that order, his feaste is there yeerly Celebrated,

[*51 St John florentin*][641] The Churche of St John florentin was builded by the florentines, and is verie well maintained and adorned by them, on the xxiiiith of June greate indullgences are there to be gained[642]

[*52 St Lawrence*[643] *in damaso*] The Churche of Saint Lawrence in Damasoe was builded by Pope Damasus whoe gave many ritche giftes unto it, the life and deathe of ye said[644] St[645] is artificially painted aboute it, it is of title of aCardinall, and hath stations on ye tuisday after ye fourthe sonday in lent[646]

[*53 Or Ladies churche de anima*] The churche of our Lady De anima pertinethe to the Dutche nation, in this Churche is buried the bodie of Pope Adriane the sixt,[647] whoe was generallie holden to be afleminge, it is called DeAnima because in it are ordinarilie masses said for the dead, there is to be seene two of ye thornes wch were thrust unto our Saviours head and divers other relicks of great account[648]

[*54 St Nicholas*[649] *in Carcere*][650] The Churche of Saint Nicholas in Carser [u] standethe in a place wherein times paste there was a prison kepte,

---

[639] 'on the said Apostles Dai .... Inocent ye eight' inserted.
[640] 'churche' deleted.
[641] 'his churche' deleted.
[642] 'on the xxiiiith ... to be gained' inserted.
[643] 'his churche' deleted.
[644] 'ye said' inserted.
[645] 'Lawrence' deleted.
[646] 'it is of title ... fourth Sonday in lent' inserted.
[647] Pope Adrian VI, reigned 1522–1523.
[648] 'there is to be found ... relicks of great account' inserted.
[649] 'his churche' deleted.
[650] 'Tuliano' deleted.

by the antient Romaines, in it is to be sene one of St Nicholas his hands and many other relickes, there are stations ye Saturday after ye fourth sonday in lent, e on St Nichlas is day there are plenary indulgence[s] ther to be obtayned[651]

[55 *Or Ladies churche called Ara Caeli*] The Churche of our Ladie called Ara caeli standethe on agreat height uppon the hill of the Capitoll, in wch place heretofore stoode ye Temple of Jupiter, and the Pallace of Augustus Ceasare it[652] belongethe to the franciscan fryers, on the days of St Anthony of Padua, St Bernard, and ye feasts of our blessed Lady plenary indullgencs is graunted unto those wch then shall be present and doe desarve ye same[653]

(70) [*56 St Peter is churche in Carcere tuliano*] The Churche of Saint Peeter in Carcere tulliano, in the place where it standethe was a prisonn where Saint Peter and St Paule were kepte in, whoe havinge converted Processus and Martinanous,[654] there did miraculusly sprunge up a fountaine wthin the prison, in the wch the saide Jaylors were baptized by them,

[*57 St Peter his churche ad vinculum*][655] The Churche of Saint Peter advinculum[656] pertainethe unto the Cannon Regulers, in it is to be seene the chaine where wth Saint Peter was tied in prison at Iherusalem, and many other relickes, it is acardinall is tytle, and hath stations on the first munday in lent, and on the first of August plenary indullgence is graunted to the devout visitors thereof[657]

[*58 St Constance his churche*] The Churche of Saint Constance standethe in the place wherein somtime, the Temple of Bacchus stood and in itt[658] liethe the body of St Agnes, on whose festivall day greate indullgence are there to be obtayned[659]

[*59 St Lawrence*[660] *in Palisperma*] The Churche of Saint Lawrence in Palisperma, standethe upon the hill Viminall, in the wch

---

[651] 'there are stations … ther to be obtayned' inserted.
[652] 'yt' deleted.
[653] 'on the days of St Anthony of Padua … and doe desarve ye same' inserted.
[654] Change from 'm' to 'M'.
[655] 'g' between 'n' and 'c' deleted.
[656] 'g' between 'n' and 'c' deleted.
[657] 'it is acardinall is … devout visitors thereof' inserted.
[658] 'itt' inserted.
[659] 'on whose festivall … are there to be obtayned' inserted.
[660] 'his churche' deleted.

place St Lawrence was martered. Here in times paste stoode the Pallace of Detius the Emperor, it goeth in the rancke of Cardinalls tytles, e hath stations the thirsday after the first sonday in lent, and pertayneth to the Franciscans in the wch is to be seene an arme of St Lawrence and many other relicks of greate account[661]

[60 *St Potentianas*][662] The Churche of Saint Potentiana standethe in the place wherein stoode hir dwellinge house. this woman was one of the moste glorious sts wch lived in hir time, in it[663] is a hallowe cave[664] wherein shee kept parte of the bloode of three thowsande martirs, there are stations on tuesday after ye therd Sonday in lent, and it is acardinalls tytle[665]

[61 *St Martins*][666] The Churche of Saint Martine is builded upon the mount Esquilin in it liethe the bodies of ye said[667] Saint[668] and of[669] Saint Silvester and divers other Saints, it belongeth to the Carmalitt Friers being allsoe acardinall is tytle and hath stations on thursday after ye fourth sonday in lent[670]

(71) [62 *St Praxcedes*][671] The Churche of Saint Praxcedes was consecrated unto hir[672] by Pope pascall the firste,[673] in it liethe hir body; there is also the bodies of fortie martires, whereof aleven were Popes, there is to be seene apeece of the piller whereunto our Saviour was tied, when he was whipped wth many other relicks e aplace wherein is contained parts of ye blood of infinit martirs, there are stations on holy monday it is graced wth acardinalls tytle e inriched wth greate indullgences wch there are to be gained at hir festival day[674]

---

[661] 'it goeth in the ... of greate account' inserted.
[662] 'churche' deleted.
[663] 'that Churche there' deleted.
[664] 'cave' inserted.
[665] 'there are stations ... acardinalls tytle' inserted.
[666] 'churche' deleted.
[667] 'ye said' inserted.
[668] 'Martin' deleted.
[669] 'of' inserted.
[670] 'it belongethe to ... fourth sonday in lent' inserted.
[671] 'churche' deleted.
[672] 'unto hir' inserted.
[673] Pope Pascal I, reigned 817–824.
[674] 'wth many other relicks ... at her festival day' inserted.

[*63 St Anthonie*][675] The Churche of Saint Anthony standethe nieghe unto the fornamed church adioyning unto the wch is[676] averie fayer hospitall and Rownde aboute it is the life of the said[677] Saint[678] moste curiously painted, on whose day plenary indullgence is there acquired[679]

[*64 St Justina*][680] The Churche of Saint Justina standethe in the mounte Cavallo, and upon the same hill the Pope hathe a Princely Pallace builded by Pope Sextus Quintus, on her festivall day there are noe indullgences there wanting[681]

[*65 St Gregorie*][682] The Churche of Saint Gregorie was consecrated[683] by himself, to the honnour of St Andrewe[684] and nowe belongethe to the monckes of his order, in the place where it standethe was the howse wherein he himself[685] and his Father dwelled on the day of all Soules and during ye octaves therof full remission of sins are then to be purchased by true penitent people[686]

[66[687] *St John and Saint Paule*] The Churche of Saint John and St Paule standethe upon mount Celio, in it lie there bodies buried; The religious men of this Churche doe never take the holie order of priesthoode, but have masse saide unto them by the monckes of Saint Gregorie his churche, they spende the greateste part of there time, in stillinge[688] of medisinable matters the wch theie bestowe upon suche as hathe moste neede of them, there are stations on ye first tuisday of lent and it is the tytular church of acardinall[689]

(72) [*67 St George his churche*] The Churche of Saint George is acardinalls tytle[690] in the wch is to be seene his owne heade, the heade of his

---

[675] 'his church' deleted.
[676] 'unto the fornamed ... the wch is' inserted.
[677] 'the said' inserted.
[678] 'Anthony' deleted.
[679] 'on whose day ... there acquired' inserted.
[680] 'is churche' deleted.
[681] 'on her festivall day ... there wanting' inserted.
[682] 'his churche' deleted.
[683] Changed from 'concecrated' to 'consecrated'.
[684] 'to the honnour of St Andrewe' inserted.
[685] 'Saint Gregorie' deleted.
[686] 'on the day of all Soules ... by true penitent people' inserted.
[687] 'A churche of' deleted.
[688] 'stilling': 'distilling', *OED*.
[689] 'there are stations ... of acardinall' inserted.
[690] 'is acardinalls tytle' inserted.

sonne, and aparte of his standard, there are stations ye second day of lent, and on his festivall day manie pardons are there gained[691]

[68 St Sabina[692] churche] The Churche of Saint Sabina is builded in the place where heretofor was the Temple of Diana, in it she[693] and manie other saints are buried, it standethe upon the mounte Aventine, on ashwensdaye the Pope and Cardinalls doe sollemnly Ryde unto it[694] and then dothe he[695] himself give asshes, unto those wch then be presente, it is woorthely intitled to a Cardinall [and] hath stations on the said wanesday[696]

[69 St Anastatius][697] The Churche of Saint Anastatius standethe two myles at leaste wthout the gates of Rome in the waye Ostia, it was concecrated unto his honnour[698] by Pope Honorius the firste[699] in the yeere 622, at the Concecration whereof there were 21 Cardinalls present, there is the piller upon the wch St Paule his heade was cutt of, wch did leape threyse after it was severed from his[700] bodie, and in[701] eatche of the three places where the heade fell, there sprung up afontaine of milke and soe Continued for the space of four and twenty houres, the wch fontaines at this daye are there to be seene full of verie sweete waters, neighe unto it is a Chappell Called Scala caeli[702] where there is an altare under the wch lie the bones of ten thowesande martires, and on ye day of ye said St plenary indullgence was there be gained[703]

[70 St Bonaventar][704] The Chuche[705] dedicated unto Saint bonaventur nowe belongethe[706] unto the Caputchine fryers, there I did see Father Fraunces Nugente Sonn unto (73) Edward Nugent of the

---

[691] 'there are stations … are there gained' inserted.
[692] 'hir' deleted.
[693] 'she' inserted; 'Saint Sabina' deleted.
[694] 'this Churche' deleted.
[695] 'he' inserted.
[696] 'it is woorthely … the said wanesday' inserted.
[697] 'churche' deleted.
[698] 'unto his honnour' inserted.
[699] Pope Honorius I, reigned 625–638.
[700] 'the' deleted; 'his' inserted.
[701] 'the' deleted.
[702] 'caely' deleted.
[703] 'and on the day of the said St … there be gained' inserted.
[704] 'his church' deleted.
[705] Recte 'churche'.
[706] Change from 'belonginge' to 'belongethe'.

Diserte,[707] [*The deserved praise of frauncis nugent*] whoe for learninge good liffe and sufficientie in preatchinge is accounted one of the beste in the contryes wherin he is imployed[708] His extraordinarie perfection is suche as well in the knowledge of divers tonges as also in his eloquent deliverance of his speeche and other rare giftes, as he maie be well termede, the precious pearle of the honorable[709] house from the wch he is descended, and the inestimable ornamente of his native Contrie, heere at ye day of the saint are many pardons graunted to pious catholickes[710]

[*71 A chappell called domine quovadis*] The Chappell called domine quovadis standethe in the waie apia [via Appia], and the reason whie it is called by that name is, as followethe, Saint Peter in the time of persecution fearinge of the Crueltie of the wicked Emperor Nero, flede for his safetie from Rome and in the verie same place where this Chappell standethe our Savior appeered unto him[711] to whom Saint Peeter saide, domine quovadis, in Englishe lorde wheether goeste thowe, unto whom our Savior answered I will goe to Rome to be offered[712] once againe, whereupon Saint Peter wente backe and shortlie after was apprehended and crucifiede, on whose festifall dayes tho[s] sowles have greate benefitt, wch wth godlie intent doe resorte theether[713]

[*72 St John[714] wtout ye gate called portus Latinus*] Without the gate called Portus Latinus is a alitle Chappell in the wch place Saint John Evangeliste was throwen into aboillinge kettle of oyle, out of the wch he came, the oyle havinge noe power to hurte hime. this was

---

[707] 'a man descended from an honorable house' deleted; Dysart, Co. Westmeath; Francis Lavalin Nugent (1569–1635), founder of the Irish Capuchins; son of Sir Edward Nugent of Walshestown, Mullingar, and his wife Margaret O'Connor; studied at Pont-à-Mousson from 1582; by 1590, MA of Louvain University; lecturer in philosophy at Louvain; entered Capuchin order at Brussels, 1591; was appointed superior at Béthune [west of Lille] Aug. 1595, *DIB*. Left Low Countries in July–Aug. 1596 for banishment to Rome, because his superiors viewed him as a representative of the 'Spirituals', or mystical movement in the order. Had returned to Low Countries by July 1598; on the circumstances of Nugent's Roman exile, 1596–8, see F.X. Martin, *Friar Nugent: A Study of Francis Lavalin Nugent (1569–1635), Agent of the Counter-Reformation* (Rome and London, 1962), 47–50.

[708] 'the contryes .. imployed' inserted; 'that order' deleted.

[709] 'honorable' inserted.

[710] 'people' deleted; 'heere at ye day ... catholickes' inserted; 'people' deleted, 'catholickes' inserted.

[711] 'Saint Peter' deleted; 'him' inserted.

[712] 'crucified' deleted; 'offered' inserted.

[713] 'on whose festifall dayes ... theether' inserted.

[714] 'is chappell' deleted.

done by (74) the comaundement of Domitian the Emperor there are
stations on saterdaie next after the fift sondaie in lent, and on the sixt
of maye plenarie remisstion of sinnes is given there unto all complet
beleevers[715]

[*73 A chappell dedicated to St peter and St paule*] In the waye of Ostia is a
Chappell in the wch place Saint Peter and Saint Paule did take there
leave the one of the other, the verie same daie that theie were bothe
martired, this and manie other testimonies befor rehearsed by me
doe make a perfect demonstration of Saint Peter his beinge at
Rome, wch notwthstandinge is gainsaiede by many of the heretickes
of this time,

[*the number of the churches in Rome*] Rome dothe containte in all one
hondred fortie and two Churches, but these wch I have named are
the principaleste of them, all thes churches at everie of there festivall
dayes and stations have excellentte musicke, and those wch dovoutly
doe visite them, at those times doe gaine indullgences for the same as
in particular hath beene mentioned[716] but espetiallie suche as doe
confesse and receave the blessed sacramente, there is not anie one
daie in the yeere one the wch you shall not finde either solemn stations or festivall dayes in som one of them at the leaste, the wch dothe
settle a habite of devotion in all suche good Christians, as doe repaire
unto that holie Cittie,

Heere it is convenient that ye[717] reader doe make a pawse and
Consider wth himself of the moste magnificente estate of the
Churche of Rome, of her incomparable governmt, and Celestiall
doctrine and then maie he wth religious admiration proclaime wth
a zelous sperite and an exalted (75) voyce, affirminge wth the
Patriarcke Jacob. [*Ge. 28*] Vere non est hic aliud nisi domus dei et
porta caeli. verily this can bi noe other then the house of god and
gate of heaven,[718] and of necessitie it muste be soe, for that our
Saviour hathe promissed, [*mathe: 16*][719] quod portae inferi non prae-
valebunt adversus eam. that the gates of hell shall not prevaile
againste her, wch is demostrativlie verified in these words of our
Redimer vid[ ]: Oravi pro te petre[720] ut fides tua nunquam deficiet

---

[715] 'there are stations ... complet beleevers' inserted.
[716] 'as in particular ... mentioned' inserted.
[717] 'ye' inserted.
[718] Genesis 28:17.
[719] Matthew 16:18.
[720] 'quod' deleted.

I have praiede for this Peter that thy faithe shall never faile,[721] the wch
as Cardinall Bellarmyne sufficientlie makethe manifeste at Lardge (in
his bookes, De summo Pontifice[722]) is meante by Saint Peter and his
successors. And for the infallible testimonie hereof we maie examyne
the Ecclesiasticall histories, and we shall finde that the bisshoppes
wch did succeede the reste of the apostles, in there particular
Seats, did intracke of time, fall either into Scisme or heresie, but it
Cannot in[723] any sorte be prowede, that ever any Pope of Rome (laufully placed) did prevaricatt or falle from his firste faithe. By the
wch[724] It dothe evidently appeere whate was the intente of or Lord
Jesus Christe when he made that praier unto his (76) father, and it
is not to be doubted if the Sonn of god had saide, oravi pro vobis
Apostolis, I have praied for you my apostles, but that all theire successors had continuede in ther puritie untill this daye, as the
Romaine Busshoppes have don. To Conclude if it were possible
that any of the true successors of Saint Peeter shoulde declyne
from the right faithe, then dothe it Concequently followe that our
Savior his petition was furstrat and made in vaine, the wch to be
affirmed were moste execrable blasphemy;

There are many godly Customes and infinit motivs used in Rome for
the sturringe of[725] men up unto devotion, of the wch I will discribe
some of the beste, soe far forthe as my slender memorie shall give
me leave,

A Description of certaine processions wch I sawe when I was at Rome

[*A maiesticall prcession*] On Palme Sondaie one of the Cardinales dothe
singe masse in the Popes Chappell, and on that daie there is great
resorte thether as well of Cardinalls Embassadors Dukes and other
noble men, as also of the meaner sorte, the Pope at that daie
dothe sitte upon a throne of ma[jes]tie, and dothe deliver Palme
wth his owne hands (77) unto the Cardinalls noble men and others
wch there be presente, the Cardinalls as they assende up the throne,

---

[721] 'Ego . . . rogavi pro te ut non deficiat fides tua', Luke 22:32.
[722] Robert Bellarmine, *Disputationes ... De controversiis Christianae fidei: Tertia controversia generalis: De summo pontifice* ([Ingolstadt, 1587]), listed in Carlos Sommervogel, *Bibliothèque de la
Compagnie de Jésus* (Brussels and Paris, 1890), I, column 1156; Robert Bellarmine SJ (1542–
1621), created cardinal 1599, *Diccionario Histórico de la Compañía de Jésus*, sub nomine.
[723] 'bi' deleted; 'in' inserted.
[724] 'he' deleted.
[725] 'of' inserted.

doe reverence wth the bendinge of there bodies thrice, and then kissinge of his Cope, doe receave the palme, in verie dutifull maner, the
noblemen and others doe kneele thrice, and kisse his fotte at the
receavinge of the same, wth as great reverence as possible maie be
usede, then dothe the Pope descende from his Throne and havinge
a quire of hevenly musicke singinge before him doth pass in prosses-
sion wth all the Cardinalls throughe the Chappell, and soe Rounde
about a fayere Roome wch is before the Chappell doore; at there
returne they finde the[726] doore shutte, whereuppon he that imediatly
goethe befor the Pope saithe this verse of the prophett David, [*Psa:
23*] Attollite portas principes vestras elevamini portae aeternales et
introibit rex glori[a]e, lifte ye up yor gattes you princes and oppen
yor everlastinge dooes,[727] and the kinge of glorie shall enter in; then
he wch standethe wthin answerethe, quis est iste rex gloriae, whoe
is the kinge of glorie then dothe the other replie, dominus fortis et
potens dominus potens in praelio, Oure lord[728] stronge and mightie,
our Lord potente in battaile, then doe they goe in procession rounde
aboute the same place againe, and[729] the same wordes, Attollite portas etc[730] are repeated and answered unto[731] as before; but at the Laste
(78) replie he wch knocked at the dore saithe, dominus virtutum ipse
est rex glorie our lord of all vertue he is the kinge of glorie,[732] whereupon the dores were opened, and the Pope havinge ascended up to
his throne, all the Cardinalls and others performinge Ceremonies of
dutie to the highe altare and to his holines, doe in orderly and decent
maner take there places, then dothe the highe masse goe forward wth
great sollemnty; the passion of our Savior beinge sunge in it in suche
a dolefull[733] maner, as woulde move devotion in the harte of any man
wch is not obdurat or obstinate [*A worthy Spectacle*] On mandaie thursdaie[734] the Pope himself dothe minister the blessed Sacrament unto
Cardinalls, and that beinge done, bothe he and they doe passe in
procession from the chappell up unto astately gallerie wch is over
Saint Peeter his steares, and there in the sight and hearinge of thowsandes of people wch stande[735] in the Courte under him, he dothe

[726] 'Chappell' deleted.
[727] *Recte* 'doors'.
[728] 'is' deleted.
[729] 'then' deleted.
[730] 'etc' inserted.
[731] 'unto' inserted.
[732] Psalm 23 (24):7-10.
[733] Word erased: possibly 'sorte'.
[734] Maundy Thursday, the Thursday preceding Easter Sunday.
[735] 'the' deleted from 'standethe'.

pronounce sentences of blessinges and Cursinges upon suche as
moste deserve them

[*Spetiall motives of devotion*] In this time of the holy weecke there are
many other processions used, Ritchly sett forthe wth divers motives
of pietie and devotion, but specially on holy thursdaie at night, at
the wch time I sawe passinge throughe the Cittie to Saint Peeters
Churche, thirteene severall (79) processions, sett forthe by the
devoute Companies of Rome, (as that of the trinitie, the holie ghoste,
the Sacrament of the altare, our blessed lady; The deade, Saint martin, and the reste, everie one of the wch Companies havinge there
severall Chappells served wth verie good musicke did strive to excell
one another in settinge forthe of ther processions, in sorte as followethe. firste there was Caried a fayre Crosse of Silver gilt wth
golde, imediatly after were borne certaine Silken flagges sett upon silver staves, then five Curious and well Carved Imadges of our Savior,
gilt wth gold, declaringe his deathe and passion. The firste figured
accordinge as he swette water and blode in the Garden, The seconde
shewinge howe he was whippede and scurged by the Jewes, The third
did represent there scorninge and Crowninge him wth thornes. The
fourthe his Caryinge of a heavie Crosse upon his bloudie and tormented shoulders, The fifte did manifeste the Crucifinge of his
moste innocente bodie, and sheddinge of his moste pretious blode
for or sines, and after them an Imadge of our Lady mornefully sett
forthe in blacke, all these were soe li[ve]lie sett forthe as the sight
of them did breede great Compunction of harte, and devout pietie
in the (80) beholders, betwixt everie of these Imadges were borne
divers ritche Crosses wth flages and banners wherin were to be
sene draven verie faierly the instrumts of his deathe, as the Crowne
whipe speare nailes spoonge, and one eche syde, and after them
were Caried many fayer lights of wax, and then[736] followed discupli-
nants[737] to the number of five hundred, or there abouts in there severall processions[738] two in everie Rancke; whippinge of themselves.
there you might beholde there bodies all gored and there blode runninge downe on[739] the streets, som of there whipes havinge smale
spurres in the ende of them wch did ravell and teare there fleashe,
to the great chastisinge of there bodies and subduinge of badd affections, after them wente in order religious men beinge som three ore

---

[736] 'then' inserted.
[737] *Recte* 'disciplinants': cf. members of a religious order in Spain, who publicly scourged
themselves by way of discipline, *OED*.
[738] 'in there severall processions' inserted; different hand.
[739] 'e' deleted.

four hundred in everie procession, singinge of theire litanies and
sainge of devoute praiers, and laste of all som of the best
Cardinalls in Rome accompanied wth many noblemen and
Sittizence, and an infinitt Companie of Common people wch did
thronge after them thorowe the streetes, In this sorte they toke
there waye over Pontangelo [Ponte Sant'Angelo], other wyse called
Saint Michaell his bridge; and soe throughe the Popes Pallace in
wch is a Chappell dedicated to Saint Paule, wherein at that time[740]
was erected a similitude (81) of the Sepullcher of our Saviour
verie mornefully sett forthe, the Chappell beinge all hanged wth
blacke velvett, and at leaste five hundred wax Candles and
Lampes burninge in it, after they had devoutly visited the
Sepullcher, from thence they descended downe a statelie payer of
steares into Saint Peeters Churche, and there did visite the altare
over the wch are kepte the handkercher wch our Savior did wipe
his face wthall, in the Garden when he swette water and blode,
in the wch[741] the perfecte picture of his heavenly face, at this daie
maie be seene, there is also the heade of the speare wch was thruste
into his moste glorious syde, as before I have spetified, at the sheawinge of wch relickes the disciplinants doe soe[742] whipe themselves
and the whole people there assembled on there knees doe soe zeal-
ously and pittifully Crie unto god for mercie, as it woulde move the
harte of any good Christian to extraordinarie devotion; from
thence theie departed in suche order and maner as theie Came
theether unto the churches from out of wch theie begane there
procession[s],

[*An example of humilitie*] On good frydaye the Pope and Cardinalls doe
goe to the Chappell in mornefull maner, all somteous ornaments that
daie are sett aside, the altare lyinge bare, and the Imadges all (82)[743]
Covered, and one that daie in the afternoone as also, on the two
daies before is tenebre[744] songe wth dolefull tunes; but leaste that
the meaninge of this might seeme difficulte to men not experienced
in those matters, I thought it not amisse to make som particular relation thereof. Lett it therefor be understoode that on the wensdaie
thursday and frydaie in the afternoone before Easter, all musicke

---

[740] 'time' inserted.

[741] 'is' deleted.

[742] 'wipe' deleted.

[743] In MS '32' – *recte* '82'.

[744] Tenebrae: liturgical office, 'usually sung in afternoon or evening of Wednesday,
Thursday, and Friday in Holy Week, at which the candles ... are extinguished one by
one after each psalm, in memory of the darkness at the time of the Crucifixion', *OED*.

as well of voyces as of instruments is layde asyde, and then is the office of ye Churche songe in a lowe lamentable fashion, and wth great deliberation, wthout the ordinarie ceremonies wch at other times are used, thereby gyvinge us to witt[745] howe shee dothe morne in remembrance of the passion of or Savior. where this service is songe there is placed before the highe altare a great Candlesticke made three Corner wyse, wch Containethe fifteene wax Candles, whereof there are seaven one eache side standinge a slope the one above the other, and the laste is sett in the topp, the wch doe represente our blessed Lady and the apostles of or Lord; In those daies the lessons of the nocturnes[746] are reade oute of the Lamentations of the prophett Jeramie, verie distinctlie wth a sadd and sorowfull voyce, and at the endinge of everie psalme[747] of that office one of those lights are extinguished[748] wch dothe signifie howe Christe his disciples in his greateste afliction (83) did one after another forsake him but the upper taper (by the wch was domonstrated the mother of god) remained untouched.

[*The unmatchable vertues of the blessed virgin marie*] by this is meante hir incomparable Constancie towardes hir onlie sonn our redimer. but when that Candle was taken downe, and putt underneathe the altare, then the night beinge fallen, ther was nothinge but darcknes. Whereby we maie learne that althoughe her reputation did seeme accedentallie dimmed, by the unthanckefull Jewes and ignorant gentiles yet was shee essentially illuminated wth the unquenshable fiere of the holie ghoste. alludinge unto this that althoughe her persevirance did seeme unto them (morallie speakeinge)[749] in shewe to[750] vanishe, yet did it remaine in full force and vigor, under ye altare[751] of gods protection. And surelie we maie verie well saie, that even as the defect of that visible light did worcke sencible darcknes in the materiall Churche, soe in a spirituall sence, there muste nedes be blacke obscuritie in there Congregation wch remove from it, the bright and cleere light of the intercession of the blessed virgin marie. This taper as aforesaide beinge taken awaye, the abbott Prior or cheefe prelatt there, dothe prononce the spalme miserere[752]

---

[745] 'to witt': 'to know', *OED*.
[746] One of the divisions of the liturgical office of matins, *OED*.
[747] 's' before 'psalme' deleted.
[748] 'do' deleted.
[749] 'seeme … (morallie speakeinge)' inserted.
[750] 'to' inserted.
[751] 'ye altare' inserted.
[752] 'Miserere': the 50th (51st) psalm, beginning 'Miserere mei Deus' 'Have mercy on me, o God': 'one of the Penitential Psalms', *OED*.

wth a slowe and submisse[753] voyce, and duringe that time the religious men or women or secular preistes of that place and divers others doe whipp (84) themselves wth suche an admirable devotion and severe pietie, as the moste Stonie hartes might there wth bi mollified; this maner of Service is appointed by the Churche to imprinte in or hartes, howe the face of the whole earthe was covered wth darcknes at the time of the puttinge to deathe of the Sonn of god, as is mentioned in these wordes of the sacred gospelles of those daies [*Luc. 22.*] vid[ ]: et tenebrae factae sunt. etc.[754] All the wch beinge ended there is the taper of ye blessed virgin discovered and sett upon the highe altar wch gyvethe light unto the whole Churche, signifyinge unto us that hir exceedinge great splendor was of suche incomparable cleernes, that it coulde not in anie sorte be longe shaddowed, and as that Candle did give great comforte unto those wch hade remained there for atime in darcknes, soe did her unmatchable virtues and spottles life, send forthe suche shininge beames of infinitt goode example, as did illustratt the whole millitante Churche in earthe. and there is noe doubt but that in the triumphant Churche shee dothe nowe moste gloriously illuminate the angells and Saints in heaven, in a higher degr[e]e then Can be Comprehended by mens understandinge, havinge (by reason of hir unspeakable merites) receaved that power from the blessed Trinitie by whom shee is[755] seated in an everlastinge throne of maiestie above angells and archangells, and Crowned Queene (85) of the higheste heavens,

Moreover it is to be noted that on[756] Maundaie Thursdaie and good fridaie, ther is in everie Churche placed a patterne of the Sepullchere of our Savior sett out wth mani lights and blacke Coverings, all wch is don to woorke an impression in our minds of his deathe and passion Suffred for us.

[*A heavenly sight*] On Easter even after the blessinge of the fier reedinge of the profices wch doe fortell the Cominge of or Savior, the blessinge of the Pascall Candle and the performinge of many other stately ritts and Ceremonies, highe masse dothe begine, and then is all the Churche served in white, wth Costly Clothe of Silver and Satten in token of the resurrection of or Savior, and when the priste dothe singe, Gloria in excelsis, then are the pictures in the Churche

---

[753] 'submisse': of voice: low, subdued, *OED*.
[754] The correct reference is Luke 23:44: 'It was now about the sixth hour, and darkness came over the whole land until the ninth hour.'
[755] 'is' inserted.
[756] Originally 'one': 'e' erased.

discovered[757] wth many lights burninge by them, and at the verie same
instante dothe the Organs Sackbutts[758] Cornetts and voyces sounde out
moste heavenly melodie together, at the wch time alsoe the bells doe
ringe and the great Ordinance of Castle St Angello doe shootte of,
everie thinge in his kinde gyvinge Laude and praise unto god, and reioycinge in his presents for the glorious Ressurrection of his imaculatte
Sonn our Redimer and advocatt Jesus Christe;

And for the more sollimnization of this triumphant feaste there
dothe use yeerely (86) to Com forthe out of[759] Saint James his
churche wch standethe in the markett place Called Piatsanavona,
[*A triumphant procession*] a worethie and well settforthe procession,
betwene twelve and one a Clocke on Easter daie in the morninge,
and is don upon the Coste and Chardges of the Spaniards wch
be[760] Residente in Rome, the wch is performed to my remembrance
in maner and forme as followethe; And[761] for that it makethe fitlie for
my purpose, I muste give the reader to understand, that this[762] markett place aforesaide, Cannot be noe lesse then fower or five hundred
yardes longe and two hundred broade, in the wch are scituated towe
verie faiere and Lardge Conduits, wherein there are many Cuninge
and Costlie devices, for apte Conveyance of wateres, and are wth an
extraordinarie and Rare worckemanshipp builte of a great height; in
the tope of the wch Conduits there were framed, for the better celebratinge of that glorious feaste, as it were two litle Castles. betwixt
them are diveres Cordes tyed, and sundrie other cordes and ropes
fastned betwixt the Pallaces wch stande in that markett place, and
those towres, upon the wch there were divers and strange fyere
worckes used, as also there were then erected in that place, three double Quires for musicke mounted upon stately Skaffolds, as heere will
(87) in particular appeere.

Firste there isshued from the Churche, sundrie motives of devotion
as the Crosse and suche lyke[763] wth as good as a thowsande lights of
wax, borne by men of good Rancke. then a Spanishe busshoppe in a
Costlie Cope bearinge the blissed Sacrament in a pix of great

[757] 'discovered': uncovered, *OED*.
[758] 'sackbutt': a brass musical instrument, *OED*.
[759] 'of' inserted; for a discussion of the Easter procession of the 'Confraternità della SS.
Resurrezione', see Luigi Fiorani, 'Processioni tra devozione e politica', in Marcello Fagiolo
(ed.), *La festa a Roma: Dal rinascimento al 1870* (Turin, 1997), 70. For two contemporary images
of the Easter festivities in Piazza Navona (from 1589 and 1592), see Michael Rak, 'Piazza
Navona: Trionfi, feste da gioco, feste stellari', in Fagiolo (ed.), *La festa a Roma*, 183.
[760] 'there' deleted.
[761] Changed from 'and' to 'And'.
[762] 'worcke' deleted.
[763] 'lyke' inserted.

vallewe, and after him followed manie great prelats and a wonderfull
number of religious men in suche order as hathe bene sett downe in
the former processions. at whose entringe into the markett place,
there appeared an angell to Com downe from the tope of one of
the Pallaces, wth a light in his hande, wch descendinge, did sett on
fyer an artifitiall divell, wch stoode towards the nether ende of the
Corde, whereupon the firste double Quire did singe out laud[e]
and praise unto god for the distruction of Sattan and did sounde
forthe manie instruments of musicke fillinge the ayer wth the[764]
noise thereof, and it is to be noted that by reason that it was darcke
and the Quires far assunder, the directors of the musicke were fayne
to kepe time wth torches; Then did devices of fyere worcke runn
betwixt the two Castles to the greate admiration of suche as were presente; when as theie had proceeded towardes the mideste of the markett place the Gallies of the kinge (88) of Spaine and Turckes galleys
did appeere to meete, and had a Cruell fight upon the Cordes, where
the turcke receaved as it shoulde seeme agreate foyle and overthrowe,
by the blowinge up of his forces. At wch time the seconde quire did
wth reioycinge mellodie give heavenlie thancks unto god for that victorie. Havinge passed towardes the ende of ye[765] Piatsa, there might
be seene a Rounde Compassed thinge representinge the worlde,
wch then turninge rounde about was sett on fyere, the wch made
resemblance unto us of the laste daie of iudgement. – whereupon
the third Quire wth lamentable tunes did expresse the afflicted estate
that men shalbe in at that dredfull daie; And in there returne while
theie were passinge on the other side of the marckett place, bothe the
towres did[766] shoote of in there maner, manie peales of shotte the one
at the other, And there wth[767] did all the Quires of musicke ioyntly
wth there voyces and instrumts sownde out a melodious and ioyfull
songe for the victorious resurrection of the only Sonn of god, the
wch continued untill suche time as the busshopppe was assendinge
up the staires wch leade up unto the Churche, and then were both
the Castles sodenly turned into scorchinge (89) flames, wherewthall
a number of great ordinance and many small Pices were shotte of,
puttinge us in minde[768] howe the Lyon of the tribe of Juda wch
descended from the stocke of David,[769] did as that daie, breake

---

[764] 'the' inserted.
[765] 'ye' inserted.
[766] 'in there' deleted.
[767] 'all' deleted.
[768] Original 's' at end of 'minde' deleted.
[769] 'See, the Lion of the Tribe of Judah, the Root of David, has triumphed', Revelation
5:5.

open the gattes of hell, conquer the dragon, and redeeme the Soules wch were in prison

[*A laudabl Custom*] There is also a procession used on Saint Marcke his daie, of the moste parte of all the religious men in Rome, wch beginnethe at Saint Marcke his Churche and passethe to Saint Peeter his Churche, this is don[770] yeerely in remembrance of the procession wch was commaunded to be Sollemnized by Saint Gregorie the greate,[771] at the wch time there was agreat plage in Rome, wch principallie by his intercession was sodenlie sceased, for it is saide for Certaine that as Saint Gregorie passed over the bridge of Saint michell in procession, there was seene an angell shethinge a blodie sworde, in the tope of Adrian his moule wch sithence that time is Called Castle Saint Angello, and never since as I harde for truthe reported[772] the plage hathe bene in Rome, I did also see at my beinge there the translatinge of the bodies of Saint [V]areus Archeleus and Pancratius unto a newe churche wch was made (90) in there honnor by the renowned Cardinall Sporsan,[773] at the wch were assembled in procession above ten thousande religious men and priests, moste of the Cardinalls in Rome and an unspekeable number of laie people flockinge after them; hereunto might be added the stately ceremonies wch are used in Creatinge of Cardinalls, whereof at my beinge there, in one daie there were seventine created,[774] also the reverente ceremonies wch I me self have seene Pope Clemente the eight use in concecratinge of a bishoppe whoe then was Called Cardinall Burgetius and nowe dothe succeede him[775] in the sea apostolicke,

[*An incomparabl precession*] But the moste stately and maiesticall procession there used is on Corpus Christie daie,[776] and Comethe forthe from Saint Peeter his Churche, the Crosse beinge Caried befor it,

[770] 'neighe unto the hospitall of the holie goste, which is a myle' deleted.

[771] Pope Gregory I, reigned 590–604.

[772] 'that' deleted.

[773] Presumably Cardinal Francesco Sforza (1562–1618), Miranda, *The Cardinals of the Holy Roman Church* http://www2.fiu.edu/~mirandas/bios1583.htm#Sforza, accessed 24 Nov. 2017.

[774] At the consistory held by Clement VIII on 5 June 1596 sixteen cardinals were created, Miranda, *The Cardinals of the Holy Roman Church* http://www2.fiu.edu/~mirandas/consistories-xvi.htm#ClementVIII, accessed 22 Nov. 2017.

[775] 'him' inserted; 'Camillus Burghesius' (Camillo Borghese), created cardinal Sept. 1593; consecrated bishop by Clement VIII in Sistine Chapel, 27 May 1597; elected pope (Paul V), 16 May 1605. Miranda, *The Cardinals of the Holy Roman Church* http://www2.fiu.edu/~mirandas/bios1596.htm#Borghese, accessed 22 Nov. 2017.

[776] For a discussion of the 'Corpus Domini' procession in 16th-century Rome, see Fiorani, 'Processioni tra devozione e politica', 73–78.

and many other dovout motives, and not soe fewe as a thowsande lights of wax borne by Cittizence of good account, Then the Pope himself bare headded wth a Canapie of Clothe of golde borne up over him by eight noblemen wth silver and gilt Staves, Carreinge the blessed Sacrament moste reverently in a Costlie pix of gold, the teares by reason of the abondance of his[777] devotion tricklinge downe his cheekes, havinge aboute him a ritche Cope (91) of Clothe of gold wth buttons of pearle and pretious stones, and the licke upon the Cardinalls wch one everie side did assiste him, then folllowed after him four and fortie Cardinalls in costlie Copes two in everie Raancke, and after them in licke order som fortie Archbusshoppes and bushoppes, a hundred mount seniors[778] (beinge men Capable of bishoprickes) the beste of the Popes houshoulde in Reade gownes to the number of seven score or thereabout, three thousande at the leaste of religious men, wth divers Quires of musicke and an inumerable Companie of noblemen cittizence and Comon people whiche thither did resorte to see that incomparable procession, wch was of suche greatnes that scante were the laste of them gone oute of the Churche when the pope was com backe and assendinge up the statlie Stayeres of Saint Peetres, after he had passed towards Pontangello [Ponte Sant'Angelo] and soe Rounde about, nighe unto[779] the hospitall of the holy ghoste, wch is a myle and a half in Compas, all the streets beinge hanged wth Clothe of arras and other Ritche hanginges, and over there heades great sailes and sheetes of Canvas tied wth ropes (92) to great pillers and mastes of timber, the mastes and Sailes are sett up at the Coste and Chardges of the Jewes, wch is inflicted as a punishmt upon them, for there is nothinge wch theie more hatte then the body of our Savior, wch that daie is in particular extraordinarielie adored; and soe returninge unto St Peeter his Churche wente unto the highe altar of the blessed Sacramente wch is over the bodies of Saint Simon and Saint Jude, at the dore of the wch altar the Pope did Elevate the consecrated hoste in the presence of the people whoe all doe kneele downe and adore the royall[780] presence of our Redimer, then did he putt it into a tabernackle of great Coste wch is in the backe of that altare, Provided for that purpose, and from thence dothe passe unto his Pallace beinge then Carried in avelvett chayere upon twelve mens shoulderes blessinge the people as he passethe by them, and[781] sheddinge of humble teares upon his

---

[777] 'his' inserted.
[778] Presumably a rendition of the Italian 'monsignori'.
[779] 'it' deleted.
[780] 'royall' inserted.
[781] 'and' inserted.

goulden Cope, wth his triple Crowne upon his heade besett wth diamonds rubies Saphieres and other pretious stones; This honnor is don
unto him for that he is helde here vicegerent unto our[782] Savior of his
universall Churche in earthe, and therfor if wee give honnor and reverence unto the deputies[783] of mortall princes wthin there (93) particular governmts, of force it muste followe that wee shoulde give and
atribute exceedinge and all possible honnor and reverence unto him
wch dothe houlde his deputation from that immortall and eternall
kinge or Savior Jesus Christe.

[*A godlye invention*] Nowe for as muche as the processions Stations and
festivall dayes are celebrated for the greateste parte in the daie time
Pope Clemente the eight for that he woulde have Continuall praier
wthout intermission in the Churche, of his extraordinarie pietie and
devotion, hathe instituted a Solemne[784] procession in Rome everie
eight and fortie howres, wherein the blessed Sacrament is Caried
by som Cardinall bisshoppe or prelatt, wth great reverence and at
there returne backe to the Churche from whence the procession
issued forthe, the Concecrated hoste is placed upon the highe altar
or upon som other altar moste convenient of the same, in a Costlie
pix to be seene by all that are present. at that time all the windowes
are shutt and the Churche hanged wth blacke, and duringe that eight
and fortie howres, there are great store of lights and lampes burninge
as well upon the highe altare, as upon manie other places in the
Churche wth Continuall pretchinge praier and meditation; wch is
performed by the religious (94) men or preists of the Churche
wherein the procession hapnethe at that time, everie one of them
in his Course accordinge as there superors dothe directe them; this
devoute Custom dothe begine at Saint Peeters, and then everie
Churche of importance takethe his turne, everie one of them stryvinge to excell one another in settinge forthe of the same, accordinge
as there abillitie dothe extende, this quaranthore as in Itallian it is[785]
called was instituted to prevente the divell; followinge therein the
Councell of Saint Peter wch exorted us sayinge, [*i petri: 5*] fratres[786]
sobrii estote et vigilate be sober and watche my brethren and show-
ethe the Cause in these wordes, quia adversarius vester diabolus tan-
quam leo rugens circuit quaerens quem devorett,[787] for that yor

---

[782] 'Ladie' deleted.
[783] 'and' deleted; 'of' inserted.
[784] Abbreviated form of 'procession' deleted.
[785] 'was' deleted; 'it is' inserted; 'quarant'ore': forty hours.
[786] 'a' inserted in 'fratres'.
[787] I Peter 5:8.

adversarie the divell licke a roaringe Lion compassinge, seekethe whom he maie devour, and therefor it is necessarie that wth the wyse virgines wee have or lampes Continually burninge attendinge for the Comminge of the bridegroome[788] our lord and redimer the Consubstantiall Sonn of the eternall god his father.[789]

Theise pius Costomes and[790] dovout processions ioyned wth severe discipline are the beste meanes to merite favor at gods handes for the shortninge or time in Purgatorie, soe as the inwarde intente be Correspondente unto the Common receavd[791] meaninge of the outwarde acction, and that theie be not in dedli sin[n]e wch perform the same; [*Certaine observations*] And trulie I have seriously observed (95) that where the doctrine of merit is nott[792] preched there actes of mortification are neglected, and but fewe good worckes effected, for of necessitie there muste nedes be great loyttringe where ther[793] is noe exspectation of recompence for painfull labor, on the other side, I have diligently taken note, that where this antient doctrine[794] is published there doe proceed from it wholesom fruites, aptly fittinge for the nurishment of mens soules, as for example[795] the buildinge of monestaries wherein many true servantes and Saints of god have lived and dyed. the erectinge of Colleges wch have bene the nursseries for the bringinge up of learned devines and g[od]ly preistes. the makinge of bridges and highe waies for the Common good of travelleres. and the Cause of intyre chastetie wch is the higheste worcke of supererogation. by the wch many holie men and women have bene advaunced to the fruition of the moste blessed visadge of the everlastinge god.

[*Matthaei cap. 7.*] And therefor wee maie verie well saie, ex operibus eorum cognoscetis eos. ye shall knowe them by there worckes[796] and for the better manifestation hereof, if wee doe observe there actions it will appeere unto us, that the Coste and travell wch was in times paste bestowed for the service of god, is nowe Converted

---

[788] Parable of the ten virgins, Matthew 25:1–13.

[789] 'his father' inserted; with reference to Jesus Christ, 'consubstantial with the Father' occurs in the Nicene Creed.

[790] 'and' inserted.

[791] Letters deleted.

[792] 'is nott' inserted.

[793] Erasure marks; 'ei' possibly deleted; from 'either' to 'ther'.

[794] Final 's' slightly erased.

[795] 'for' deleted.

[796] Here Piers changes the gospel wording so as to emphasize the theological case for works, 'A fructibus eorum cognoscetis eos', 'By their fruits you shall know them', Matthew 7:16.

to the pleasure of men; as for example. In steede of faier Churches they make (96) stately pallaces, in place of Ritche Copes and vestments and other Churche stufe, Somteaus apparell for there owne uses; In lewe of hospitallitie and lardges to the poore, deyntie dishes for the pleasinge of there owne appetites; Finallie[797] whereas in olde time there was great bountie bestowed in there hales, for the Common good, nowe have they withdrawen themselves into ther inner roomes for there private profitte and pleasure, The wch things are soe apparant as they themselves Cannott denie the same; [*other observations*] Other observations maie be taken note of for the Convinceinge of there innovations, and amongeste other things som oathes[798] wch theie usualie sweare, wch by them are kepte in practis, in a kinde of Careles fashion, not respectinge the originall Cause for the wch theie were firste intented.

For whoe Can gainsaie, but that ye[799] swearinge by[800] the holie masse, the Crosse of Christe, or by oure blissed Ladie, were done in regarde of the sacred reverence wch was due to everie of them, to thende that men takinge oathes of suche great account and waieght, might have there affirmations the[801] better believed; But nowe the sacred Sacrafice of the masse is forbidden as unlawfull, the glorious signe of the Crosse accounted superstition, and the blissed mother of god litle esteemed of by them.

Also they maie perceave the antiquitie of (97) Catholicke religion, if they will but marke the names of som of oure holie dayes[802] allowed of by them, to witt Christe his masse daie, on the wch everie preiste is licensed to saie three masses to the honnor of the birthe of the Sonn of god. Candlemas daie wch signifieth a masse saide as that daie wherein Candles are blissed, holie masse daie by the wch is to be understoode the masse saide to the honnor of all the saintes. Morover if theie please to Consider, the returnes of there tearmes,[803] theie shall not finde them voyde of matter of inducemente to ancient religion. for whate can be mente by: Crastina Animarum, but the daie after the office saide for the Soules departed. the wch thinge

---

[797] 'here' deleted.
[798] 'a' inserted.
[799] 'ye' inserted.
[800] 'by' inserted; different ink and hand.
[801] 'the' inserted.
[802] 'dayes' inserted; different ink and hand.
[803] 'the returns of there tearmes': 'return' refers to a sheriff's report upon a writ directed to him; by extension the word refers to the days within a legal term when returns were made, *OED*.

theie nowe thincke[804] verie vaine and needlesse; And what maie be insinuated[805] by the returnes Called the octaves of the blissed trinitie the purification of the virgin marie, and suche others, but that the firste inventors of the lawe knowinge them to be dayes of note in the Churche of god, did sett them downe rather then other dayes, for the better direction of the people wch were sommoned to appeere in there severall Courtes. But surely I muste needes saie that theie have either forgotten, or maliciously neglected, the true use of octaves for that it is the ordinarie time allotted for the (98) celebra-tinge of principall feastes, wch howe well theie doe observe there Churche men Can beste wittnes.

It maie also be noted howe in there bookes theie doe sett downe Ember weecke,[806] in lattin called, quatuor tempora, at the wch times in Catholicke Contries the busshoppes doe use to give holie orderes as also the orders called minores, and then[807] doe they ordi-narilie faste accordinge to the prceptes[808] of the Churche, but amon-geste them the imagenarie consecration of there supposed preestes now by them used is nott att those tymes appointed.[809] as for ye lesser orderes there is noe suche thinge named in theire Churche, and as toutchinge fastinge in generall theie are contented to here it spoken of, but not to make use of it.

I cannot heere omitt the Rogation weecke[810] mentioned by them, in the wch solemn processions in olde time have bene used, for the increase of the fruites of the earthe, and abstinence from fleashe com-maunded, but howe this is parformed by them I neede not make anie relation, for the breache hereof doth manifestlie and dailie appeere as well in there dyett as in there abrogatinge of those processions.

To be bri[e]fe lett us observe that Callender and it will easilie be seene, that all the (99) Saints mentioned in it, were (as they tearme us) papistes, and moste of them priestes wch saide masse as Saint Gregorie Saint Augustin Saint ambros, etc. And therefor seeinge

---

[804] 'nowe' deleted.

[805] 'And what' deleted.

[806] Denotes the four periods of fasting and prayer observed respectively in the four sea-sons of the year; each fast occupied three days, and the weeks in which they occurred were called Ember weeks; on Ember Saturdays ordinations usually took place, *OED*.

[807] Second 'then' deleted.

[808] *Recte* 'precepts'.

[809] 'the imagenarie consecration … tymes appoynted', inserted, different hand; 'there are noe lawfull busshoppes and therefor noe consecration of preestes' deleted.

[810] In the season after Easter, refers to 'the week in which Ascension day falls', *OED*.

that theie acknowledge them to be Saints it muste of force followe
that theie are in a miserable estate, for theire soules, wch be not of
that religion wch those holy men weare of, and consequently in
state of perpetuall damnation (unles that in time theie submitt themselves unto that Churche, of the wch those Saints weare members,
the wch is perspicuously proved to be the Churche of Rome by infinitt good aucthorities. and amongeste them by blissed Saint Jeram,
whoe in his Epistle dedicatorie of the newe Testamente written
to[811] Pope Damasus callethe him by these wordes, tu qui summus
es sacerdos, in Englishe, thowe wch arte the higheste prieste,[812] the
wch dothe include, that[813] the sea of Rome was then ye[814] cheefest bisshopricke in the whole worlde, and so dothe continue to this daie as
is well made knowen by Cardinall Bellarmyn, in his bookes, de
summo pontifice, and divers other learned men whose testimonies
maie well be obstinatlie denyed, but shall never be iustlie refel[t]ed
These thinges beinge by men of ordinarie capacitie (100) considered
of, doe worcke litle impression in them, but if prudent and iuste
respecte be putt in practis, by those wch are of ripe iudgmt (and
not willefullie blinded) usinge due reflexion upon there understandinge, theie shall finde that these observations are of verie great consequence, and that the parlementarians[815] have muche overseene
themselves, for that theie made not another callender when theie
framed there newe religion, in soe muche as therein is evidently
seene, by circumstances the antiquitie of the Catholicke faithe, wch
by there innovations is as muche as in them liethe suppressed and
extinguished.+

+ [816] Thus much I thought coveniant as not impertinent to be
added hereunto to thende that it might the better appeere unto
the diligent reader howe by the evident testimonie of antient recorde
(manifestlie specifiead in the allowead bookes of oure newe
instructers) it is cleerlie perceyved, that the religious actes tendinge
to mortification and pietie wch nowe are used in the moste holy
Cittie and in all other Catholicke places, have bene in effecte put
in practis in these oure Christian Contries from the time of there

---

[811] 'by' erased.
[812] This letter of St Jerome to Pope Damasus I (reigned 366–384) was included in the
introductory material of the Vulgate Bible; what became the standard edition of the
Vulgate was first published under Clement VIII in 1592.
[813] 'then' deleted.
[814] 'ye' inserted.
[815] One who 'accepts a religion or church ordained or ruled by parliament', *OED*.
[816] Separate page, not numbered; inserted after the main text was completed; see
Introduction, pp. 44–45.

firste Conoertions[817] unto the true faithe, untill suche time as the
Lutherans Calvenistes and other suche sectories did by there vaine
and pernitious inventions hinder the laudable continuance of the
same,[818]

[*The magnificence of ye churche of Rome*][819] The ceremonies used in Rome
as well in there churches, as also at there publicke processions are soe
heavenly there musicke soe excellent, there relickes soe exceedinge in
nomber and coste, there Churche stuffe and other ornaments soe
ritche and Somteous, as the vallewe of them woulde in a maner
seeme inistemable to be rehearsed, and the repeatinge of the partic-
ulars prove tedious, and therefor I will at this time omitt to use any
further discourse of them. but nowe I shall by gods permition proceede to make

A description of the chifest Colleadges in Rome

(101) [*i the Roman Colledge*] The faireste and beste is named the Roman
Colledge, builded by Pope gregorie the thirttenthe for the use of the
Jesuits, here be the schooles[820] wherein they reede devinitie,
Philosophie, the mathimattickes, humanitie, grammer, and suche
licke, there Scooles are verie lardge and fayer, and yett notwthstandinge the resorte of scollers is suche unto them, as they have scante
roome to write in; the methode wch they use in teat[ch]inge is soe
substantiall compendious and exact, and performed by them soe diligently, as aman shall learne as muche there in seven yeeres as in
manie other places he shall doe in twentie, and it is not to be won-
dred that there doctrine doth prosper, for there rules are soe virtuous
and there liffe soe exemp[i]llear, as makethe them at this daie to be
beloved of all the zelous Catholickes, and hated by all pollitcke[821]
worldlinges. At the deathe of Gregorie the xiiith this Colleadge
was unfinished and soe yett remainethe, there is livinge gyven by
him unto it[822] sufficient to mantaine two hundred and fiftie Jesuits,
but had he lived he had doubled there revenues,

[*2 the novitiat*] Ther is another howse in maner of a Colledge dedicated unto Saint Androwe wch belongethe unto the Jesuits, this is

---

[817] Conversions.
[818] End of inserted material.
[819] Text continues on p. 100.
[820] 'Scollers' deleted: 'schooles' inserted; different ink and hand.
[821] *Recte* 'polliticke'.
[822] 'yt' deleted; 'it' inserted.

there[823] house of probation. heare all suche as enter into the Societie muste (102) be trayned up for two yeeres, in all pious exceccies as praynge fastinge meditation discipline[824] and suche other acts of mortification, and if in that time they trie themselves, valiant soldiors in resistinge there owne appetitts, then are they further admitted, but if theie doe not satisfie the expectation of there Superiors[,][825] they are quietly dismist; The Jesuits are very choise[826] in receavinge of any Scollers into ther novitat, soe as lightly there is noe Jesuitt but is borne of averie great house[,][827] hathe som rare gyfte of witt and learninge[,][828] or is excellent in som suche qualitie or occupation as maie be for ther creditt or profitte of there order; [*A spirituall exercise*] There is in[829] the novitiatt as[830] also in other Colledges wheres the Jesuits beare rule agodly exercyse used, wch is ordered in sorte as followethe.[831] First the Scholler[832] is putt into aprivatt Chamber where noe bodie comes at him exceptinge his ghostlie Father (wch instructethe him howe and upon whate matter he shoulde meditate) and he wch bringethe him meate wth whom he muste use no[833] idle speeches duringe the time of his restrainthe. The time wch ordinarilie theie use[834] is eight daies at leaste the wch[835] is augmented by theire superiors, according as they shall finde the strainthe and pietie of ye exercysed. Duringe this time theie muste kepe averie spare diett and not sleepe above five or six houres (103) in fowre and twentie, theie muste use discipline and muche prayers, and meditatt som five houres at diverse times in the daie;

At there first entrance theie muste meditatt on there Creation redemtion and preservation, wherein theie shall consider of the miraculous worckes of god, and of his lowe[836] towards mankinde, that

---

[823] Change from 'the' to 'there'; the novitiate was at Sant'Andrea al Quirinale.

[824] 'discipline': the mortification of the flesh by penance; by extension, a whip or scourge, especially one used for religious penance, *OED*.

[825] Stroke similar to comma.

[826] 'choise': of persons, 'careful or nice in choosing; selective, discriminative', *OED*.

[827] Stroke similar to comma.

[828] Stroke similar to comma.

[829] 'in' inserted.

[830] 'as' inserted.

[831] Here Piers refers to the meditations of the First Week of the Spiritual Exercises of St Ignatius Loyola, see Joseph Munitiz and Philip Endean (eds), *Saint Ignatius of Loyola: Personal Writings* (London, 1996), 289–302.

[832] 'h' inserted.

[833] Change from 'noe' to 'no'.

[834] 'theie use' inserted; different ink and hand.

[835] 'time' deleted.

[836] i.e. love.

consideringe the ende for the wch the[y] were made,[837] theie shoulde give all honnor and dewe glorie unto there maker,

The seconde meditation is to consider of the torments of hell and of the endlesse paine wch theie shoulde endure, if they doe not by a perfect faithe and good life prevente the same,

The thirde meditation is[838] of Purgatorie, in the wch they muste consider howe to make there time shorte, by meanes of there godly cariadge in this liffe, for the fiere of it never leavethe burninge, untill it hathe purified soe muche of the Soule as was putrified by Sinn, for there is noe uncleane thinge that cann[839] enter into the kingdom of heaven,

The fourthe meditation is of there deathe, or departure oute of this worlde, wch beinge considered of, dothe breede great remorse of Conscience, and of oure liffe lewdly paste, and at that instante to imagine howe many millions of worldes woulde be given by them for one houre of true repentance,

(104) The fifte meditation is of Sinn in the wch theie are to collect as nighe as they can, the true number of all there sinnes comitted, wch they can remember, wth the quallitie nature and degree of everie one of them, and other circumstances thereunto belonginge, wch thinge will breede great compunction of harte and hatred of former bad affections,

The other meditations sett downe by there ghostly fathers[840] are moste of the mercyes of god, as that of the prodigall childe[841] and others. Duringe the time that they doe meditatt upon hell Purgatorie deathe and Sinn the windowes of the Chamber are for the moste parte closed, to the ende that they maie the better Consider in what horrible darcknes there soules are in, soe longe as they are inwrapped within either of them; soe havinge Considered of gods iudgmts the[y] oppen the windowes of there Chambers and of there mindes, and doe looke cheerefully upon the mercyes of god, then they doe make agennerall confesson of all there Sinnes unto

---

[837] Here Piers refers to the 'Principle and foundation' meditation of the Spiritual Exercises, Munitiz and Endean, *Saint Ignatius of Loyola*, 289.

[838] 'is' inserted; different ink.

[839] 'cann' inserted; word deleted.

[840] 'father' deleted; 'fathers' is the following word.

[841] The parable of the prodigal son is given in Luke 15:11–32.

there ghostly father, and soe receavinge of the blissed Sacramente, theie are restored to there former libertie,

[*Howe grace and free will are placed in man,*] By this spirituall exercis it dothe appeere howe a man havinge the grace of god, maie benefitt the estate of his Soule by the well application of his free will, for the better (105) understandinge whereof; lett any man Imagin that he dothe lie danger-ously sicke in his bedd, and that ye Phisition dothe prescribe unto him a medicin, and leavethe the same in his Chamber prepared for him, there is noe doubt but he maie choose wheether he will receave the same or no, soe as it liethe in his sure disposition whether he will live by applyinge of it, or perishe, by doinge the contrarie. Jo[in]e soe speakinge in a spirituall sence we maie conceave god to be the Phisition, the grace of god the medicen, a mary Soule the patiente, and his free will the application, wch beinge proporcionallie consid-ered, we maie by good consequence gather that as a skillfull Phisition perceavinge his prescribed remedie to be reiected by his patient, dothe worthely with drawe his help from him, Soe will the heavenly Phisition take his grace, from those wch doe neglecte the applieinge of the same, by good worckes and other actes of pietie, for the curinge of there deseased Soules. And therefor the studients of these Colledges by the direction of there Superiors the Jesuits, doe use this Custom of restreinthe, and many other godlie rules, havinge confidence that by suche meanes the grace of god, wilbe continwed, in them and applied as an everlastinge benefitt unto there soules.

(106) And surely it cannott be but that the wante of understandinge, howe grace and free will are in man, is the cause whie manie in these dayes run mainlie into desperatt estate, shrowdinge themselves under the Collor of predestination, the wch[842] theie wreste and misconster[843] accordinge there particular fancies. and will alleadge the scriptures for the same, but if they be questioned wthall wch is the booke of god they will saie the olde and newe Testament wch nowe they use, unto the wch maie be replied that they have no infallible argumt to prove, that thos bookes be the true scriptures for the better man-ifestinge whereof, I muste toorne the pointe of there owne weapon againste themselves: Firste it muste be supposed accordinge there doctrine, that the Churche of Rome fell into heresie or scisme about six hundred yeeres after Christe. althoughe they cannott assigne wch was the firste Pope or Bisshopp of that Sea that did declyne, in what yeere this hapned, in what matteriall pointe he

[842] Second 'wch' deleted.
[843] i.e. misconstrue, *OED*.

differe[t]he from his predicessors, or by what generall Conncell laufully called he was condemned; Butt if the westerne churche did prevaricatt and become atichristian (as theie doe teache and give forthe)
I then demaunde where there bible hathe bene ever (107) since kepte,
For firste there was not one Creature intirlie of there religion[,] borne
in nyne hundred yeeres after this imaginarie falle of the Pope, wch
might preserve the same, And the reason is for that there was not
in all that[844] time any man wch agreed wth them in all substantiall
pointes of faithe, Secondly it dothe nott[845] appeere that theye
receaved it by mirackle, or that it was delivered unto them by the
handes of Angells, This beinge true (as it might easilie be prooved)
they cannot then denie but that they received the same either
from the Latin or greeke Churche, or from the Synagoge of the
Jewes. If they saie theie had it from the Latin Churche, whie shoulde
theie[846] beleeve any worde wch is in it, seeinge it was soe many[847] hundred yeeres, in the custodie of him whom theie[848] beleve to be ante-
christe. whoe might change alter and corrupt the same as pleased
him; if they doe averr that the scripture came to them from the
Greeke Churche, they muste give noe creditt thereunto, for that
the Easterne Churche hathe bene infected wth scisme and heresie
many yeeres befor the time assigned by them, of the decaye of the
Churche of Rome, and I thincke theie will not saie that it was delivered unto them by the Jewes Sinagoge, for that they be the[849] oppositt
enememyes of Christe (108) And therefor noe truste to be had in any
booke kepte by them,

Soe as to conclude (everie thinge beinge equallie and dailie considered) they cannot demonstrativlie knowe, that they have the true written worde of god in there possession, for that theie have no infallible
meanes to iudge of the certaintie thereof, And therefor it followethe
that[850] whosoever dothe not beleve the apostolicke Sea of Rome, to
be the true and unspotted Churche of god, hathe noe reason to
putt his confidence in the olde or newe Testament, for that[851] he
hathe no[852] sufficentt or evident grounde to[853] enduce him, for to

[844] 'that ' inserted.
[845] 'nott' inserted; different ink and hand.
[846] 'woulde' deleted.
[847] 'yeere' deleted.
[848] 'woulde' deleted.
[849] 'the' inserted.
[850] 'that' inserted.
[851] 'that' inserted.
[852] 'no' inserted.
[853] Word deleted.

conceave that those weare the bookes wch weare lefte unto us by or
Saviour and his apostles; and consequently there is noe sure waie
lefte by them wherebie a man maie be saved. This muche I thought
fitt as by the waie to speake of this matter, accordinge my litle skill
and learninge, but nowe I shall (godwillinge) make som reporte of
the other Colledges as far forthe as my knowledge dothe extend.

[*3 The Englishe Colledge*] The Englishe Colledge dothe containe
twenty[854] seaven chambers beside the halle refectory lyberarie[855]
wardcrob[es] kitchen and other houses of office, the Churche there
is dedicated to the blissed Trinitie and to Saint Thomas of
Canterbury;[856] one of whose armes is to be seene there as befor
(109) I have specified; there are belonginge to the house two faier
courtes, aboute the wch the churche and lodginges are builded, in
the mideste of one of them is a verie lardge Sesterne into wch runnethe throughe gutteres and pipes[857] of leade all the raine water,
wch for the more parte fallethe upon the churche and lodginges
rounde aboute it, wch water dothe serve to drincke wth there
wine, and for other necessarie uses, the licke is to be seene in
many other places in Rome, there is belonginge to the colledge
agood Garden and a fayer viniard wch standethe wthin the
Compas of Nero, his decayed Pallace, where wee[858] did use to recre-
ate our selves one daie in the weeke, On the[859] eves of there patrone
dayes the Schollers[860] doe discipline themselves and doe use other
extraordinary devotions. The revineves of the Colledge doth
amounte at the leaste to eight thowsande crownes yeerely

[*4 The German Colledge*] The[861] Colledge belonginge unto the Germans
Pollonians[862] and hungarians, is farr greater then the Englishe,[863] but
my knowledge of it and the others followinge is not sufficient for the
makinge of any lardge discription of them, the revenues of it doe
amount to twentie thousande crownes ayeere, it hathe a verie fayer
and lardge vineyard belonginge unto it, and many other thinges

---

[854] 'twenty' inserted; different ink.
[855] 'lyberarie' inserted; 'and' deleted; different ink.
[856] Thomas Becket [St Thomas of Canterbury, Thomas of London] (?1120–1170), archbishop of Canterbury, saint and martyr, *ODNB*.
[857] 'and pipes' inserted.
[858] Final 'e' inserted; different ink.
[859] Change from 'ther' to 'the'; 'r' deleted using different ink.
[860] 'h' inserted; different ink.
[861] The ink changes here.
[862] 'Pollonians': natives of Poland, *OED*.
[863] 'Colledge' deleted.

fitt and necessarie for them; the wch I cannott inparticular manner resite;

(110) [5 *The Gretian Colleadge*] There is a fayer colledge adioyninge unto Saint Athanatius Churche wch was builded of purpose for the great-ians, it hathe manie good comodities belonginge unto it; of the wch I have receaved no certen notis[864]

[6 *The Neofit Colleadge*] Neighe unto Saint Androwe his churche where the Thiatins[865] doe dwell, is a colledge for the bringine up of suche Turckes. Jewes and infidells, as in there youthe are converted unto Christian religion;

[7 *The maretine*[866] *Colleadge*] There is another Colledge, for the bring-inge up of the maretines, apeople wch dwell beyonde Jherusalem, all these colleadges and divers others in Rome, and else where, have bene erected by Pope Gregorie the xiiith whose zeale and prov-idence for the estate of the Churche of god, may easely be perceaved, by those notable worckes wch he hathe lefte behinde him, The gover[n]ment of those Colleadges he comitted unto the Jesuitts wch as yett doe remaine in there handes. and for that the maner[867] thereof[868] may be the better understoode I will as neighe as I can sett downe the Rulles wch theie have instituted for that purpos. and for as muche as in Rome and other places of Italie, they doe recken the clocke forwarde to the foure and twenteethe houre, and doe still soe sett there clockes as at the Sonn settinge it shall alwayes stricke foure and twentie, I will therefor for the better understanding of those wch dwell in these partes, devide there times (111) and houres of studie and other exercises into that manner of countinge of houres wch wee doe use in these contries, in maner and forme as followethe,

[*i The Rulles of the Colleadges*] Half an houre after fowre of the clocke by computation, in the morninge, a bell doth ringe wch dothe warne all the Scollers to ryse, wch they muste doe speedely and wth Sylence,

[2] At five the bell ringethe, and then everie one in his studie dothe meditatt upon som devout matter fittinge the daie and time,

---

[864] 'of the wch … no certen notis' inserted; different ink and hand.
[865] The Theatines: a religious order founded in Rome in 1524, F.L. Cross and E.A. Livingstone (eds), *The Oxford Dictionary of the Christian Church* (Oxford, 1997), sub nomine.
[866] Referring to the Maronites, a sect of Syrian Christians, living in Lebanon, *OED*.
[867] 'of' deleted.
[868] 'of' added to 'there', different ink; 'Government' deleted.

accordinge ye direction gyven by the prefecte of the chamber wherein he liethe;

[3] Half an houre befor six the bell warnethe them to goe to churche, where all devoutly doe here masse together, after masse, it is laufull for them to talke one wth another, but not before,

[4] Betweene six and seaven of the clocke they goe all to⁸⁶⁹ ther studies, and for the space of two houres doe dilligently imploy themselves, unto there divinitie, and Philosophie, everie one accordinge his capacitie;

[5] Soone after eight⁸⁷⁰ the bell ringethe and then doe theie all goe to the buttrie hatche⁸⁷¹ where everie one hathe a glasse of wine and a peece of a mangett⁸⁷² for his breakefast, then doe they assemble at the colledge doore, and from thence doe walk, two and two together wth a decente and sober pace untill they com unto the Romane Colledge where the artes and sciences are openlie read,

(112) [6] Beinge com thether they take there places in the Scooles accordinge the classe where eache of them dothe use to studie, and doe write there, for one whole houre suche matter as the reader doth dictatt unto them. after the maister hathe don readinge the younge Jesuits doe devide all ther Scollers wch com theether to write, into sundrie companies and doe cause them to make rehearsall of that wch they had written the day befor, wherein they diligently examine them for half an houre,

[7] By the time that this examination is don it⁸⁷³ is som half an houre after ten of the Clocke at the wch time theie doe all meete at the Romane Colledge gate and doe take there waie homewarde in suche⁸⁷⁴ manner as theie came forthe; the yongest Scollers goinge foremoste, and soe in order everie one accordinge his place, when they com home if there be any time befor aleven of the clocke, they bestowe it in mendinge⁸⁷⁵ of there lessons by there books wch write best and spidieste,

[8] At aleaven of the clocke the bell warnethe⁸⁷⁶ them to dynner, and beinge com unto the dyninge place, standinge rounde about it in

---

⁸⁶⁹ 'to' inserted.

⁸⁷⁰ 'of the clocke' deleted.

⁸⁷¹ 'buttery': in colleges, the place where food was kept; 'buttery-hatch': the half-door over which food was served, *OED*.

⁸⁷² Probably 'manchet': 'a small ... loaf or roll of the finest wheaten bread', *OED*.

⁸⁷³ 'yt' deleted; 'it' inserted.

⁸⁷⁴ 'grave' deleted.

⁸⁷⁵ Mend: to improve, ameliorate, or render more excellent, *OED*.

⁸⁷⁶ 'Ringethe' deleted; 'warnethe' inserted.

grave maner, Father Rector appointethe one of the priestes to saie grace, wch beinge don they sitt all downe at severall tables everie one accordinge his place, and doe eate ther meate wth silence, and while they sitt at dinner one of the (113) Scollers as his tourne fallethe out, dothe reade som parte of the Scriptures the Ecletiasticall historie or som other dovout booke accordinge the appointmt of the Superiors; there commons[877] of meat is competent everie one havinge his portion by himself, there wyne is good, there bread verie white and newe, whereof they have at meale time as muche as they will use, there is also water gyven them wth there wyne of the wch everie one takethe a quantitie accordinge his affection,

[9] After there meale tyme[878] is don wch continuethe som half houre or there abouts, grace beinge saide, they have licence to recreat themselves, in som commendable exercyse for the space of ane houre, provided that they goe not out of the sighte of there Superiors, nor use exercyses wch are two violente, wch in that hote contrie is verie dangerous for breakinge vaines,

[10] About one of the clocke everie one goethe to his studie and there appliethe his booke for the space of two houres,

[11] At three[879] they goe to the Scooles accordinge as they did in the fornoone, and there doe write there dictatts an houre, and dispute half an houre[880] cominge[881] home to there owne Colledge alitle before five;[882]

(114) [12] At five of the clocke everie one dothe repayre unto his repititer apointed for the examination of them, and doe dispute upon suche matter as was Comprehended in the dictatts wch they tooke in the daie befor, for the space of an houre, after the wch som doe studie there mathimaticks others mende there lessons and move doubts in matters of difficultie;

[13] At seaven[883] the bell dothe ringe to Supper at the wch they doe use suche order as they did at dinner;

[14] Then have they one houres recreation as they had after dynner, wch continuethe untill half an houre past eight.

---

[877] 'commons': share of a common table; board; rations, *OED*.
[878] 'meale tyme' inserted; 'dinner' deleted.
[879] 'of the clocke' deleted.
[880] 'and' deleted.
[881] 'inge' inserted after 'com'; different hand.
[882] 'of the clocke' deleted.
[883] 'of the clocke' deleted.

[*15*] After the wch they doe all kneele downe in the halle and one of the priestes in his torne doth saye the litanies wth som other prayers;[884]

[*16*] At nyne of the Clocke everie one departethe wth silence unto his chamber and receavethe instruction of som grave preiste wch is there prefect,[885] whatt matter he shoulde meditatt upon, the next morninge,

[*17*] Half an houre before ten they goe to there rest[886] everie one[887] beinge alone in a bedd by himself, and soe are allowed to sleepe untill four[888] and a half the next morninge, wch allowance commethe iuste to seaven houres,

[*18*] On Sondayes and great hollidayes they bestowe the fornoone in confession receavinge (115) of the blessed Sacrament, the readinge of sts lives hearing of masse helpinge to singe highe masse, and other devout exercyses,

[*19*] In the after noone ordinarie recreation beinge don theie doe accustom to exercyse there Singinge untill toward foure of the clocke, at wch time they singe evensonge, wch beinge ended[889] they walke altogether by the river of Tyber or by som other convenient place, to take the ayre, and to refreshe there spirites, on those dayes there commones are[890] mended accordinge the greatness of the feaste,

[*20*] The cheefe time of recreation wch is used by them is[891] on viniarde dayes wch commonly is on wensdaye and then[892] in the fornoone doe they ordinarily visitt the seven principall churches of Rome wch are som twelve myles in compas asonder and[893] doe[894] meete at there viniarde where they are[895] licenced to use all honest sportes and recreatione; there they have a hansom howse wherein they eate ther dinner, and duringe the longe doaies[896] there supper,

---

[884] 'and meditation' deleted.
[885] Change from 'the' to 'there'; 'of the chamber' deleted.
[886] 'bed' deleted; 'there rest' inserted; different hand.
[887] 'one' inserted.
[888] 'a clocke' deleted.
[889] 'ended' inserted, different ink; 'done' deleted.
[890] 'are' inserted; 'it' deleted.
[891] 'is' inserted.
[892] 'then' inserted, different ink; 'on that daie' deleted.
[893] 'there' deleted.
[894] 'they' deleted.
[895] 'are' inserted.
[896] days.

in the wch[897] they have double commons; while they are in the viniarde they ought not to studie on there dictat[898] bookes, uppon
such apayne as shall be thought fitt by there superiors.

[21] The Scollers maie not walke abroade about any occation wthout
licence, wch they cannot have but for som devout purpose as the visitinge (116) of som churches where are stations or great feastes, and
then dothe a whole chamber goe together wth there prefect, or if
it happen that there goe but two together, the one of them muste
be agrave preiste,

[22] There are none admitted unto thes colleadges but suche as have
comendations from som good Catholickes and are fytte to heare
lodgicke wch is reade unto them in one yeere,

[23] After theire hearinge of lodgicke if they be founde capable they
doe studie Phisicke and methaphisicke for two yeere, and Scoole
divinitie wch is reade unto them in four yeeres,

[24] If there capacities be not of the beste, or that they be farr in
yeeres when they com thether, then after the hearinge of there lodgicke they are turned to the studinge of cases of Consciens, wch they
doe practise them selves in, for two yeeres.

[25] One yeere befor the endinge of there course they doe common-
lie take holy orders, in the wch time theie doe exercyse themselves (on
holy daies) in the afternoone and at other convenient oportunities[899]
appointed be there superiors to preatche in there naturall tonge to
the ende that they maye be the more fitt to doe good in there severall
contries,

[26] In lent they use at aleaven of the clocke to goe to som principall
Churche to heere a Sermon wch duringe that time[900] they shall (117)
not misse of in any churche of account wthin Rome, and then for
that they eate but [one] meale a daye, they doe not dyne untill
twellve of the clocke, and have som light Colation of fruite at night,

[27] On Saint Steven his daye one of the Englishe Colleadge dothe
allwyes preatche in Latin in the presence of the Pope and
Cardinalls, and after them doe the German and other Colleadges
take there turne in preatchinge duringe the holy dayes,

---

[897] 'in the wch' inserted; 'where' deleted.
[898] 'dictat' inserted, different ink.
[899] 'oportunities' inserted; 'times' deleted.
[900] 'of lent' deleted.

[*28*] All the Scollers of these Colleadges wch are erected for strangers have ther manitenance and teatchinge at the chardge of the Colledge untill the expiration of there courses, wch the Casuists doe ende in three yeere and the Scoole devine in seaven,

[*29*] At the expiration of there course theie are brought unto the Popes presence whoe givethe them his benediction, and three score crownes to everie one of them in there purses, to carrie them home to there contries,

[*30*] From Saint Peeters day untill the Nativitie of our blissed Lady,[901] they take there dicta[tatt]s in the common Scooles, onely in the forenoone by reason of the extreame heate that be in the afternoones,

[*31*] From the daye of the nativitie of oure Lady untill the daye of all Soules,[902] there are (118) generall vacations in all the Colleadges, and then have the Scollers allowed them an houre extraordynarie of sleepe, in this tyme they doe often visitt the seaven churches of greatest priviledge, and other places of devotion[903] and doe use that holy exercyse the wch I have already partly discribed, the Scollers in this tyme doe accustome[904] to make repitition of there whole yeers worcke unto the repetitors of the Colledge, and the pristes doe moste give themselves unto preatchinge, if any of the Scollers doe offende in makinge breatche of any of these rules then are they penanst for there offence, accordinge to the qualitie of the fact, as som by tellinge there owne faults openly; others by restrayninge of there libertie demynishinge of there commons, and suche licke, as it shall seeme fitt to there superiors, About ayeere after I was receaved into ye Englishe Colledge, I harde of my Fathers deathe wch was noe smale greiff unto me. after the receavinge of the wch Sorrowfull tedinges,[905] I did the rather enter into the exercise beforenamed that thereby I might learne patience to endure crosses,

[*A true reporte of the English scollers in Rome*] Duringe my tyme of lyveinge amongst[906] them,[907] I cannot but testifie, that I sawe not any other practise amongest them, towardes the estate of Englande, but that[908] wch was

---

[901] That is, from 29 June to 8 Sep.
[902] Feast of All Souls, 2 Nov.
[903] 'of devotion' inserted, different ink.
[904] 'accustome' inserted; 'use' deleted.
[905] 'newes' cancelled.
[906] 'amongst' inserted, different ink; 'in' deleted.
[907] 'Englishe Colledge' deleted.
[908] 'it' deleted.

vertuous and honeste, neither did I ever heer them confer or talke of any matter wch might (119) concerne the stirringe up of rebellion or troble wthin there native contrie, but they did often praie for the conversion of there prince, and restoringe of religion, and trulye there is no man of indifferent iudgement, that can iustlie conceave, howe men (followinge these aforenamed rules as they doe) can have leysure for the contrivinge of matters soe impertinent unto there vocation; This I speake for that I knowe theye are muche chardged by there adversaries for the contrivinge there of conspiracies and rebellions;

[*The penetentiaria or Colleadge of Ghostly fathers*] There is aplace in manner of a colledge called the Penetenciarie[909] wch also belongethe to the Jesuits. in it doe dwell som of the gravest and antientest Fathers of the Societie, of everie kingdom in Christendum, one or more, wch are appointed to heare the confessions of all suche strangers as com to Rome, it standethe neighe unto Saint Peeters Churche, in the wch those Fathers doe exercyse ther function;

[*The holy house of inquisition*] There is a fayere Pallace in the manner alsoe of a colledge, nighe unto the hospitall of the holy ghoste called the holy house of inquisition, of the wch the Domynicans have the chardge; it was moste of it built by Pope Pius Quintus whoe was himself a Domyncan fryer. and[910] averie severe man againste all heretickes, and agreat reformer (120) of religious orderes; Havinge spoken thuys briefly of the colleadges I shall (godwillinge) sett downe in fewe wordes,

A description of the seaven hills wheruppon Rome is builte

[*1 Mons capitolynus*] The principall of them is called monscapitolynus where yett the olde capitall is to be sene, of avery stately and fayre buildinge, in it the antient Senators of Rome were wonte to keepe there councell house, but nowe there is only one Senator in Rome wch sittethe there as a iudge to here and deside ordinary matters of controversie, betwixt partie and partie, but if there be any matter of great importance it is determyned by one wch is appointed by the Pope Governor of Rome,[911] as wee enter up to the topp of the capitoll

---

[909] Spelling altered by addition of several letters; different hand.

[910] 'He was' deleted; 'and' inserted; Pope Pius V, reigned 1566–1572.

[911] On the role of governor of Rome in the 16th century, see Miles Pattenden, 'Governor and government in sixteenth-century Rome', *Papers of the British School at Rome*, 77 (2009), 257–272.

hill, there stande two fayre pinacles, in the tope of wch are two brasen boules, in the one of wch are conteined the ashes of Julius
Ceasar, and in the other the ashes of Pompie, In the courte of the
Capitoll is the Statua of Morforius[912] leaninge upon his elbowe wth
a goodly conditt of water runninge from him, Right before the capitoll doore is a fayre and lardge courte, in the mideste of wch is the
Statua of Marcus Aurelius on horse backe, all of copper verie artificially (121) framed, his attyer and furniture beinge fashioned after the
Irishe manner. the Venetians did offer, to have gyven for it soe
muche Silver as it did waye, wch by reason of the love that the
Romanes bore to Marcus Aurellious his morall verteous, was by
them[913] refused, In this place Cicero and other Orators in tymes
paste did use to declayme there pers[ua]tive and invective orations,
upon this hill stoode in olde tyme the great Temple of the god
Jupiter, into the wch the Romanes did use to triumphe, and give
thanckes for suche victories as they then receaved; adioyninge unto
this hill is Arvinous[914] house in the wch Cicero heretofor dwelled;
At the footte of the Steares as ye passe up to the Senate house
there is a stately piller erected in the honnor of Duke Collumna[915]
whoe was generall for the Pope, at the great overthrowe gyven by
the[916] Christians upon the Turckes at the battle of Lepanto;

[*The battell of Lepanto*][917] And for as muche as this batle was verie
famous and exceedinge profitable for the whole estate of
Christendum, I have thought fitt to make a compendious reporte
thereof;

Be it therefore understoode that the firste of the Confederatt[918]
Christians wch putt into the adriaticke Sea, was Venerius the vene-
tian admirall, and wth him[919] fiftie Gallyes whoe attended at
Messana for the comminge of Don John[920] of (122) Austria, generall
of the Spanishe forces and of the whole Fleete, where Marcus
Anthonius Collumna whoe was admirall of twelve Gallyes for the

---

[912] Initial letter altered from 'm' to 'M'.
[913] 'by them' inserted, different hand.
[914] 'u' inserted.
[915] Marcantonio Colonna (1535–1584), *Dizionario Biografico degli Italiani*, http://www.trec-cani.it/enciclopedia/marcantonio-colonna_(Dizionario-Biografico)/, accessed 23 Nov. 2017.
[916] 'Turckes' deleted.
[917] Different hand.
[918] 'de' inserted.
[919] 'him' inserted; different ink, different hand.
[920] 'de' deleted; Don John of Austria (1547–1578), half-brother of Philip II of Spain.

Pope, and of twelve more wch were sente thether from the great
Duke of Florence and three Gallyes of Malta mett him, then came
thether Anthonius Currynus[921] wth three score and[922] twoe venesian
Gallyes, and shortly after them the Gallyes of Sciscill, Naples, Pisa,
and Genua aryved there, and in ye[923] ende of august Don John
whoe then[924] was not above fowre and twentye yeeres olde,[925] was
verie triumphantly receaved by the Pope and venetian admirals.[926]
The venetian Fleete consisted of a hundred and eight Gallyes, six
Gallyasses, two tale shipps and agreat number of smale Gallyotts
unto them were ioyned Colluminus wth his forces, and Auria the
Spanishe admirall[927] wth fowre score and one Gallyes, Soe as in all,
there were two hundred twenty one vessells for fight, In this Fleete
were twenty thowsande fightinge men of well experienced Soldiors,
besides mariners, and agreat number of noble men, namely
Alexander fornecio Prince of Parma,[928] franciscus maria Prince of
Urbin,[929] Jordanus Ossinus[930] of the honnorable famely of the ursinge
in Rome, and divers others[931] wch volontarily undertooke that
voiadge for the deffence of the Christian faithe;

they beinge thus mett together, (123) called a councell wherein it
was debated whether they shoulde presently sett upon[932] the
Turckes forces or hover there abouts untill suche time as his Fleete

[921] Probably referring to Marco Querini, a Venetian admiral at Lepanto, *Enciclopedia
Italiana* (Roma, 1935), *sub* Querini; 'Antonius Quirinus', Richard Knolles, *The generall historie
of the Turkes, from the first beginning of that nation to the rising of the Othoman familie: With all the
notable expeditions of the Christian princes against them: Together with lives and conquests of the
Othoman kings and emperours faithfullie collected out of the best histories, both auntient and modern,
and digested into one continuat historie until this present yeare 1603* (London, 1603), 870; Knolles published the first significant work on Turkish history in English, comprising 1152 pages,
renowned for its style and its popularity. A recurrent theme was the need for Christian
unity in order to combat the Turkish threat; Richard Knolles (late 1540s–1610), *ODNB*.
[922] 'three' deleted.
[923] 'ye' inserted.
[924] 'then' inserted.
[925] 'and' deleted.
[926] Don John was received by 'the Venetian and Popes Admirals', Knolles, *Generall
Historie of the Turkes*, 870.
[927] Probably referring to Gian Andrea Doria (1540–1606), Genovese admiral at Lepanto,
Dizionario Biografico degli Italiani, http://www.treccani.it/enciclopedia/giovanni-andrea-
doria_(Dizionario-Biografico)/, accessed 23 Nov. 2017.
[928] Alessandro Farnese (1545–1592), duke of Parma.
[929] Francesco Maria della Rovere di Urbino.
[930] Paolo Giordano Orsini (1541–1585), *Dizionario Biografico degli Italiani*, http://www.trec-
cani.it/enciclopedia/paolo-giordano-orsini_res-aco68daf-373d-11e3-97d5-00271042e8d9_
(Dizionario-Biografico), accessed 23 Nov. 2017; 'Pau. Iordanus Ursinus', Knolles, *Generall
Historie*, 870.
[931] 'wth' deleted.
[932] 'hover there abouts' deleted; 'presently sett upon' inserted.

shoulde make towards them, [*The Christians resolution for ioyninge of bat-tell wt ye Turcks*] but after alonge consultation wherein there were many differente opinions, they resolved to sett forwarde, and putt there Fleetes in order martiallinge the same as if they were readye to ioyne battell; passinge this by Paxo one Mutius Fortina a Spanishe capten, raysed a quarrell amongeste the venetians wch grewe to suche a mutinie,[933] as had almoste bene the overthrowe of the whole armye, for Venerius the venetian admyrall[934] sente the capten of his owne Gallye for to patifie them, whoe was ill intreated by Mutius Fortina,[935] And therefor for preventinge of further incon-veniences, Venerius caused him to be hanged upon the crosse yarde of a gallie, wherewth Don John beinge greatly discontented sharply reproved Venerius for the same, so as there had licke to have byne agreat slaghter made betwene the Spaniardes and the venetians, had not Collumnius by his grave councell and good advice, diswaded them from the same;

from thence the Christians Fleete passed to Cephalyna where they receaved advertisment that the Turckishe Fleete (wch were to the number of three hundred thirtie and three Sayle of one sorte and other) laye in the Gulphe of Lepanto otherwise called the Gulphe of Corinthe, That the Turckes (124) Bassas Haly and Partan hearinge of the Christians Fleete approched neere unto them, consulted together whether it were[936] more conveniente to issiue forthe and give them batle, or to staie wthin the gulphe at there owne deffence, and havinge agreat while bene in controversie betwene themselves, what were[937] beste to be don, in that action. [*The Turcks resolve to fight wth ye christians*] at leinght they agreed to fight wth our forces, beinge pufte up wth pride by reason of the victorie wch they had (not longe before that time obtained,) by wininge of the kingdom of Ciprus and other Christian territories, whereupon Pertan Bassa made an exhortatio[n][938] speeche unto his armye, encouradginge them by manie examples of former victories, had againste the Christians, to prosecute there enemyes, assuringe them that there number of men and vallor in performance of warlicke exployetes, was not to be compared wthall by the servants of Christe, on the other side, don John wth effectuall perswations procured his Fleete

---

[933] 'mutanie' altered to 'mutinie'.

[934] Sebastian Venier (Veniero) (1499–1578), Venetian admiral at Lepanto.

[935] 'M' and 'F': altered from lower case to upper case, different ink; 'Mutius Tortona', Knolles, *Generall Historie*, 873.

[936] 'were' inserted.

[937] 'were' inserted; different ink.

[938] Last letters altered.

(wch fought under the banner of our Saviour) valiantly to venture there lyves as well for the deffence of Christian religion, as also to be revenged upon the Turckes for many iniuries wch the[939] had don unto there severall kingdomes, sheawinge them thereby, that they shoulde please god by vanquishinge of his enemyes, deliver the whole body of the comon welthe from emynent danger, wine everlastinge fame unto them and there posterities, and gett eccee-dinge (125) great booties for the betteringe of ther privatt estates;

[*The battell beginnethe*] Which wordes beinge uttered by these famous comanders soe inflamed the myndes of the captens and Soldiors of bothe the armyes, that wth cheerefull shoutes (the apparent witt-nesses of there willinge hartes) the Christians couragiously gave the onsett, wch was as resolutly intertained by the Turckes.

Betwene bothe the Fleetes there laye six great Galliasses[940] of the Christiane navie, placed there by the Generall, wch wth there great artillery did ecceedingly annoye the Turckes gallies, whoe in respecte of there multitude lay soe thicke that noe shott was spente in vaine.

And nowe the Ordinance begann to plaie on either side, the roaringe noyse whereof together wth the warlicke soundes of dromes Trompetts and other martiall instruments, as also the hedious cries of the maimed and wounded Soldiors was suche, that the verie neighboringe hills resounded wth the echo thereof. the abondance of arrowes and dartes fell licke showers of winters haile, soe thicke as they seemed to dim the Skyeyes. the Sease all neere thereabouts beinge even died wth the efusion of blode, and spred over wth the corpes of slaghtered men, but herein manifestly appeered the mightie and miraculous hande of god, feightinge for his Servants, for where in the beginninge of the daye befor the battle, the wynde wth agentle (126) pleasinge galt brought on the Turckishe navie in suche forme and order as they desired.

The fight was noe sooner begun but the allmightie god ever myndfull of his promise wch he hathe made for the deffence and protection of his Churche, and Chosen, againste there enemyes, caused the winde wth a stiffe gale to turne directly againste the Turckes, whereby the smoke of there great Ordinance and smaler shott was caried directly in there faces, and the Sunn where as[941] the moste parte of that

---

[939] *Recte* 'they'.

[940] Galliasse: 'a heavy, low-built vessel, larger than a galley, impelled both by sail and oars, chiefly employed in war', *OED*.

[941] 'as' inserted.

daye itt[942] had bene overcaste wth cloudes nowe cleerd himself, and shone soe bright upon the waters that by the reflection thereof, and the continuall smoke of ther artillerye they were not able to discerne what they had to doe, wch ecceedingly daunted the Turckes and muche animated the Christians.

Divers terrible Skirmisses paste between them in sundrie places, here the Turckes overcom, ther the Christians repulsed, either generall carefully observinge where any of there partie was destressed, and still releevinge them wth freshe suplies, ever presentinge there owne persons in places of greatest danger for the hartninge of ther Soldiors. Soe as fortune seemed yet uncertaine on whether side to bestowe the honnor of soe great a[943] daye.

[*A crueall incounter betwixt ye Generalls gallies*].[944] In the middest of wch cruell and doubtfull fight, the generall gallyes of either side havinge discovered the one the thother, after mutuall (127) dischardge of divers peales of shott, bothe of them eagerly thirstinge for the glorie of the victorie, commaunded there Gallyes to be grapled together, when as if the battell had even nowe begune a freshe either side coragiously assaulted the other, wth eger furie sheathinge there Swordes in the bodies of there adversuries, and coveringe the deckes wth the carkasses of the mangled Soldiors, continwinge thus for the space of three houres, oure generall Gallye beinge overlaide wth the multitude of the Turckes, and havinge loste many of his beste and approved Soldiors. Begann to fainte, wch animated the enemyes, that beinge now confidente of the victorie wth cheerefull shootes they pressed into the Gallye[945] nothinge doubtinge but that they shoulde easily surprise her, wch fell out farr contrarie to there expectation.

For Don John noe lesse polliticke then valiant wyselye castinge all doubtes and stryvinge to prevent all danger, that might occur. had befor the fight, stowead fowre hundred of his choyse Soldiors under hatches, wth intent to reserve them, as his laste refuge, whereof he nowe standinge in neede, and the expected signall gyven, that concealed supplye wth ecceedinge celerity; lepte upon the hatches and wth a ioyffull shoote of victorie fiercly assaulted the almoste

---

[942] 'itt' inserted.

[943] 'a' inserted.

[944] Different hand; the editor has placed this heading here; in the MS it is on the margin at top of p. 127.

[945] 's' erased.

(128) wearyed Turcks that wthin shorte tyme they had not only cleered there owne gallye from the enemy but wth incredible vallor and couradge they boarded the turckishe galley in wch encounter Haly Bassa himself plainge the part not only of an expert generall but of a valiant Soldior was hurte and taken. [*Haly Bassa slayne*] whoe beinge brought befor Don John seinge him to be mortally wounded caused his heade presently to be strucken of, and upon apicke to be raysed up into the ayere, holdinge the same a while wth his owne handes. wch being seene by the turckes and knowen to be the heade of ther generall strucke suche a sudden amazament into ye harts of the reste of the turkishe armie, [*The Christians obtaine the victorie*] that those turckes wch in other places of the battell remained as victorious, wth the exceedinge horror of that wofull sight lefte of the victorie to the vanquished, strievinge nowe to save themselves by flight. whoe lately thought of [i] nothinge lesse. of suche exceedinge vallor is the life and presence of a worthie and experte generall.

Amongest whom Partan Bassa was one of the first that fled. whoe leavinge his galley wth a fewe more in a longe boate runn himself a shore and soe escaped. Also Uluza[le] one[946] of the admiralls of there navie perceavinge that Don John, Colluminus, and Venerius, made towards him fled wth xx[v] galleys backe into the gulphe of Lepanto and was persued by them untill it was allmoste night. (129) Uluzales thus escapinge wthin eight dayes[947] aryved at Adryanople where Selimus then kepte his Courte, whoe understandinge of the defeat of that royall fleete, the overthrowe of soe manie experte commaunders and valiant Soldiors what wth the losse thereof, and the disgrace wch he had thereby receaved, was dryven into suche an excessive mallenchollie that for the space of certaine dayes, he permitted noe man to speake wth him, and his anger and hatred soe increased againste the Christians that he was purposed to have putt them all to the sword wthin his dominions, fearinge leaste they woulde have usede the benefitt of this occation and have taken up armes againste them for the recoverie of there libertie.

[*The number of ye turckes wch were slayne and taken at this battell*] The number of the Turckes slayne[948] and drowned in this battle was 32000

---

[946] 'one' inserted.

[947] 'dayes' inserted.

[948] 'd' at end of word erased; Knolles gives one estimate (naming the author) of 32,000 Turks killed, while adding that other authors give less than half that number, Knolles, *Generall Historie*, 883.

there weare taken prisoners 3500, and 12000 Christians prisoners released wch weare gallie slaves wth the Turckes. and of the turkishe gallies weare taken 162 and suncke or burnte 40 and of galliotts[949] and other small vessells weare taken aboute 60. prisoners of note taken weare Achamatt and Mahomett the Sonnes of Haly Bassa, bothe afterwardes sente as prisoners to the Pope, there weare divers other principall commaunders of the enemyes forces made captives that daye whom I omitt to name.

(130) Don John wth the reste of the generalls of the Christian armye beinge returned from pursuinge of the dispersed Turkishe natian[950] wth one consente upon there knees rendred immortall thanckes to god the only anchor of that memorable overthrowe, wch beinge done letters weare imediatly dispatched to the severall princes and states whoe had bene confederatt in this famous act[i]on, whoe wth universall signes of Joye expressed the contentment they receaved for that triumphant victorie, wch was obteyned on the viith daye of October 1571;

[*The number of ye christians wch were slayne at that feight*] Of the Christians there was Slaine that daye 7566 amongste whom the cheefe men were, John Barnardinus of the honnorable family of Cordua[951] in Spaine. Horatius Carraffa and Ferantes Bizballius. Virginius and Horatius noble Romaines of the honnorable famely of Ursini[952] of the venetian Nobillitie. Agustinus Barbadicus Benedictus Superantius, [Vin]centius[953] Quirinus Johanes Lawreta[n]us. wth divers other as well Itallians as Germans, This muche I have thought fitt to speake of this moste famous overthrowe, but whoesoever shall desire to knowe at lardge thereof, lett him enquire for the Turkishe historie written by Richard Knolles[954] whoe hathe sett downe the same at Lardge.

The consideracion[955] wch principally moved me to reherse[956] the manner of this victorius batle, was to give occation to the reader to

---

[949] Galliott: 'a small galley or boat, propelled by sails and oars, used for swift navigation; in English applied esp. to Spanish and Mediterranean vessels', *OED*.

[950] Word possibly altered: from 'natio' to 'natian'.

[951] 'Cardona', Knolles, *Generall Historie*, 884.

[952] 'of the honourable family of Ursini. Of the Venetian nobilitie, Augustinus Barbadicus', Knolles, *Generall Historie*, 884.

[953] 'Vincentius Quirinus', Knolles, *Generall Historie*, 884.

[954] Richard Knolles, *Generall Historie* (London, 1603).

[955] 'consideracion' inserted, different ink; 'cause' deleted.

[956] 'reherse' inserted, different ink; 'sett downe' deleted.

consider howe easie a matter it weare for the Christians (131) to recover ther territories wonn by the Turckes if they did ioyne together in a firme knott of frendshipp, for if soe great a disstruction were made of the enemyes of god, by the forces of theise Catholicke Princes ther assembled, surely⁹⁵⁷ it may well be coniectured, that had the reste of the Christian kinges ioyned wth them in that honnorable act[i]on, there might have bene a full conqueste in shorte tyme made upon those hatefull wreatches, whereby the holy lande had bene restored, Greece gayned, many other regions brought unto there former estate, Catholicke religion generally embrased, and the whole Christian Common welthe settled in perfecte peace and trannquillitie, manny more instances might be sheawed as that of Skanderbegge⁹⁵⁸ (whoe is renowned for his deadly warr made uppon him) and of the moste valiant Capten Huniades⁹⁵⁹ in there time, as also of the worthie Transilvanian Prince in our dayes wth divers others whoe doubtles had dryven that cruell tyrant out of all his dominions had they bene Seconded by those whom the cause did conserne. but if the reason thereof be deeply wayed it will appeere to be the wante of unitie in faithe amongeste men baptized. for it is manifest that they wch rente themselves from the body of the knowen churche of god, have bene leaste forward in gyvinge ther ayde for the persecution of this professed enemy of Christe and as the Prophett Jeremy saithe [*Cap. 2.*] Dereliquerunt fontem aquae vivae et foderunt sibi cisternas⁹⁶⁰ (132) dissipatas quae Continerae non valent aquas. they have forsaken the fontaine of the water of life, and have digged unto themselves cesterns, yea scattered cesterns, wch are not able to containe any water;⁹⁶¹ And therefor it is not to be wondered at, if they be overwhelmed wth the swallowinge waves of gods wrathfull displeasure, and carried headlonge throughe the gapinge gulphe of his dreadfull iudgmte, even to the dipeste pitt of horrible confusion, wch willfully doe departe out of his blessed arke in the wch they might be safely transported by the calme seas of his Fatherly mercy unto the happie haven of eternall salvation;

---

⁹⁵⁷ Word following deleted.

⁹⁵⁸ George Castriot (1405–1468), known as Skanderbeg, Albanian military commander, *Enciclopedia Treccani* http://www.treccani.it/enciclopedia/scanderbeg/, accessed 23 Nov. 2017.

⁹⁵⁹ Janos Hunyadi (*c.*1387–1456), Hungarian military commander, *Enciclopedia Treccani* http://www.treccani.it/enciclopedia/hunyadi-giovanni-reggente-di-ungheria, accessed 23 Nov. 2017.

⁹⁶⁰ Word 'cisternas' repeated.

⁹⁶¹ Jeremiah 2:13.

Nowe I thincke it not amisse here to relate howe that I have hearde
for an undoubted truthe that the Christians wch weare drowned at
this famous feight, weare knowen by there faces lyinge upward in
the water, and the Turkes by the contrarie, whereby may be iustlie
gathered that the continances of the children of god weare derected
towards the heavenly habitation wherein ther soules are for ever
placed, and the ofspringe of Satan towards the infernall lake, in
the wch they[962] shalbe perpetually tormented. I did also heere by
the reporte of verie credible parsons[963] when I was in Rome that
Pius Quintus[964] wch then was Pope used and caused to be exersysed
suche (133) extraordinarie devotion as well of prainge and fastinge, as
other actes of Pietie, for the good successe of the Catholicke armye,
That god did miraculously reveale unto him the day and tyme of this
triumphant victorie the wch he for toulde as well to the Cardinalls
wch then were presente as also to divers others, whereby we maie
understand howe avaylable the petitions of holy men are in the
sight of god. I have insisted the longer uppon this particular discours
for that it concernethe as beste is specified[965] the greateste and moste
fortunate battell wch was ever fought by Sea, betwixt the Christians
and the Turckes, but nowe I shall (god willinge) saie somwhat of the
other hills.

[2 *Mons Pallatinus*] The second hill is called Mons Pallatinus
and hathe under it a myle in compas of lande, here in tymes
paste was the statlye Pallace of Nero, wch nowe is altogether ruinated, and wthin that compas, at this daye are manye fayre
vyniards planted, wch have in them many faire and costlye
pondes replenished wth divers kinde of fyshes, many statly conditts and verie Princely walkes, garnished wth the Statuas of the
false gods verie artificially sett forthe. Upon aparte of this hill
standethe the vinyard belonginge to the Englishe Colledge
under the wch at this Day are to be seene divers wauts of this
decayed Pallace.

(134) [3 *Mons Aventinus*] The third hill is called Mons Aventinus it containethe under it as good as two myle of grownde in compas, upon it
doth stande many fayre Churches and other buildinges.

---

[962] Altered from 'the' to 'they'.
[963] That is, 'persons'.
[964] Pope Pius V, reigned 1566–1572.
[965] 'as beste is specified' interlined; different ink.

[*4 Mons Cellius*] The fourthe is called Mons Cellius uppon the wch standethe Saint John Lateran his churche and many other monuments.

[*5 Mons Esquelinus*] The fifte is named Mons Esquelinus upon the wch standethe Saint Maria Maiores churche and many others.

[*6 Mons Vimiales*] The sixt is named Mons Viminales[966] upon the wch nowe standethe Saint Lawrence his churche, in Pallisperna, Saint Potentilmos churche, wth divers others edifices of accounte.

[*7 Mons quirinalis*] The seaventhe is named Mons Quirrinales, at this daye it is called the monte cavallo of the wch I have already made som discription, upon this hill are the statuas of two men on horsbacke all of marble sett up by Pope Sextus Quintus, they were made by two sundrie workemen and yett noe man can discerne any defference betwixt them. There are divers other hills in Rome amongst the wch I cannott omitt to saye somwhate of [*Potters hill*] Potters hill[967] wch is of agreat bignes, and is all of suche potts of earthe as the subiectes of the Romains have broght there tribute in; after the deliverie of wch into the treasurie they broke the potts wherein they broght the same in that place, wch in processe of time grewe into that bulke of great wonder wch is to be seene not farr distante (135) from the gate of Ostia; of the wch I doe speake by my owne experience for that I have my selfe discovered the same by cuttinge of a sodd in the tope of the hill wch at the moste was but three inches thicke This beinge deeply considered of, a man maye thereby gather howe great and inestimable the reveneus of the antient Romans weare and howe mightie and lardge theire Empier.[968]

There are divers other lesse hills in Rome, the writinge of everie of wch[969] in particular woulde be to tedious; In[970] the time of ye prosperous estate of the antient Empier of Rome (the whole worlde in a maner beinge then at there comaunde) theise hills weare throwly inhabited but nowe they are for the moste parte waste.

Havinge nowe spoken of these hills soe muche as I have thought convenient I shall by gods leave proceede breeflie to rehearse,

[966] 'Viminales': 'n' inserted.
[967] 'hill' inserted; different ink and hand.
[968] 'weare' erased.
[969] 'wch' inserted; different hand.
[970] Altered from 'i' to 'I'.

The Discription of other antiquities in Rome and first of the thearms and bathinge houses

[*1*] The faireste and moste Sumteous of that sorte was builded by Alexander Severus and Nero, the ruins whereof is to be seene where Saint Eustatius his churche is builded.

(136) [*2*] There was another builded by Anthonie Carra[c]alla[971] upon the mounte Aventine,

[*3*] The third builded by Aurellius the Emperor

[*4*] The fourthe wch passed all theise in greatnes was builded by Diocleasian, nighe unto the place where nowe Saint Susana her[972] churche standethe, at the buildinge of wch Dioclesian did ose[973] the labor agreat while of 140 thowsand christians wch weare forced to worcke there,

[*5*] The fifte was builte by Domytian the Emperor the ruins of wch is to be seene, nighe unto Snt Silvester his churche, it[974] was borne up wth two hundred statly pillers of moste costly worckmanshipp

[*6*] The sixt made by Trayane uppon the mounte Esquilen, nighe unto the place where nowe Saint martine his churche standethe, these houses and many others of the same sorte, weare builded by the heathen Emperors, and weare moste ritchly sett forthe wth curions[975] pillers, and marble pavemts, but nowe where moste of them stoode are verie fayre churches since the tyme of Christianitie erected.

The principall gattes of Rome

(137) [*1*] The firste gatte of moste account in Rome is nowe called Porte Populo, in old tyme it was named the gate Flamynia

[*2*] The second Pinciana then called Collatiana[976]

---

[971] Final 'alla' inserted, different ink.
[972] 'his' in MS.
[973] Probably 'use' intended.
[974] 'it' inserted; 'yt' deleted.
[975] Probably 'curious' intended.
[976] Possibly 'Collatina'.

[*3*] The third Solaria then called Quirniall

[*4*] The fourthe Saint Agnes gate then called amentana or[977] vemynall,

[*5*] The fifte Saint Lawrence his gate then called Tibuytina and Taurina.

[*6*] The sixt gate of Saint maria maiore then called Libicana or Prenestina.

[*7*] The seaventhe Saint John his gate then called Celi montana or asinaria.

[*8*] The eight is the Lattin gate then called the florentine

[*9*] The ixth Saint Sabastine his gate then called apia or Capena into this gate the Romans did comonly inter in there greatest tryumphes.

[*10*] The tenthe Saint Paule his gate then called Ostience or Trygemia;

[*11*] The xi [Ry]pa gate then called Portuence,

[*12*] The xii Saint Pancratio his gate then called Aurellia or Pancratiana.

(138) [*13*] The xiiith Setymyana then called fontinalle

[*14*] The xiiiith Torione then called Postrula

[*15*] The xvth gate is named Pertusa.

[*16*] The xvi gate is that of the holy ghoste

[*17*] The xvii gate is that of Belvider

[*18*] The xviii gate is named Celeno in olde tyme called Ena, all these gattes for the more parte were made wth verie fayre free stones and full of artifitiall statuas

---

[977] 'or' inserted.

The highe wayes of Rome

From eatche of these gates above named were made verie fayre wayes of good pavemt upon the coste of the antient Romans, but the moste principall of them are these wch followeth,

[*1*] The waye Flaminia builded by the consull Flamynius wch beginnethe at Porte Populo and reatchethe to A[r]ymyne [Rimini] wch is ii c myles at least,

[*2*] The waye Emilia made by Lepedus and Flamynius consulls, and reatchethe to Bolonia wch is ii c myles from Rome.

[*3*] The waye Apia made by Apius Claudius Censore it reatchethe from Saint Sabastin his gate to Capua.

(139) [*4*] The holy waye beginnethe at the arke of Constantine and soe by the Romane markett into Campidolia.

[*5*] The waye of Vitelia beginnethe at the hill Janiculo and reatchethe to the Sea wch is fiftene myles in leinthe.

[*6*] The waye Ostia reatchethe from Saint Paule his gate to Ostia.

[*7*] The triumphant waye beginethe at the vaticano and leadethe to Capidolio.

[*8*] The straight waye wch passethe thorowe the fieldes of mars, in the wch feildes the antient Romans did use to trayne their Soldiors. there are belonginge to Rome divers other wayes of lesse account wch I have omitted to speake of,

The Bridges of Rome

[*1*] The firste Bridge wch ever was builded over the Ryver Tyber (wch runnethe from Rome) was called Sublissio, and was at the foote of mounte Eventine it was firste builded by Ancrus[978] Martius, and afterwarde fell often to decaye, and was lastlye reedified by the Emperor Anthonius Pius of a great height all of marble.

---

[978] 'n' inserted; 'x' deleted.

(140) [2] The triumphant Bridge passed over right againste the hospitall of the holy ghoste but it is nowe decaided.

[3] Saint Bartlmewe his Bridge builded by Sestus and Esquilinus,

[4] The Bridge of Sixtus builded by Anthonius Pius but beinge ruinated, was repayred by Pope Sixtus the fourthe.[979]

[5] The Bridge of Saint Angello builded by Adryan the Emperor, and brought into better forme by Pope Nicholas the fifte.[980]

[6] The Bridge milvious is som two myle wthout Porte populo and was builded by Emilius Sta[v]cus, nighe unto this Bridge Constantine the greate did overthrowe Maxentius the Tyrant, the self same daye in the wch Constantine gave this overthrowe to maxentius, he sawe in the ayere a crosse, and harde a voyce wch saide unto him these wordes in hoc signo vinces,[981] that is to saye in this signe thowe shalt overcom, whereby we may understand that as Constantine in the signe of the Crosse did overcom the Tyrante maxentious soe maye we thereby vanquishe the divell wch continually laiethe snares for our destruction

(141) There is alsoe builded over Tyber the Bridge mamelus three myles wthout Rome (named soe from mamia mother unto Alexander Seaverus.

The Aquaeductes of Rome

[i] Of these there weare seaven in number whereof the moste famous was called Aqua marsia the ruines whereof maie be seene as wee passe to Sainte Lawrence his churche wthout the walles, The beginninge of this aquaducte is thyrtie seavene[982] myles beyonde Rome,

[2] The aquaducte begune by Julius Ceasar and ended by Claudius, and it is to be seene nowe partlye ruinated as you passe by mounte Celius[983] to mounte aventine divers arches[984] of that aquaducte weare a hundred footte in height a peece, the makinge of it did

---

[979] Pope Sixtus IV, reigned 1471–1484.
[980] Pope Nicholas V, reigned 1447–1455.
[981] Latin quote possibly in different hand.
[982] Word erased; 'seavene' inserted.
[983] Altered from 'Celio' to 'Celius'.
[984] 't' inserted above 'c'; change from 'archers' to 'arches'.

coste a million of golde and two hundred ny[n]itie five thowsande crownes of golde,

The other aquaducte of Rome are, muche licke unto those wch I have named and are nowe in decaie, [*A faire and costly aquaducte builded by Pope Sixtus Quintus*] This aquaducte last named[985] dothe take his beginninge 36 myles from Rome; But[986] there is a newe aquaducte lately made by Pope Sixtus Quintus, wch is brought out of the contrie agreat waye upon a wale of (142) bryke throghe pipes of lead, at the ende of wch aquaducte, wthin the cittie standethe the Imadges of Moyses and Aron ingraven in marble, wch wth rodes in theire handes dothe seeme to stricke a rocke, out of the wch dothe gushe throwe the mouthes of two lyons abondance of excellent sweete water,[987] wch by conveniences from them thorowe pipes of leade dothe[988] serve a great parte of the cittie,

The Amphitheators and other theators of Rome.

In the Amphitheators of Rome the wch weare verie hoodge and lardge, the Romans did use to houlde there sworde plaies, and kepte theire wilde beastes, the ruins of two of them doe yett remaine, The one of them was nighe unto the Pallace of Nero, and was builded by Vaspasian the Emperor, and dedicated by Tytus his Sonn, in the dedication of wch weare killed five thowsande wilde beastes of divers Sortes, the forme of it wthout is rounde, but wthin it is framed licke an egge and is of suche a mightie height and bignes as it woulde have contained wthin it[989] foure skore 1000 and 5000[990] persons, I did my self measure the breadthe of it and did fynde it (143) to be xii[xx][991] yardes,[992] in this place the wicked Emperors did martir many Christians for their consciences, by throinge them to lyons and other wilde beastes wch there were kepte,

The other amphiteator stoode, in the place where the Churche of the holy Crosse of Jherusalem, nowe standethe but was not of suche greatnes as the other,

[985] 'last named' inserted; different ink and hand.
[986] Altered from 'b' to 'B'.
[987] 'and' deleted.
[988] Altered from 'doe' to 'dothe'.
[989] 'five thowsande and' deleted: here Piers describes the Colosseum.
[990] '1000 and 5000' interlined; '1000' different ink.
[991] 'xx' above 'xii' i.e. 20 x 12, namely 240 yards.
[992] 'longe' deleted.

There were three principall theators in Rome, the firste made by Pompeii, the seconde by Marcellus, the theerd by Cornelius Balbo, in these places the Romans did use to celebrate there feastes and comedies everie of these might containe foure skore thousande parsons, that of Pompei stoode in Campafiore[993] where standethe the Pallace of the moste worthie famely of Ursino, That of marcellus begun by Julius Ceasare, and ended by Augustus, stoode where nowe is the Pallace of the moste noble famely of Savella, that of Cornelius Balbo stoode nighe unto the gate of Flamynius,

The markett places of Rome

There weare in Rome seaventine markett places, but the faireste weare those of Julius Ceasare, Augustus Nero and Trayon and[994] the Roman markett at the footte of the Capidolio (144) where nowe standethe the Arke of Septimio and reatchethe to Saint Cosma and Damyanus Churche, nighe unto the wch stoode the Temple of Vesta, that of Ceasur was wthin the porte Faustina,

That of Augustus was in the place where nowe standethe the Churche of Saint Andre[w]e,[995] That of Trayan was where nowe his Pillar standethe

The markett places nowe in greateste requeste are Piatsanavona[996] and Camphio[re] of the first I have already[997] made som relation nighe unto the wch is[998] an olde Statua called Pasqui upon wch many libells are sette, In the other there is aplace of execution appointed for the burninge of suche persons as are condemned for hereasye,

The triumphant Arkes of Rome

There was in Rome thirtie six Triumphant arkes, wch weare made in the honnor of thos Emperors wch subdued under the Empier of the Romans[999] any kingdom province or Cittie but ther remaine but six of them, That of Septimyus Ceverus in Campidolie wch was made

---

[993] i.e. Campo dei Fiori.
[994] 'and' inserted.
[995] Altered from 'Andrea' to 'Andrewe'.
[996] 'is' deleted.
[997] 'already' inserted, then crossed out.
[998] 'the' deleted.
[999] 'in' deleted.

upon his conqueste, had upon the Parthiente, That of Constantine the great made upon the overthrowe wch he gave to Maxensius, That wch was made by (145) Vespatian and Tytus after there winninge[1000] of Iherusalem these and the reste made by Domytian and others upon the licke occation, weare verie sumteous made of free Stone, wherein weare ingraven ye[1001] som of there victori,[1002]

The pallaces of Rome

There were many antient Pallaces verie sumteously builded but nowe utterly decayed as that of Romulus wch was builded upon the mount Pallatine, those of Augustus, Claudius, Nero, Vespatian, Tytus, Constantine, and manie others,

But the faireste nowe remayninge is that of Saint Peters of the wch I have in another place made some mention. From this stately Pallace there passethe a gallery made of Stone, wch leadethe to the Castle Saint Angello. wch standethe at the ende of Saint Michaell his bridge[1003] this castle is verie lardge beinge builded as rounde as any balle and was in olde tyme tearmed Adrian his moule, The reason of the changinge of the name whereof I have related in the discours of processions, This place is verie strongly fortified. here the Pope kepethe great store of artillerie and provision for warr, amongst the wch there is one pyce of great ordinance wch hathe (146) seaven boares in it for ye receavinge of shotte. this buildinge standethe in suche sorte as it is able to comaunde all Rome, At the celebration of there principall feasts there are[1004] shotte out of yt[1005] castle many peales of great Ordinance and many rare fyre worckes usede as also at the dayes of the Election and coronation of the pope; On the outmoste wall of the same is the[1006] visadge of our Savior moste exactly graven in stone. There are other faire Pallaces belonginge unto his holynes, as those of St Marcke, St John Lateran and montecavallo. Next unto them nowe in account is the Pallace of Cardinall Ferneso,[1007] verie faierly builded beinge of a iuste square and equall in breadthe and height.

[1000] 'there winninge' inserted, different hand.
[1001] 'ye' inserted, different hand.
[1002] Four letters erased.
[1003] 'Churche' deleted; 'bridge' inserted, different hand.
[1004] 'are' inserted, different hand.
[1005] 'yt' inserted, different hand.
[1006] 'the' inserted, different hand.
[1007] i.e. Palazzo Farnese.

There is another fayre Pallace belonginge unto Cardinall Mounte Alto,[1008] whoe is Lord Chauncellor unto the Pope; There are divers others verie lardge and fayre, as that of Cardinall Caiettan whoe is lord Treasurer unto the Pope, and protector[1009] of the Englishe. That of Cardinall Penelle whoe is averye papall man, and cheefe of the inquisitione. That of Cardinall Rusticouche[1010] whoe is generall vickar unto the Pope, nighe unto the wch is averye lardge and fayere Pallace wch in tymes when Catholicke religion florished in England did belonge unto the Embassador (147) wch came from thence to Rome. There is also a fayre Pallace wherein Cardinall Mathias dwell-ethe whoe was protector of the Irishe. Upon the hill Pincio is a stately Pallace belonginge unto the Duke of Florence, by the wch is a curious Garden full of exquisitt water worckes, verie fayre walkes, and manie[1011] antient statutas of the olde gods;

[*A rare and costlye concept*].[1012] Amongste those rare devises there was one extraordinary conceite worthie to be noted, the wch wthout doubt was performed wth greate arte and infinitt labor, for in an out corner of the Garden there were to be seene the statuas of a number of[1013] men, women, and children, all made of white marble, wch weare as it weare behouldinge of a fearfull eclipes of the Sunn, one of them did seeme to stare and loke soe gastly as if he weare beside him-self, another appeered to be strucken downe wth feare to the earthe, others by pointinge wth[1014] there fingers and makinge strange coun-tenances, did demonstratt howe muche they did wonder at that u[n]usuall[1015] sight, there was one wch was deemed to be falinge from his horse wth the terror wch he conceaved thereof, and lokinge alitle farther there might be sene the livlye representation of divers women, wch beinge possessed wth feare and tremblinge, sought as it weare to heyde them selves in a growe[1016] nighe unto them adioyninge, as also the perfecte resemblances of

---

[1008] Alessandro Damasceni Peretti (1571–1623), also known as Cardinal di Montalto, cre-ated cardinal 1585; vice chancellor of the Holy Roman Church, 1589–1623. Miranda, *The Cardinals of the Holy Roman Church* http://www2.fiu.edu/~mirandas/bios1585.htm, accessed 25 Nov. 2017.

[1009] 'unto' deleted.

[1010] Girolamo Rusticucci (1537–1603), created cardinal 1570; vicar general of Rome, 1588–1603. Miranda, *The Cardinals of the Holy Roman Church* http://www2.fiu.edu/~miran-das/bios1570.htm#Rusticucci, accessed 25 Nov. 2017.

[1011] 'manie' inserted, different hand and ink.

[1012] Different hand, different ink – black ink, in contrast to brown ink of body of text.

[1013] 'of' inserted.

[1014] 'wth' inserted, different hand.

[1015] Altered from 'usuall' to 'unusuall'.

[1016] Probably 'grove' intended.

certaine[1017] (148) yonge children wch beinge frighted wth that horrible spectackle did make as if they did rune to there mothers for
succor, wth many other moste admirable apparances, the wch
weare soe exactly carved and artificially sett forthe as my witt cannott possibl[ie] compas the sufficient desiferinge of them,

Nighe unto the gate of Ostia are the viewes of Pontius Pilatt his
Pallace, and not far distante from thence are the ruines of 2[1018] two
Temples wch weare dedicated unto the Sonn and the moone,
there are soe[1019] many goodly Pallaces in Rome belonginge unto
the Cardinalls, Dukes, markuesses, Earles, and other great cittizens,
as the rehearsinge of them in particular woulde prove tedious, and
therefor I will seace to name any more of them; It is founde by antient recorde that there weare in Rome a thowsand seaven hundred 97
fayre Pallaces builded by the antient Romans.

The Courtes and Senackles of Rome

There weare in Rome in the tyme of the antient Romans 35 courte
houses, som of them pertaininge unto the priestes of that tyme, where
they handled matters belonginge unto there place, the reste pertained
to the Senators, wherein they hard publicke causes, (149) but the
moste curious of all theise, (exceptinge the Capitall) was that where
nowe standethe the churche of Saint Peeter ad vinculum; in the
wch the heathen priestes did make their false divinations; There
weare three Senackles in Rome wheare the Senators did meete to
deliberatt upon ther serious affaires. one of them was in the
Temple of Concorde, another at Saint Sabastine his gatte, the
third in the Temple of Bellona, in the wch they receaved suche
Embassadors as com from theire Enemyes, the wch weare not suffred
to enter wthin the cittie.

The maiestratts of Rome

Rome had only seaven kinges, and after that they weare governed be
two consulles, whoe had full power and aucthoritty only for one
yeere; there weare officers called preturs wch did keepe the lawes,
the one of them did iudge of privatt matters, and the other of the
causes of strangers. There weare fourteene wch weare called

[1017] 'also the perfect … certaine': continuous line under last line of text on this page, at
right angle to line indicating left-hand margin of the page.
[1018] '2' inserted.
[1019] 'may' deleted.

Trybuns of the people. theise had aucthorittie to lett and staye the decrees of the Senatt or Consulls, every Trybon had power to imprison a consull, The questors had the chardge of the Treasurie and of readinge letters in the Senatt. The Edilles had care of the cittie and of ther (150) publicke plea[c]es; The Sensors did enquire and take care of the behavior of the people, another sort of Sensors had the care of the Temples, of the common rents of the customes of the cittie, and did chastice vices. The Tryumvirio[1020] had the chardge of punishinge mallefactors, especeally of those wch coyned mony; and of suche people as did walke at unseasonable tymes in the Night, and to take heed that noe mischaunce shoulde com to the cittie by fyer, There weare pretors and other officers wch weare to longe to be rehearsed,

There are many other thinges of account to be resited the wch I will breefly pass over, as for example, there great lybreraries, ther triumphant pillers, the goulden house of Nero, the ritche buildinge whereof woulde seeme increadible to be[1021] rehearsed[e]:

The Campidolio, there trybes wch amount to 35, there treasure houses, wch weare verie lardge and ritche, there places for receavinge of strangers, the filde of mars, there hospitalls for decayed Soldiors, the vinyards, there Gardens, there Publicke gernells[1022] for keepinge of graine, wch weare verie lardge and capatious, there Sollemne celebratinge of there festivall dayes, there Tables of brasse and copper, of the wch there weare three thowsande, in the wch the antient lawes of the Romans weare written, ther prisons, ther (151) maner of buriall, there Temples, ther priestes, and vestall virgins the[1023] crownes and recoardes as they did use to give unto suche as deserved well at ther hands, and the number of there people, wch in Servious Tulius tyme amounted to 84 thowsand persons, and at the firste warr made againste Charthadge, there weare founde in Rome twentye hundred and nynetie thowsand three hundred and theertie soules,[1024] in the tyme of Tyberius Ceasare there weare 16 hundred thowsande 2 hundred and 92 soules, nowe lately in the tyme of Pope Sixtus Quintus there weare soules dwellinge in Rome to the

---

[1020] Letters in italics inserted.

[1021] 'he' deleted.

[1022] A form of 'garnel': a granary or barn, *OED*.

[1023] 'the' inserted.

[1024] The translation of the population figures from Italian to English is unclear; see the original Italian, as given by Palladio, in Girolamo Francini [Francino], *Le Cose Maravigliose dell'Alma Città di Roma* (Venice, 1588), 122–123; here in the margin of the 'Discourse' there is a cross, indicating a reader's perplexity regarding this passage.

number of fowre hundred thousande and somwhat more, the liber-
alitie and ritches of the antient Romans was inestimable and
incomparable.

The Antiquitie of Rome

Rome was builded by Romulus in the yeere of the worlde 4447. and
after the destruction of Troye 405 yeares, and was increased after
wardes by suche kinges,[1025] consulls, and Emperors as had aucthoritie
over it, many aucthors doe write of the greatnes of Rome, som saye it
was fiftye myles about, som saye 32, and som 28, but as it is nowe in
our tyme, it is accounted but 16 myles in compas, it standethe by the
ryver Tyber, the water of the wch ryver[1026] (152) is verie muddy; and of
a darcke collor, but beinge kepte in a sweete vessell it growethe verie
cleere and medicinable.

Rome standethe som fifteene myles from the sea, and is invironed
wth great montaines. The Romans from the firste buildinge of
there cittie untill the raigne of Augustus ceasure weare the greateste
Idollators absollutly in the whole worlde, in his tyme there was a generall peace betwixt all nations, and then the prince of peace our
Saviour was borne, and yett the Romans beleeved not in Christe
untill abut the raigne of Tyberious ceasure in whose tyme he was crucified. There is an antient letter remayninge nowe in the liberarie of
the vaticano written by Pontius Pilatt, wherein he certified, Tyberius
Ceasure, that the Jewes did soe importune him that he was enforced
to putt to a moste cruell deathe one Jesus of Nazarethe whoe as he
parswaded himself was an inocente and giltles man, this letter dothe
soe concurr wth the scriptures that I thought it not amisse to resite
this muche of it.

Upon the reporte of the myraculous dedes don by our Saviour in his
liffe, and of his deathe and glorious resurrection, many of the
Romans and of divers other nations,[1027] receaved the Christian faithe,
but weare mightily persecuted and martered for the same by the (153)
wicked Emperors, soe as from the tyme of the crucifyinge of Saint
Peeter whoe was the firste Pope untill the raigne of Constantine
the greate, there weare martered 32 Popes besids thowsandes of
other Christians,

[1025] 'and' deleted.
[1026] 'by the ryver Tyber ... wch ryver' underlined.
[1027] 'receavethe' deleted.

[*The miraculous conversion of Constantine the great.*][1028] This Constantine
after he had overthrowen maxensius the Tyrant, in sorte as I have
allredy partly touched, had the quiett possession of the Romane
Empeer, and chaunced to fall into a leprosye for the cueringe
whereof he assembled together his Southesainge Phisitions and
other cunninge men, whoe havinge conferred thereof they did conclude that he coulde not be holpen unlesse he had washed himself
in the bloode of inocents, the wch accordinge unto there advice he
intended to performe, but before that this matter was putt in execution there appeared in avition unto Constantine in the night, two
grave and antient men wch exorted him to flee the develishe consaile
of his wicked Phisitions, and to sende wth all speede for Saint
Silvester then Pope (whoe at that tyme did heede himself[1029] in
caves and other secreatt places for estuinge of ye[1030] persecution
wch his predesessors had tasted of) and to be adviced by him for
the recovery of his healthe, the next morninge followinge he sente
his protection for St Silvester, and havinge debated the matter wth
him he founde (154) by the sight of a picture wch St silvester had,
that the[y] wch appeared unto him weare Saint Peeter and Saint
Paule, wch he tearmed to have bene two of the Christians gods,
but upon further conference wth Saint Silvester, lickinge of his zealus
speaches and grave councell he was contented for the curinge of his
lyprosie to be christened by him, and thereupon recovered his former
helthe and cleanes. The Fonte wherein he was Baptized is at this daye
to be seene in a chappell adioyninge unto Saint John Latrans
churche, in the wch they doe nowe use to christen all suche turckes
and Jewes as are in Rome converted to the Christian faithe, After
that Constantine the great was thus myraculously converted by
Saint Silvester he gave Rome and all Itally unto the sea apostolicke,
he threwe downe the Temples of the false gods and erected many
churches (as befor is resited,) to the honnor of god and his Saints,
and leavinge Rome wente himself into Greece and builded a fayre
cittie at Bizantiom, callinge it Constantinople according to his
owne name, and there kept his imperiall Seate; We maye well here
note a wonderfull worcke of god in makinge Rome the heade of
all true religion wch heretofor was the cheefe ringleader of all
Idollatries, from that time untill this daye, (wch amountethe to som
(155) 13 hundred yeares) ye Popes have succeeded eatche other in
Rome preatchinge and teatchinge the doctrine wch there predicessors receaved of Saint Peeter, as is sufficiently proved by Father

---

[1028] In the MS this heading is on the margin towards the top of p. 154.
[1029] Start of new word deleted.
[1030] 'ye' inserted; different hand and ink.

Bellarmyne in his books of the Controversies of this tyme, whoe for his exceedinge great learninge and vertue is exalted unto the place of a Cardinall.[1031]

The Pope wch at my beinge in Rome lyved was worthely for his Clemencie called Clemente the eight of that name beinge a Florentine descended of the house of Al[o]brandino, befor whom there have succeeded one another in Rome the number of 234 popes.+

[*The virtuouse life and worthie acctions of Pope Clement the eyght*].[1032] This Clement was a moste verteous and devout man as I my self can testifie, for when he was caried in his greateste maiestie blessinge of the people, he ordinarily shedd tears, and in sainge of masse he did the licke, morover I have knowen that he hathe walked privatly from his house of Montecavallo[1033] unto Saint Marye Maiores churche divers tymes (wch is nighe a myle in lenight, and as it was tolde me bare footte) upon devotion to saye masse at an alter dedicated unto our Lady; wthin that churche, in the backe of wch is a picture of hirs wch was painted by Sainte Luke in the tyme of his beinge Pope, he did matters of great consequence as the bringinge in of the kinge of Fraunce to the unitie of the Churche, after whose (156) reconsiliation his imbassador cominge to Rome was mett wthall by at the leaste five thowsande Romans whereof the moste parte weare noblemen Bushoppes, and cittizens of great accounte rydinge of gallant horsses on costly footte clothes. also the agreeinge of Fraunce and Spaine to gether wch befor weare at warres; the makinge of atonemt, and peace betwixt the kinges of Transilvania and Polonia, the convertinge of the mightie regions of Japonia, by the Jesuits,[1034] wch for a great parte was done in his tyme, beside many overthrowes gyven by his armye and the Emperors forces upon the Turcke, againste whom he did mantaine eight thowsande men continually under the Emperor his leadinge) upon his[1035] owne coste and chardges; he kept a hundred horse and two hundred footte of sweechers[1036] wch did serve him as his garde, and had a stronge

---

[1031] Robert Bellarmine SJ, created cardinal 3 Mar. 1599. Miranda, *The Cardinals of the Holy Roman Church* http://www2.fiu.edu/~mirandas/bios1599.htm, accessed 21 Jan. 2018.

[1032] For a survey of Clement VIII's pontificate (1592–1605), see entry by Agostino Borromeo, in Massimo Bray et al. (eds), *Enciclopedia dei Papi* ([Roma], 2000), III, 249–269.

[1033] 'ca' inserted.

[1034] For an outline of Jesuit activity in Japan at the end of the 16th century, see *Diccionario histórico de la Compañía de Jésus*, sub 'Japón'.

[1035] Previous 'his' written in faint ink.

[1036] Swiss guards; probably a variant of 'Switzer', *OED*.

warde of men in the castle of St Angello, he was daylie buildinge of Saint Peeters churche wch is soe hoodge that it will not be[1037] in many years finished, and did repayre many Churches, Bridges, and highe wayes wch weare decayed, his bountye towards men wch flye thether for ther consciences was verie great, his hospitallytie kepte for Pillgreems exceedinge[1038] plentifully extended,[1039] he did give mony to beare there chardges of those, wch for devotion (157) sake doe undertake to visitte the Sepullcher of our Savior in Iherusalem, he bestowed agreat deale of mony in pentions, and relived an infinitt nomber of poore people. many other good thinges he performed, the wch for brevetye sake I omitt to speake of, [*The revenues of the Sea Apostolick*] In this sorte he distributed the revenues of the Sea apostolicke wch amount to 24 thowsande crownes a daye, In all his actions shewinge bothe charitie and bountie wch weare deeds correspondente unto his holie[1040] profossion[1041] and princely callinge.[1042]

And amongste other his laudable actions it shall not be amisse heere to sett downe howe that we were[1043] certified in Spaine after my departure out of Italy that upon the Duke of Farrara his deathe, his Base Sonn did indevor to houlde the Cittie and Dukedom by force, of the wch his holynesse beinge enformede, did sent perswasitive letters unto him wishinge him to resigne and give up the cittie, the wch he refused to doe, whereupon he was excummunicated, and yet not wth standinge he persisted in his rebellious disobedience, by meanes whereof all the Citties and Townes wch he helde were interdicted,[1044] but the Pope perceavinge that he continued in persecutinge his wicked determynation for the furtherance of the aucthoritie wch he exercisethe by Saint Peters keyes he, drwe out Saint Paule his sworde gathered an armye of fortie thowsande men, at (158) leaste, and tooke his Jorney himself from Rome in parson, in maner and forme followinge.

Firste there passed before him dyvers noble men and captaines wth many troupes of horse and companies of footte, then dyvers of the beste cardinalls wth many Archbishoppes and bushoppes and there

[1037] 'be' inserted.
[1038] 'exceedinge' inserted; 'verie' deleted.
[1039] 'and' deleted.
[1040] 'holie' inserted.
[1041] *Recte* 'profession'.
[1042] From here, change of ink.
[1043] 'we were' inserted; different ink and hand.
[1044] Cut off authoritatively from religious offices or privileges; regarding a place or person, 'lay … under an interdict', *OED*.

attendants, in the midest of whom was carried the blessed Sacramt in a ritche cheeste or Truncke wth many lights borne aboute it, and in the rereward wente the Pope himself wth noe suche pompe or maiestie, nor suche nombers of honnorable personadges as he sente before him, therein shewinge what honnor and reverence he did beare unto the blessed Euchariste wherein is containede the glorious body and precious blode of or Savior Jesus Christe; In whatsoever cittie or Towne they happened to take ther lodginge duringe that iorney the blessed Sacrament was taken out of the Truncke wth great reverence and caried in moste heavenly maner unto the cheefe churche ther, and sett upon the highe altar of the same, the churche beinge hanged wth blacke and many lights placed in it, unto wch then did resorte an infinite number of people wch for a great parte did praie there all night, for the wch they receaved great indulgences. in this sorte his holynes passed alonge untill he came to Bolonya, wch is som two hundred myles from Rome and thertie myles from Farrara, where he receaved a submission from the Dukes base (159) Sonn whoe wth great repentance and humillitie was content to be censured by the Churche for his wicked acte, whereupon the Pope perceavinge the great sorrowe and greeffe he sustayned for his unadvised atempt[1045] moste gratiously bestowed upon him the citties of Modenar [Modena] and Regium [Reggio] and married him to a kinswoman of his owne, at the wch tyme he dismissed his armye, and Jornyed forward to Farrara, where he was receaved wth inestimable ioye in moste magnificient maner, and there tooke quiett possession of the same, and for the establishinge and settlinge whereof unto his successors, he dwelt there for the space of a whole yeare at the leaste, and did enacte a lawe wth the consent of the Cardinalls, that henceforward there should noe more dukedomes or other principall signories be gyven in state of inheritance by the Churche to anye man, but that they shoulde be governed by deputies, wch shoulde have noe intreste in them but duringe the Popes pleasure.

Then did he returne to Rome in moste maiesticall maner and was mett in his waye by many worthie noblemen as well of the spirituall as temporall callinge wch came wth exceedinge great reverence and alacretie to congratulate his good successe, and was wth unspeakable applause of the whole multitude receaved at Rome, where in verie Saintctlicke[1046] fashion he spente the remaynder of his dayes, havinge in most holye and prudent maner governed (160) the Sea apostolicke for the space of sixteene years,[1047] to the highe advancement of god his

[1045] 'and' deleted.
[1046] Altered from 'fam' to 'Sainctlicke'.
[1047] Pope Clement VIII reigned from 1592–1605.

glorie and wonderfull benefitt of his Churche for the wch wthout doubt he hathe receaved a Crowne of aeternall felicitie.

And as in his spirituall government he was moste happie, soe was he[1048] surpassinge wyse and carefull in exercisinge of his temporall aucthoritie, as well did appeere in all suche citties and contries as weare under his domynion and namely in preservinge of graine for the use of the common welthe, not only in Castle Saint Angello but also in many other fayre and lardge garnells, soe usinge the matter in suche sorte as it was not perceaved in Rome, whether corne were deere or good cheape, by reason that the price of breade still continued at one rate, for an order was taken that the bakers shoulde still have wheate out of his store allwayes in a reasonable manner, howsoever deere it weare in other places, wth condition that when it did happen to be cheape in other regions, theie shoulde buy his provition at the wonted rate, before theie did bestowe there mony else wheare, and for this cause the bakers weare tyed that they shoulde use noe alteration either in the size or price of breade many other suche wholesom lawes were enacted and confirmed by him, for the good of the common welthe the wch weare to longe heere to be resited.[1049] After whose deathe was chosen Leo the eleventh[1050] who lyved butt a short tyme, and then[1051] succeeded Paule the fifte[1052] of whome I have allreddie made som mention, who is a verie personable man [in]duead wth great wisedom and understandinge[1053]

(161) [*A strange monster*] Amongste other things wch might be added to this discourse I have thought good to sett downe howe I did see at my being there astrange monster wch was two children, the heade of the one being in[1054] the breaste of the other, and bothe his hands hidden wthin his brothers[1055] sides[1056] all his other members beinge perfecte and hanginge wth suche a weight as it was verie greavous unto the bigger boye.

[1048] 'moste' deleted; 'surpassinge' inserted, different hand.
[1049] New hand to end of page.
[1050] Pope Leo XI, elected 1 Apr. 1605; d. 27 Apr. 1605.
[1051] 'then' inserted.
[1052] Pope Paul V reigned from 1605–1621.
[1053] 'After whose deathe … great wisedom and understandinge' inserted in new hand.
[1054] 'in' inserted.
[1055] 'brothers' inserted – new hand, as previous insertion on p. 160 of MS.
[1056] 'and' deleted.

There was also a man in Rome wch alwayes daunced from Sonn rysinge untill Sonn settinge wch as I harde was a punishment layde by god upon the grand Father of that man and his posteritie; the reason was for that he beinge dauncinge amonge other companie did not that reverence unto the blessed Sacrament (wch passede by them) as the reste of his company did. moreover I did see one carrie a woman in a basket, wch he showed for mony; shee beinge not three footte hye in statur. And a man wch was all covered wth heare wch grewe out of his body:

Last of all I have not thought it not amisse[1057] to declare somthinge as toutchinge the Jewes. wch since the deathe of or Savior have bene scattered as vacabons and slaves upon the face of the whole earthe, in Rome they have a place alotted them to dwell in by the ryver of Tyber wch is inclosed in the manner of a Towne wth stone wales, and[1058] are there som 30 thowsande in nomber they have there Synagoges sett out wth lampes and lights, wherein they use ther hebrue service, (162) and there olde ceremonies, not far from there dwellinge is a peece of land inclosed wherein they bury there deade, there hate towardes Christians is suche, that if a christian childe doe goe under the beare as they carrie a Jue towardes the place of buriall, they will presently goe backe againe wth the corse to use some ceremonies unto it, affirminge that he was by that meanes[1059] poluted by the Christian, his passinge under it,[1060] they live for the more parte by buinge and sellinge of caste apparell and other oulde stuffe, there men and women are knowen by there yallowe hatts and heade tyere, wch theie are[1061] tyed upon paine to weare, the cheefe cause whye theye are suffred to dwell amonge Christians is for that divers of them are yearly converted unto the Christian faithe, and noe Christians perverted by them.

There is a churche not farr from them unto the wch theye do use[1062] to sende, one out of everie house on Saturdayes to heare a cermon wch is preched by a Jesuite or som other religious persone, wch dothe worcke greate and good effecte amongeste them, for I have sene me self som of them wch weare converted at those cermons cristened at Constantine the greate his fonte.

[1057] The sense is 'I have thought it not amiss'; probably a copyist's error.
[1058] 'and' inserted, new hand, as previous insertions; 'they' deleted.
[1059] 'by that meanes' inserted; new hand.
[1060] 'by the Christian, his passinge under it' – line through, but legible.
[1061] 'are' inserted; new hand, as previous insertions.
[1062] 'doe use' inserted, new hand; 'are bounde' deleted.

They wch doe desire to knowe more at lardge in matters [beine] related[1063] of the antient and modern[1064] Romans,[1065] lett them enquire for a booke called the antiquities and mervellous things of Rome written by Hierom Francis. before mentioned.[1066] and they shall see at full that wch I have heere breefly sett downe.

(163) Upon my departure from Rome, Father Parsons and Doctor Haddocke (whoe bothe weare in great credit wth the Pope) brought me unto his holynes his presents and used suche commendations of me to him as I receaved his benediction kissed his footte and hade a helpe of some crownes of him towardes my iorney homewards.

My Jornie from Rome hom[e]wads

I begane my Jorneye from Rome in the company of certaine Englishe priestes on the 15 daye of October accordinge to the newe computation and in the yeare of our Lorde 1597 and left Phillip Draycott in the Englishe Colledge whoe sheawed himself verie obedient unto his superiours, and did daily increase bothe in vertue and learninge, usinge always suche offices of gratitude and faithfulnes towards me self as he was able to performe. After my departure he intred into the Novitiat of the Jesuits and there dyed, to the great Edification of all suche as were presente, the wch was signified unto[1067] (164) me by Doctor Haddocke (I then beinge in the Englishe Colledge of Cyvill [Seville] in Spaine.) That daye wee passed over Pontmillvio and that same[1068] night we lay at Regnata.

The xvi daye by Burgetto where we passed by Tyber and soe by Utriquelye [Otricoli], and the cittie Arnye [Narni], and then to Turnye [Terni].

The xviith[1069] by the cittie Spoleta [Spoleto] to Vercana [Verchiano].

[1063] 'in matters related' inserted, new hand; word deleted.
[1064] 'and modern' inserted; new hand.
[1065] 'and the notable things wch they have done' deleted.
[1066] 'written by … before mentioned' inserted; new hand; Francini, *Le Cose Maravigliose*.
[1067] 'as were presente, the wch was signified' – line under last line of page (as before).
[1068] 'same' inserted.
[1069] 'daye' deleted.

The xviiith[1070] to the cittie Torentine [Tolentino] where the body of St Nicholas of Torentine[1071] lyethe

[*The principallitie of Marca.*] The xixth[1072] to the cittie Marcereta [Macerata] where lyethe the Popes legatt for ye Territories of Marca.

The xxth daye to the holye house of our blessed Lady in Loretta [Loreto], and for that it is a place of great devotion unto the wch doe resorte in pillgreemadge an infinitt namber of zealous Catholickes I have thought it expediente to make som shorte relation of the principall matters concerninge the same.

[*An abridgement of the holy house of Laurettas historie*] The reader muste therefor understande that this holie house firste stoode in Nazerethe and that in it was borne and brought up the sanctefied mother of god, where also by the Omnipotente power of the holye goste shee was saluted by the Angell Gabriell, and conceaved of the Redeemer of mankynde, in the wch shee did after his blessed birthe carefully for dyvers yeares nurishe him. [*Our Ladies howse much honored by ye Apostles.*] After the deathe of oure Saviour and of the spottles virgin marie this howse was muche honnored by the apostles beinge then used by them as a[1073] churche (165) and soe continued in estimation untill the raigne of Constantine the great, [*A faire churche builded by St Helina over our[1074] Ladies howse.*] at the wch tyme the Empresse Saint Helyna about three hundred yeares after the birthe of Christe, builded a verie fayre[1075] churche over it unto the wch there daily resorted agreat multitude of godly Christians, wch beinge possessed wth pious affections, did visite that angelicall habitation, the wch concourse of pillgrimes was religiously continued untill the yeare 700 or thereabouts at the wch tyme the Saricens did wynn Iherusalem, and the territories thereunto adioyninge; but not wthstandinge did suffer the Christians to visit the holye places untill that the Turckes in the yeare 1050, havinge conquered the holy land, did exceedinglye vex and persecute them, whereupon Pope urban the seconde[1076] stirred up Godfrie of Bullin and other Christian

---

[1070] 'daye' deleted.
[1071] St Nicholas of Tolentino (c.1245–1306), Augustinian friar, Cross and Livingstone, *Oxford Dictionary of the Christian Church*, sub nomine.
[1072] 'daye' deleted.
[1073] 'as a' inserted.
[1074] 'our' inserted.
[1075] 'house' deleted.
[1076] Pope Urban II, reigned 1088–1099.

princes for the recoverie of the same, the wch they accordinglie performed in the yeare 1100.

After the wch[1077] victorie obteyned, the fame of that holy howse still
increasede, in soe muche, as the great Christian Champion
Tancred did indowe the same wth verie riche[1078] giftes, [*A metrapolitan
Sea establishead in Nazereth.*] and did procure that Nazerethe shoulde be
established the seate of a metropolitan Bisshopricke. But in processe
of tyme (the Christian princes fallinge into contention amongste
themselves) weare not able to maintaine sufficient forces, to bridle
the dailye incurtions of the (166) Turckes into the holy land, [*The
waye to Nazerethe stopped by the Turcke.*] soe as by peece meales the enemyes of god gatte it all into there possession insomuche as the holy
places coulde not wth safetye be visited, and not wthout greate
coste unto the pillgrimes. This insolencie of the Turckes governments
in those partes seemed to be established before and in the yeare,
1291. and then the barbarous, crueltie of these tyrants grewe to
suche a heade, as the waye to the blissed howse was cleane shutte up.

[*The miraculouse removeinge of the holye howse into Dalmatia.*] But god by his
omnipotente power in the saide yeare 1291, and on the eight of maye
in the tyme of Pope Nicholas the fourthe[1079] did miraculously remowe
the same into Europe, and placed it in Dalmatia in the side of a mon-
tayne right over the Adriaticke sea, wch hapeninge in the night tyme,
did supernaturally sende forthe shininge beames of light, the wch did
breede suche[1080] wonder in the inhabitants thereabouts as happie did
he thincke himself wch firste might visitt soe strange a spectacklle,
after the movinge whereof they tooke the measure of it to be in
lenithe fortie footte, in breadthe twentye, and in height twentie
five. havinge in it an Imadge of our blessed Lady and a Crosse
bothe of them carved by Saint Luke the Evangeliste, and the altar
upon the wch Saint Peeter said his first masse, wch thinges the
mother of god, (appeeringe unto an olde man wch for the recover-
inge of (167) his helthe cam theether) revealed unto him tellinge
him, that it was the howse wherein shee dwelte, and howe by the
power of god it was carried thither, these and divers other matters
worthie of note I me self have seene in the place where nowe the
howse standethe, of the wch after a while I shall (god willinge)
make some mention.

[1077] 'wch' inserted.
[1078] 'verie riche' inserted; new hand.
[1079] Pope Nicholas IV, reigned 1288–1292.
[1080] 'suche' inserted.

The truthe hereof beinge confirmed as well by the wonderfull recover-ie of the olde man as also by many other mirackles, bread suche devotion in all the borderinge contries as great nombers of them flocked theether in godly and pious maner to visitt the same;

[*The miracle approved by due enquirie*]¹⁰⁸¹ And for the better satisfaction of the people the magistratts of that contrie sente fowre men of greate accounte, and sufficientie into Gallelie to see if the pr[o]misses weare true, the wch they founde to be certaine, for havinge veweade the churche builded by Saint helina theie sawe there the place where this he[a]venly habitation was seated, and lackinge measure of the newe [r]ente up fondation they perceyved it to be of longitude and latitude equale wth the howse, and beheld agreat gapp in aparte of the churche, throughe the wch it¹⁰⁸² was carried, and this was also verified unto them, by the conquered Christians there remay-ninge, wch wittnessed the same; Upon the returne of these gentlmen the Dallmatians grewe (168) into suche a presumptious conceipte that theie thought themselves to be the beste deservinge nation in the whole worlde, [*The wonderfull transportation of ye blissed mantion into Italy*] for the punishment whereof it pleased god, sodainly by his angells to transporte the same into Itallie, on the fifte of December in the yeare 1294. and¹⁰⁸³ in the tyme of Pope Boniface the eight,¹⁰⁸⁴ wch as it was an infinitt greefe unto the Illirians soe was it an unspeakeable ioye to the Itallians unto whom it shoulde seeme this extraordinarie blessinge was gyven for that amongst them is erected the place where the generall deputie of heaven houldethe his dwell-inge. It happened to be lefte in the contrie called Pissinu som myle from the sea, and in a grove not far from Rakinata [Recanati]. the wch belonged to a matron called Lawreta. wch beinge once blased abroade mightie was the resorte of all sortes of¹⁰⁸⁵ people unto that happie mantion, wheare divers weare myraculously cured of ther infirmities.

[*Our Ladies howse againe removed.*] From thence it was removed som one myle unto a hill belonginge unto two bretheren, whoe used the pill-geemes in verie badd sorte, and weare soe covetous and discom[o] dious as by the iuste iudgment of god, [*A fourthe remove.*] that blissed buildinge, was carried unto another hill som flight shotte distante

---

¹⁰⁸¹ Different ink.
¹⁰⁸² 'it' inserted.
¹⁰⁸³ 'and' inserted.
¹⁰⁸⁴ Pope Boniface VIII, reigned 1294–1303.
¹⁰⁸⁵ 'sortes of' inserted; word deleted.

from thence, beinge som two myles from the Sea all wch alterations chaunced in[1086] the yeere after the (169) cominge thereof into Italye the wch soe increased the devotion of all Christian domynons wch hard thereof, as inumerable were the people wch daylie repayred theether, and an espetiall cause movinge them thereunto was for that a holy hermitt had receaved the licke revelation from the Queene of heaven as the olde man in Dallmatia had, as before is declared;

[*The certainty of ye miracle ratified by a further inquirie*] The wch when he had related unto the cittizens of Rakynata and inhabitants of Picinum [Picena], theie made agreat assemblye bothe of the cittie and contrie, and chose xvi men of the moste discretion and iudgment amongste them to undertake a iornye for Dalmatia, and from thence to Gallilie, to thende[1087] that theie might be certainly enformed, by there inquirie and dilligence of the infalybillitie hereof, Upon whose aryvall at the Illurian Porte beinge verie inquisite of the matter, they understoode by the common voyce of the sorrowfull people that all wch theie harde befor was true, and for the better ratefeinge thereof, there was sheawed unto them a chappell wch for devotion sake was builded in the verie same place, where oure blissed Ladies house stoode, wth an inscription over the doore thereof, importinge as muche;

From thence they passed by sea into Syria where theie paied a great som of mony to the Turckes officers for havinge leave to visett the holy places, wch beinge performed by them they[1088] (170) found as well by there owne vewe, as also by the reporte of the poore oppressed Christians wch dwelt at Nazerethe, that they wch weare sente from Dalmatia theether had made a faithefull returne of the busines committed to there chardge, and thereupon wth great ioye theie returned home, to the inestimable comfort of the Picenises wch wth one[1089] consente in the yeere 1296. tooke the blissed Ladie[1090] of Lawreta for theire patronis. the fame of the wch happie tydinges beinge bruted abroade was the cause of the repayringe theether of an infinit companie of pious Chrystians, the wch theie were the more incensed unto, for that there weare seene by the observation of the neighbors thereunto adioyninge divers flames of fyere

[1086] 'in' inserted.
[1087] That is, 'the end'.
[1088] 'holy places ... by them they' line inserted under final line of page, as before.
[1089] 'one' inserted.
[1090] 'Ladie' inserted.

descendinge in the night tyme from heaven uppon that holy place to the great admyration of suche as behelde the same;

And then did dyvers men builde Innes and other houses upon that hill for the receavinge of Pillgreemes, wch in great abondance did resorte thether; And for as muche as the[1091] n[e]ither parte of the wale of the house seemed by reason of the oft removinge thereof to be impaired[1092] the inhabitants thereabouts did adioyne newe butteris[1093] unto it, leaste perhappes it might in tyme for want of reparations fall into decaye, but this newe worcke did soone of it self fale from the olde, soe far as a boy wth a (171) light might easilie passe betwixt them, wch sheawed that the kepinge up and preservinge thereof was myraculous and not ordinare.

In the grove not far from this heavenly mantion there was abydinge one Paule an Hermitt, wch for ten yeares together, and namely on the ewe[1094] of the Nativitie of the blissed veirgin, did see abondance of fyere descendinge from heaven and invironinge of the same, the wch he revealed unto the great men of Rakinata, [*A churche builded by the Racanists over the howse.*] whereupon theie builded a fayre churche aboute it, and dedicated the same unto the birthe of the spottles mother of god.[1095]

Unto the wch Pope benedictus the xiith[1096] graunted manie indullgences and after that the towne beinge growen unto agood leynght. [*A market and a faire graunted unto Laureta by Pope martin the fift.*][1097] Pope martine the fifte[1098] graunted unto it a lycence for the haveinge of a marckett and a fayre. the wch was confirmed by divers Popes wch after did succeede him. And when as Pope Eugenus the fifte[1099] begane his raigne wch was in the yeere 1450 he did endowe it wth many ritche gyftes, and the indulgenges thereof weare augmented as well by him as by Pope Nicholas the fifte his immediat successor.

[1091] 'the' inserted; different ink.
[1092] 'im' inserted.
[1093] 'ther' deleted.
[1094] That is, 'eve'.
[1095] 'unto the wch' erased.
[1096] Pope Benedict XII, reigned 1334–1342.
[1097] Different ink.
[1098] Pope Martin V, reigned 1417–1431.
[1099] There is some confusion in the text regarding the sequence of the popes: in fact, Eugenius IV reigned 1431–1447, and his successor was Nicholas V, reigned 1447–1455.

In the tyme of Pope Calistinus the thirde,[1100] the Turcke haveing wone Constantinople and many other Christian territories made many incursions into Dalmatia, and not beinge content therewth sente an armye for the invadinge of (172) Italy and for the takinge and suppressinge of the churche and house of Lawreto wch then was growen to exceedinge great welthe by reason of the manie presious Jewells costly challices[1101] candellstickes and sumteous churche stuffe wth other ornaments wch as well the severall Popes, as also divers princes noblemen and others of good Rancke had bestowed uppon that sacred place.

[*The Turkes forces miraculouslie overthrowen*] Upon the wch occation the Pope sente a smale fleete of gallies for the deffence of that coste, wch meetinge wth the Turcks forces gave them soe great a foyle as moste of them weare Slayne and not a fewe taken prisoners, whereupon the generall relatinge by letters his successe unto his holynes signified that the victorie was obtained beyonde human licklyhoode, wch he attributed unto the intercession of oure blessed Lady of Laureta.

[*Pope Calistus strangelye cured for ye wiche cawse he indowead the place wth manie riche giftes*][1102] Next after Calistus, was chosen Pius the seconde,[1103] whoe falinge into a dangerous fever by prayers made unto hir, was sodenly recovered, the wch increased soe the glorie and renowne thereof as not only Pope pius him self, but many others did give presents of mightie worthe, unto that devoute habitation; [*The wonderfull recoverie of Pope Paule the Second and his buildinge of a newe churche over the holy howse.*][1104] Pope Paule the seconde beinge infected wth the plage and carried into the holye house, was[1105] incontinently delyvered thereof, whereupon as a singe of thanckes gyvinge unto the mother of god he plucked downe the old churche, and made a verie fayre and lardge one in steede thereof he (173) freed that churche from the aucthoritie of the bushopp of Rakynata,[1106] and did subiect it[1107] imediatly unto the Bisshopricke of Rome, givinge[1108] the priestes of the same, lycence to absolve men in cases reserved as well papall as episcopall.

[1100] Pope Callistus III, reigned 1455–1458.

[1101] 'foure' deleted.

[1102] The margin entry is misleading, for it was Pius II (not Pope Callistus) who was cured.

[1103] Pope Pius II, reigned 1458–1464.

[1104] Pope Paul II, reigned 1464–1471.

[1105] 'was' inserted; new hand, different ink.

[1106] Diocese of 'Racanaten' (Recanati) 'et Maceraten' (Macerata), in Italy.

[1107] 'it' inserted; new hand.

[1108] 'and' deleted; 'gave' changed to 'givinge'.

[*The Turkes againe are vanquishead by miracle*] In Pope Sixtus the fourthe his government, mahomet the great sente an armye of purpose for the robbinge and destroinge of Laureta, wch then was vallewed to be worthe six millions of gold or ther abouts, but when the Turckes came wthin sight of it, a soddene feare soe possessed them that wth all expedition they fledd and departed, beinge freighted wth great astonishment; by the wch we maye easely perceave howe avaylable the prayers of the Queene of heaven are to those wch unfaynedly putt there truste in her;

In the tyme of Pope inocente the eight,[1109] the chardge thereof was comitted unto the Carmelit fryers and abondance of ritches bestowed upon it

After his desease[1110] Pope Alexander the sixt[1111] receyved the government of the churche, in whose tyme there happened a great plage amongeste the cittizens of Rakinata, for the remedy whereof they wente wth a sollemne procession unto Laureta, humbly cravinge the asistance of the blissed virgin in there soe dangerous acase, whereupon the pestilence wthout delaye seased, and for a token of gratefullnes the Racanatists did dedicat unto hir a crowne of gold ritchly besett wth pearle and pretious stones wch nowe is to be seene upon the heade of her (174) Imadge

In the tyme of this contagious sicknes the Carmelitts departed from thence and thereupon the chardge of that sacred chappell was gyven to certaine godly priestes hired for that purpose but wthin a while after the cannons of the churche toke the care thereof upon themselves.

[*The churche finishead by Pope Julius the 2.*] The great churche there was finished by Pope Julius the seconde[1112] and fortified it after the maner of a castell for preventinge of the Turckes soddain attemptes.

[*The wales of Loretta builded by Pope*[1113] *Leo the 10th.*] The wales of the Towne were made by Pope Leo the tenthe[1114] in whose tyme many were the noble men and women wch shewede there lyberalitie towardes that pious place.

[1109] Pope Innocent VIII, reigned 1484–1492; Pope Sixtus IV, reigned 1471–1484.
[1110] i.e. after the death of Innocent VIII.
[1111] Pope Alexander VI, reigned 1492–1503.
[1112] Pope Julius II, reigned 1503–1513.
[1113] 'Pope' inserted.
[1114] Pope Leo X, reigned 1513–1521.

[*Oure Ladies house compassed by Pope Clement the vii wt marble*] After whose
deathe Pope Clement the viith[1115] caused our ladyes house to be compassed about wth costlie marble in suche sorte as nowe is to be sene,
in the wch the effect of this historie is compendiously ingraven, [*The
certainties of ye comminge of that Sacred chappell into Itally againe Ratified*] It
pleased him also while he exercised the place of generall pastor
and that for many good and godlie considerations to sende three
of his chamber beinge men of perfecte good liffe and integritie to
make a full experiment of the undoubted truthe and maner of comminge into Itallie of those happie wales. and soe accordinge as theie
were directed, they iornyed firste to Lawreta, from thence crossed
over the sea unto Slavonia, and havinge don there busines there,
they tooke Shippinge and sayled for Siria where theie aryved and
travellinge to Gallely, founde all to be moste manifestlie true wch
befor was reported (175) by the fowre men wch were sente from
Dalmatia and the sixtene unto whom the Pisonestes had committed
there truste concerneinge the exact enquiringe thereof bringinge wth
them som of the brickes of Nazerethe wch were in everie pointe licke
unto those of wch the olde howse was made, upon whose returne to
Rome they were receaved by his holynes wth exceadinge great ioye
and inestimable gladnes. In his place succeeded Pope Paule the
theerde[1116] whoe did stryve to exceede his predicessors in deckinge
and settinge forthe of that celestiall chappell, and did buy for the
use of the churchemen of the same, divers vienyeards[1117] and other
peeces of lande. [*pope paule the theerde bestowed maintenance for twelve quer-
esters to singe in ye churche and chappell*] he did also appointe yt there
shoulde be brought up in chaste and cyvill maner twelve queristers,
wch shoulde wth the cannones of the churche singe hmmes and sal-
mes unto the honnor of the blissede virgin. and suche was his
unspeakable affection to that place as wthin the space of three
years, he did wth lowly reverence thrise[1118] visitt the same, [*A
Colledge of Jesuits erre[c]ted in Loretta by pop Iulius the 3*][1119] Pope Julyus
the thirde[1120] did institute in Laureta a Colledge of Jesuits,[1121] the
wch colledge was augmented and inritched by Pope Paule the

[1115] Pope Clement VII, reigned 1523–1534.

[1116] Pope Paul III, reigned 1534–1549.

[1117] 'y' inserted; different ink.

[1118] 'thrise' inserted.

[1119] *Recte* 'pope'.

[1120] Pope Julius III, reigned 1550–1555.

[1121] 'in' deleted; the Jesuit college in Loreto was established in 1554, Alfred Hamy, *Documents pour servir à l'histoire des domiciles de la Compagnie de Jésus … [1540–1773]* (Paris, [1892]), 39.

fourthe who[1122] committed the care of that Sanctified chamber to them.[1123] in th[ose] Popes[1124] tymes there did appeere greate flames of fyer to descend in the night tyme from heaven upon the Churche as earste befor there had don, as also wonderfull great light myraculously did[1125] illuminat the whole inner parte thereof.

The Jesuits from the tyme of the firste erectinge[1126] (176) of ther Colledge have the hearinge of all the pillgrmes confessions wch come thether untill this daye the wch chardge is verie sufficiently exercysed by them.

[*Great coste bestowed by Pope Pius the fourthe upon ye pallace adioyninge to the churche*] Pope Pius the fourthe was noe lesse carefull then the reste for the settinge fourthe of the same and bestowed muche coste upon the pallace thereunto adioyninge, he did manie other meritorious works there, wch I omitt to speake of;

[*Pope Pius ye fift furnished ye church wt excellent musicke*] Pope Pius the fift came not behinde any of them for his zeale and lyberallitie towardes that holy mantione as well was perceaved by the stately order bothe of musicke and ceremonies wch there he appointed as also by the ritche[1127] churche stuffe and other ornaments wch he dedicated unto it.

[*The highe wayes leadinge to Loretta mended by pope Gregorie the 13*] Pope Gregorie the xiiith imitatinge those wch wente before him did not only confirme the indullgences alreddye graunted by other popes unto it but did muche amplifie them, he made and mended dyvers highe wayes wch leade thether, and did many other good worckes about the same verie worthie of highe commendation, amongst the wch he augmented the meanes wch was appointed for the receyvinge of pillgrimes, whereof there are many there intertained;

[*A bishopps sea established in Loretta by pope Sixtus ye 5*] Pope Sixtus the fifte for that he was borne in that contrie did strive to excell all his predicessors, in gyvinge honnor and creditt unto that religious monument, and therefor he did there establishe a Bisshopricke (177)

[1122] 'Pope Paule the fourthe who' inserted; 'him, and' deleted; Pope Paul IV, reigned 1555–1559.
[1123] 'Pope Paule the fourthe' deleted.
[1124] 'Popes' inserted.
[1125] 'did' insert.
[1126] Last line of page, line through, as before, but legible.
[1127] Word erased; 'ritche' inserted.

appointinge certaine Townes neighboringe unto it to be subiecte unto the Bisshoppes aucthoritie he converted the churche wch before was collegiall unto a cathedrall, and gave the towne of[1128] Laureta the name and liberties of a Cittie, he caused a hill wch hindred the inlardgment of the cittie to be made Equall wth the lower grownde, all the wch he performed in the yeere 1586.

[*Clement ye viiith geveth all possible indullgences unto ye holy house of or Lady.*] The other Popes wch rayned after him graunted manye great indull-gences to it. but especially Pope Clement the eight, whoe did ampli-fie them soe muche as it was to be thought that nothinge more coulde be aded thereunto, his pietie and devotion was extraordinarie and verie exemplar, as before I have mentioned.

The myracles wch have bene don by the intercession of oure Lady of Laureta are soe many and soe strange as weare wonderfull and tedious to be rehearsed, for whate deseas can any man name wch hathe not bene there[1129] cured, what numbers of lame blynde, deafe and spe[t]chles men have bene restored to there use of there severall senses and former perfection of body; and is it not a thinge worthie of admyration to consider what a sorte of people have there bene dis-possessed of divells, as also how as well great prelats as other inferior persons have escaped as it weare inevitable dangers, and uncurable deseases, by callinge upon hir moste blissed name.

The giftes wch have bene presented unto this holy house, by men and women of all estates (178) and callinges, as well of relickes Jewells ringes and chaines of golde. as also of costly crosses challices Silver Candlestickes and other ornaments are soe many and soe inestimable as it is impossible to sett downe the true number or worthe of them.

The churche stuffe sente and gyven unto it by mightie princes, and others of good account as well of clothe of golde and clothe of silver and strange needle worcke, as also of velvett and satten ritchly imb[r]odered and sett wth curious lace of great vallewe, is soe surpas-singe sumpteous, as it weare an endles labor to[1130] declare the certaine estimation thereof,

By the course of this historie it dothe appeere of whate efficacie the intercession of the mother of god hathe bene, in all antient

---

[1128] 'of' inserted.
[1129] 'there' inserted.
[1130] 'sett' deleted.

tymes[1131] amongste the servants of or Savior Jesus Christe, the wch notwthstandinge is gainsayed by or newe gospellers,[1132] as by there late devisede doctrine is made moste evident.

Whoesoever dothe desire to knowe more in particular the som of this wch I have breeflie touched concerninge the house of oure Lady of Laureta lett him reade a booke written by Horatius turselinus[1133] a Roman, and of the Societie of Jesus, whoe dothe at lardge and verie exactly discourse thereof.

[*A Relation of suche things as I took note of at my beinge there myself*] The thinges of account wch I myself tooke note of at my beinge there, weare as followethe. Firste the [s]cituation of the Towne wch standethe upon the ridge of the hill in suche sorte as (179) it is allmoste impossible in latitude[1134] to inlardge the same, it is placed[1135] right over againt[1136] Slavonia The Adriaticke Sea dothe devide that cuntrie[1137] from Italye; and thereabouts the passadge in Saylinge is som hundred myles over,

In the ende of this admyrable edifice of or ladyes is a chimney by the wch the Peerles Mayde did often warme and[1138] feede hir blissed babe, in the wch is to be seene the skillett in the wch shee warmed milke[1139] for him, This chimney is daylie visyted wth great devotion, there are manie repentant teares shedd in that place, and abondance of monye throwen into it by them wch visitt the[1140] same in soe muche as the harthe thereof is moste commonly covered over wth coine. Som ten foote from thence standethe crosse over the house, the altar and from bothe the endes thereof unto[1141] bothe the sides of

[1131] 'tymes' inserted; 'as' deleted.

[1132] Gospellers: those who claim exclusive possession of gospel truth; in 16th and 17th centuries, 'often applied derisively to Protestants, Puritans, and sectaries', *OED*.

[1133] Orazio Torsellino (Torsellini) SJ (1544–1599), writer and historian, rector of the Jesuit community, Loreto, 1591–1595; his book on the history of Loreto appeared in 21 editions (1597–1837), *Diccionario Histórico de la Compañía de Jésus*, sub nomine; *Horatii Tursellini e Societate Jesu Lauretanae Historiae Libri Quinque* (Rome, 1597); see also Paul Murphy, 'The Jesuits and the Santa Casa di Loreto: Orazio Torsellini's *Lauretanae historiae libri quinque*', in T. Lucas (ed.), *Spirit Style Story: Essays honoring John W. Padberg* (Chicago, 2002), 269–281.

[1134] 'to' placed above 'in'.

[1135] 'over' deleted.

[1136] 'againt' inserted.

[1137] 'Slavonia' deleted; 'that cuntrie' inserted.

[1138] 'and' inserted.

[1139] 'in' deleted.

[1140] 'the' inserted, different hand and ink.

[1141] 'the' deleted.

that moste honnorable lodginge and costlye plates of Silver wherein are framed manie motives of pietie and devotion, wch serve as a partition for the devidinge of the place into two distinct roomes. Upon the heade of the Imadge of or lady wch standethe in the backe[1142] of ye mideste of the alter),[1143] standethe the crowne of golde gyven unto her as in the historie is mentioned and about hir necke is a chaine of golde whereat doe hange many pretious Jewells of exceedinge great vallewe. Befor this altar are placed six angells of Silver wth lampes in there hands continually lightinge.

   at eatche ende of the same is a cheeste wth holes in the topps of them[1144] into the wch the devoute pillgrimes and good Catholickes wch[1145] com thether doe put there almes, wch doe amounte (180) yeerly to ten or twelve thowsande poundes, the care and chardge of these cofers are comitted by his hollines unto the Bisshopp of the cittie the Governor of the same, and[1146] The rector of the[1147] Jesuitts ther residente, the cofers have either of them three lockes and every one of the keepers of[1148] them hathe a severall key for the openinge of the[m][1149] soe as they muste all three be[1150] present when the treasure in them contained is taken out, for the wch as also for the whole revenues of the churche they are accountable unto the Pope or his substitute, the wch ritches is imployed for the mantenance of the churche the relivinge of poore orphants and widdowes, the redeiminge of captives, and other holy uses. On eatche side of this miraculous chappell is a[1151] great brasen doore curiously wrought wth Imagerie. The house in the iner side is poorly builded but invironed in the out parte wth most costly marble and adorned wth verie artificall statuas as in the historie thereof is mentioned the iner[1152] wales of this glorious chamber are worne smothe wth the kisses of[1153] devout Christians.

In this holy habitation those pillgrimes wch doe resorte thether doe use after the makinge of there confessions to heere masse and to

---

[1142] Originally 'backeside'; 'side' deleted.
[1143] No previous bracket.
[1144] 'wth holes in the topps of them' interlined.
[1145] 'doe' deleted.
[1146] 'and' inserted.
[1147] 'same' deleted.
[1148] 'the keepers of' inserted.
[1149] Words deleted.
[1150] 'be' inserted.
[1151] 'is a' inserted; 'ly two' deleted.
[1152] 'side' deleted.
[1153] 'the' deleted.

receave the blissed Sacramt the wch benefitt it hathe pleased god to bestowe upon mi when I was there to my unspeakable comforte.

Nowe if aman havinge behelde these hevenly motives woulde spiritu-ally exerceese his understanding (181) in that blissed oratory or in[1154] any other convenient place, [*The method to be used for ye exersisinge of Contemplation.*][1155] and meditat upon the most happie incarnation of the second person in trinitie. he shoulde receyve thereby exceedinge great inward comforte, for the better performinge whereof, he muste have a stronge imagination that he seeithe the three devine parsons sittinge in a moste splendent throne of surpassinge maiestie, beinge attended upon by the bright shininge cherubens and ceraphins [and] wth the other quires of the angelicall companie of heaven, wch wthout intermission doe singe all honnor and glorie unto him wch lyvethe for ever and ever, whoe overmatchinge the Sonn in cleernes and the Sandes of the sea in number, doe prostrate them-selves in the presence of his Omnipotencie. This beinge considered of, it is firmly to be conceyved that these eternall iudges havinge vewead all the partes of the worlde, and the mightie multitudes of peo-ple therein dwellinge, did more respecte the moste blissed virgin for hir singular humillitie, then all the great princes of the whole worlde, for the[re] regall birthe and parentadge, and thereupon it pleased god the maker of all thinges, to sende the arkangell gabriell wthe the moste hevenly imbassadge, that ever was or shalbe sente, whoe moste ioyfull for soe honnorable a preferment in an instant appeered unto the devouteste creature that ever lyved, and did salute hir wth the angeli-call salutation, shee then (as it[1156] (182) is fitt to be coniectured) exerci-singe of hir mynde in som divine meditation, and wth mylde obedience did submitt hir will unto the pleasure of god,

here the godly Christians wth admiration and reverence may use mentall discours of the myraculous conception of or Savior, and not stryve to deserve by there owne reason and capacitie, the super-naturall worcke of our hevenly father, as the Sacramentarians[1157] of oure tyme doe, wch will not beleeve the royall presence of christe in the blissed Euchariste because that sensiblye they cannot perceave the same, and it is strange that they will give creditt unto the incar-nation before mentioned to the Trinitie wherein are three persons in

---

[1154] 'in' inserted.

[1155] Here Piers refers to the contemplation on the incarnation from the Second Week of the Spiritual Exercises, Munitiz and Endean, *Saint Ignatius of Loyola*, 305–306.

[1156] 'was' deleted.

[1157] Sacramentarians: in the 16th century, used, by opponents, 'as a general name for all deniers of the doctrine of the Real Presence [of Christ in the eucharist]', *OED*.

one essence, and two natures in one person, to the birthe of the Sonn of god whose matchles mother continued a virgin before in[1158] and for ever after the same, or to the makinge of the worlde of nothinge, seeinge that they will not beleeve transubstantiation in the wch there is more possibillitie (naturallie speakinge) then in any one of these Sacred misteries, as for example sake muche more easie is it to turne one substance into another then to make the universall orbe of nothinge, many forceble arguments might be used for the due proofe of my assertion herein, the wch I omitt for that this matter is not professedly handled by me.

But to returne to or purpose inestimable is the benefitt wch is obteyned by theise holy men wch bestowe agreat parte of there tyme in this and other the licke sweete contemplations, in the wch they take suche spirituall consolation as they will nyne tymes meditate upon one[1159] thinge in (183) substance but in maner dyfferente. Firste theye consider of the same, wth applyinge bothe the powers of the Soule and sences of the body; for the better ponderinge upon this inwarde busines, Then doe they severally[1160] make use of everie distincte sence, as by takinge a perswasive vewe of the subiecte intended to be meditated upon, and namely of that alreaddy specefied that is to saie of the glorious and regall sittinge of the Father the Sonn and the holy goste, in there illuminated Seat of aeternall maiestie, the unspeakable number and brightnes of the angells of heaven, the cleere splendence and diligent dispatche of the angell gabriell concerninge the embassadge committed to his chardge, the peerles bewtie and humble behavior of the blissed virgin, and ye suprabundant ioye and gladnes wch is to be thought was amongste the heavenly companie upon the returne of the moste happie messenger. Then to exercise there eares in the full opinion of hearinge the irrevocable decree of the moste highe, the reverent wordes of the holy Salutation, and the moste humble answeare of the meeke maide.

To conceave that they doe touche the[1161] more then stately mantions of the celestiall habitation, as also the pious oratorie of the imaculat vessell of pure chastetie. To have a sweete saveringe[1162] taste of the premisses[1163] and an odoriferous inwarde smellinge thereof, After ye

---

[1158] 'in' inserted.
[1159] 'matter' deleted.
[1160] 'severally' inserted.
[1161] 'the' inserted.
[1162] Word deleted.
[1163] Words erased; 'taste of the premisses' superimposed.

wch[1164] they doe[1165] acustom to[1166] practise there understandinge in runinge deeplie into the consideration of the holy misterie, ther will in applyinge, the fruyt (184) thereof to the good of there Soules and there memorie, in preservinge the utillitie gayned thereby wthout corruption; This devine exerc[ ]ese of contemplation cannot be well executed but by suche men as have mortified there affections and have sequastred themselves from worldly affaires, for the true use thereof is soe heavenly as it makethe godly men to be lickned unto angells, for that ther Soules are lifted up as it weare into heaven wth the winges of pra[y]ers and meditation. by reason whereof in a spirituall sence they maie be well tearmed the inhabitantes of the Everlastinge kingdom the fellowe servants of thrones and potentates and the ioyfull[1167] cittizens of the glorified Ijerusalem,

Nowe if it woulde please the newe fangled men of or tyme to consider of there owne actions, theie shall finde that there suppressinge of monasteries and other religious houses hathe bene the cause of disturbinge men from usinge this celestiall practise, for that those howses of god beinge defaced there are nowe noe places lefte wherein there[1168] might be convenient opportunitie had to directe goode witts and well inclyned myndes in this soe pure and senceare acourse, [*Certaine obiections answered*] But or adversaries will obiecte that in or religious houses there have bene many bade lyvers, I answeare hereunto that althoughe that there have bene divers of or professors of religion as vicious as som of them, yett cannot they assigne any of ther companie wch[1169] have bene soe vertues[1170] vertues and of[1171] soe Sanctified a liffe as thowsands of oure churche have bene, (185) + They also averr[1172] that it was not requisite that religious places shoulde have suche great lyvinges as have bene belonginge to them, I answeare that they are beste worthye of maintenance wch doe moste service to god, but theie are of that companie therefor .et[z]. In prooffe whereof we shall in readinge of ye Saints lyves finde that ye more parte of them, were monckes cannons friers Nunes and of other religious orders wch manifestly sheawethe that they served god best and therefor weare cannonized by the aucthoritie of the

---

[1164] 'ye wch' inserted.
[1165] 'doe' inserted.
[1166] 'to' inserted.
[1167] 'ioyfull' inserted.
[1168] Word deleted; 'there' inserted.
[1169] 'wch' inserted.
[1170] New page, unnumbered; 'vertues and of ...of oure churche have bene'; remainder of page is blank.
[1171] 'of' inserted.
[1172] 'obiect' deleted; 'averr' inserted, different hand and ink.

Churche for Sanctified people; another obiection is that in these later dayes they declyned from there firste puritie and that therefor in som contries theie were iustly suppressed and there lande bestowed uppon laye men, to this I saye that althoughe som of them did err in manners yet verie fewe did slyde from the knowen faithe, the wch fewe as Luther and the reste of the apostate crewe are in higheste favor wth the newe starte up gospellers. nowe if that in respecte of the abuses wch happened in som of oure religious howses there whole fraternities weare extinguished, they might as well have forbidden marriadge for there is noe Sacrament more violated then it is, as everie daye by experience is evidently seene, and surely I maye wth good reason averr that matrimony shoulde rather have bene banished then religious vowes, for that the one is but a temporall bond wch tiethe man and woman together, the other a perfecte unitinge of god and man in¹¹⁷³ a spirituall knott of wedlocke, and therefor had the Parlementarians of or adge byne as earneste reformers as deformers theie woulde rather have punished the abuses of [se]ttaries, then rooted out there whole profession (186) but som will further alleadge that the overmuche welthe of or regular companies was the cause of there sinninge I saye that it was not there great ritches wch made them offende but want of govearment¹¹⁷⁴ for we see daily that poore men beinge not kept in awe of the lawes doe committ many bad p[ar]tes, and shall it therefor be saide that there povertie is longe of it, nowe if in removeinge of this supposed cause the effecte doe cease, whie shoulde theie not as well¹¹⁷⁵ shewe¹¹⁷⁶ there zeale in gyvinge meanes to the poore, for the¹¹⁷⁷ amendmt of there lyves, as in takinge from the ritche for the same cause, wch seeinge theie have not don wee maye perfectly perceave that this ther assertion is but a cloake for the coveringe of there covetous disposition.

They will not also sticke to give out that oure religious are¹¹⁷⁸ a needles companie of idle men. Hereunto I maye well saye that theie are altogether ignorant of the use of exerceesinge a contemplative life wch thincke that men of there sorte are idle but soe fully are there drye pates deprived of the moisture of gods grace that theie cannott have that¹¹⁷⁹ sufficiencie of the blissed dewe of heaven wch might

---

¹¹⁷³ 'in' inserted.
¹¹⁷⁴ 'but want of govearment' inserted, different hand.
¹¹⁷⁵ 'in' deleted.
¹¹⁷⁶ Change from 'sheweinge' to 'shewe'.
¹¹⁷⁷ Change from 'there' to 'the'.
¹¹⁷⁸ 'are' inserted; 'men' deleted.
¹¹⁷⁹ 'that' inserted.

water there understandinge and make there imagination apte for the
intertaininge of suche divine inspirations, as ordinarily doe floe in the
braines of those holy men, by the wch meanes theie are soe celestially
bussied as all the imployments in this worlde are but meere idlnes in
respecte thereof, And yett lett us looke somwhat further into the matter and it will easilie appeere what incoveniences have growen by
there everting and impropriatinge of[1180] monasteries, for by that
meanes the service of god is diminished, hospitallitie decayed,
and agreat number of people for lacke of meanes forced to lyve
by robbinge[1181] stealing (187) and other badd qualities wch[1182]
might have bene receaved into those happie mantions and directed
in the way of vertue[1183] and devotion. But let us examine against
whom have theie sheawed this spight, it is not against there owne
brothers and Sisters wch in those houses and by there meanes
were relyved and brought up[1184] for what Abaye Priorye or other
pious receptacle was ther wch was not replenished as well wth
noble mens Sonns as others of spetiall reckninge wch nowe are
necessitated for the more parte either to live in obscure povertie
or by badd shiftes, beinge in a sorte compelled thereunto for that
there ealder brothers thincke all to little for them selves, and therefor yealde them but smale or noe help of maintenance And as for
the possessors of those places theye[1185] turne all the profitt thereof
unto there owne privatt use convertinge[1186] ye comoditie wch was
wonte to be bestowed in lyberalitie, almes deeds and devoute
motives into pride[1187] covetetousnes parsemonie and other the
licke abuses.

To conclude it cannot be denyed but that the faults of religious
men were[1188] soe grevous unto them that they did extraordinarie
great penance for the same, but there successors wch are of the
newe rell[ya]tion[1189] doe falle into divers inormyties wthout any
due[1190] feeling thereof and doe soe little esteeme of contrition, confession and satisfaction as theye[1191] account but as[1192] a scorne and geste of

---

[1180] 'of' inserted; 'everting': to overthrow, *OED*.
[1181] 'and' deleted.
[1182] 'I' erased.
[1183] 'virtue' altered to 'vertue'.
[1184] 'up' inserted.
[1185] 'the' deleted.
[1186] 'convertinge' interlined.
[1187] 'pride' inserted, different hand.
[1188] 'were' inserted, different hand.
[1189] 'wch are of the newe rell[ya]tion' inserted, different hand.
[1190] 'great' deleted; 'due' inserted, different hand.
[1191] 'as theye' inserted, different hand.
[1192] 'account', 'as', inserted.

that holie sacrament[1193] makeinge themselves ther by[1194] uncapable of the mercies of god. + Soe as wainge everie thinge in an equalle ballance they maie perceave that there inovations and alterations are bothe in religion and pollicie to be worthily reiected and despised. I have heereby the waye endevored to answeare these obiections, hopinge thereby to satisfie som of them wch as yet are waveringe in there opinions as also have (as alitle befor dothe appeere) inv[ ]erted.

(188)[1195] som fewe wordes of contemplative exerceese haveinge[1196] accordinge my smale skill sett downe the same[1197] as well to make men to understande what[1198] pius devotion is used in the holy house of Laureta as also to showe myne owne affection towards that sacred chappell the sufficient reporte of the myracles and riches whereof is impossible by me to be related,

There are many other[1199] thinges of great accounte belonginge to this house and churche worthye here to be [resi]ted.[1200] of these the moste principall are the vestries of the wch there are two in number. in the one of them is the heade of St Gerion sente thether by the Queene of Bohemia there are inclosed the relickes, of the martires of the Thebane [re]ligions,[1201] the head is all covered wth Silver, downe to ye shoulders, and a crowne of gold besett wth pretious stones upon it, therebe twelve statuas of the twelve apostles of three spandes in height apeece, a lardge crosse of Silver gilded and inambled of fowre foote in height, two silver candlestickes of three footte in height, gyven by Pop[e] Julius the second, and fowre somwhate lesse of the same sorte,[1202] a crosse of Silver wth six Silver candlstickes bestowead[1203] by the Dutches of Florence, and two other candlstickes of five footte in lenithe apeece,[1204] another crosse of fowre footte and more gyven by the Cardinall

---

[1193] 'that holie sacrament' inserted.
[1194] 'ther by' inserted, different hand.
[1195] One and a half lines of text erased: 'vertues and of soe sanctified a life as thowsands of or church have bene +'; this material was inserted on unnumbered page between pp. 184 and 185.
[1196] 'I' erased; 'have' altered to 'haveinge', different hand.
[1197] 'the same' inserted; same hand as previous insertion.
[1198] 'what' inserted.
[1199] 'other' inserted.
[1200] Word altered by changing letter; unclear.
[1201] Initial two letters erased.
[1202] 'There is' deleted.
[1203] 'bestowead' inserted, different hand; 'gyven' deleted.
[1204] 'there is' deleted.

Gambara;[1205] (189) A thuryberum of Silver wth anavicula curiously wrought[1206] dedicated unto that holie howse[1207] by the Duke of Urbin, nyne other great candellstickes[1208] presented by sundrie other persons.

In[1209] the other vestrie is[1210] a booke bestowead[1211] by the Duke of Bavaria of one inche thicke three inches longe and two inches broade of puer golde besett wth pretious stones of the valewe of[1212] one thowsande crownes, There is a cupp gyven by Henry the Seconde kinge of Fraunce worthe twelve thowsande crownes a capp[1213] of agett stone presented[1214] by Duke Pernowne valued at two thowsande crownes, There be soondrie[1215] other gyftes offered[1216] and sent[1217] by dyvers other noble personadges amountinge to the valewe of 30 thousande crownes

More[1218] a crosse dedicated therunto[1219] by the Duke of Bavaria worthe fowre thousande crownes, I sawe[1220] there[1221] 19 great challyces of puer golde whereof one dothe waye as it was told us[1222] seaven poundes in weight[1223] In[1224] bothe the vestries are[1225] five hundred challices of Silver whereof som be gilt, wth patents and cruetts and other necessaries satable unto them,[1226] also agreat cupp of Silver to keepe the blissed Sacrament in worthe eight hundred crownes besides an incredible[1227] number of other ritche gyftes and precious Jewells the

---

[1205] Gianfrancesco Gambara (1533–1587), created cardinal 1561. Miranda, *The Cardinals of the Holy Roman Church* http://www2.fiu.edu/~mirandas/bios1561.htm#Gambara, accessed 24 Jan. 2018.

[1206] 'gyven' deleted.

[1207] 'dedicated unto that holie howse' inserted.

[1208] 'gyven' deleted; 'presented' inserted.

[1209] 'There is' deleted; 'in' altered to 'In'.

[1210] 'is' inserted.

[1211] 'bestowead' inserted; 'gyven' deleted.

[1212] 'I C' possibly deleted.

[1213] Probably 'cupp' intended; Henry II (1519–1559), king of France, r. 1547–1559.

[1214] 'presented' inserted; 'gyven' deleted.

[1215] 'soondrie' inserted; 'dyvers' deleted.

[1216] 'offered' inserted; 'sente' deleted.

[1217] 'gyven' deleted; 'sent' inserted.

[1218] 'More' inserted; 'There is' deleted.

[1219] 'gyven' deleted; 'dedicated therunto' inserted.

[1220] 'I sawe' inserted in margin.

[1221] 'by' deleted.

[1222] 'as it was told us' inserted.

[1223] 'in weight' inserted.

[1224] 'There are' deleted; 'in' altered to 'In'.

[1225] 'are' inserted.

[1226] 'there [are]' deleted; 'allso' inserted.

[1227] 'an incredible' inserted; 'a wonderfull' deleted.

wch we had noe opportunitie to peruse, and[1228] a wonderfull deale of churche stuffe as well of copes and vestments and other ornaments; there is ther to be harde verie[1229] excellente and divine[1230] musicke as well in the churche as in the chappell, at highe mass and (190) at evensonge sett out wth Organes and other sweete instruments as in effecte hathe formerly bene rehearsed in the presedente historie,

At the weste ende of the churche are two fayre brasen gattes of licke worckmanshippe to those of or Ladies howse, right. Befor the churche doore is the statua of Pope Sixtus Quintus whoe was a great benefactor thereof[1231] as before is lickwyse[1232] mentioned

Right beneathe the churche steares is a fayere courte rounde about the wch are the Pallaces of the Bishopp of the diocese and the Governor of the Cittie, as also the Colledge of the Fathers of the Societie of Jesus, in the wch there are of everie contrie in Christendom som one or more appointed for the necessarie ende already named in this discourse

I have taken som tyme more then ordinarie in[1233]discribinge this holy habitation and in settinge downe a compendium of the historie thereof for that it is one of the greateste places of pillgrimadge nowe as before I have saide[1234] in the whole worlde, but nowe I shall (god willinge) proceede to make relation of the reste of my iornye towards this kingdom of Eirland [Ireland],

One the xxiiith daye of October we came to Ancona. the cathedrall churche there is dedicated to Saint Sirianus wherein liethe his body; This saint was Pathriarke of Iherusalem, whoe wth St Helina founde the crosse of or Lorde. there also restethe the bodies of Saint Marcelynus Bishopp and Confessor of Saint Oliver Abott of St Lawrentia virgine and martire and of blessed (191) Anthony whose body we sawe under one of the altars of the same churche.

[1228] 'and' inserted; 'we also sawe there' deleted.

[1229] 'verie' inserted.

[1230] 'and divine' inserted; 'good' deleted.

[1231] 'thereof' inserted.

[1232] 'lickwyse' inserted.

[1233] 'this' deleted.

[1234] 'as before I have saide' inserted; different hand.

The xxiiiith[1235] by the cittie of Senegulla [Senigallia], unto[1236] Fano, at the wch cittie is the divition betwene Marca and Romania,

[*The kingdum of Romania*] The xxvth[1237] by[1238] Pessero [Pesaro] to the Cittie of [1239] Arimynei [Rimini],[1240]

The xxvith[1241] by[1242] Syienna to a[1243] cittie called[1244] Forum livii [Forlì] where the Popes legatt for Romania liethe,

The xxviith[1245] by Fossa to the cittie Emule [Imola] where[1246] is interred the body of St Peeter Crysolegus and St Cassianus wch is patrone of the cathedrall churche thereof[1247]

[*The Dukdum of Romania in Lombardy*] The xxviiith[1248] to the antiente cittie of Bolonia [Bologna]; in the mideste of the wch[1249] is a piller wch devidethe Romania and Lumbardy; in this cittie is the Popes legatt wch governethe those partes. in the Domynicans churche, there liethe the body of Saint Domynicke, whoe hath a sumptuous tombe over him.[1250]

[*The Dukdum of Ferara*] The xxixth[1251] to the cittie Modena in Latin called Mutinum, there liethe the body of Saint Semynianus patrone of the cathedrall churche. three myles shorte of Modena runnethe the ryver Panara [Panaro] where beginnethe the Dukedom of Ferara. All the regions wch we[1252] passed throughe betwixt Rome and the saide Dukedom belonge to the Sea apostolicke

---

[1235] 'daye' deleted; after each calendar numeral, word 'daye' deleted.
[1236] 'unto' inserted; 'the Cittie' deleted.
[1237] 'daye' deleted.
[1238] 'the Cittie' deleted.
[1239] 'of' inserted.
[1240] 'where the Councell of Arimynyne was helde' deleted.
[1241] 'daye' deleted.
[1242] 'the Cittie' deleted.
[1243] 'a' inserted; 'the' deleted.
[1244] 'called' inserted.
[1245] 'daye' deleted.
[1246] 'liethe' deleted; 'is interred' inserted.
[1247] 'there' deleted; 'thereof' inserted.
[1248] 'daye' deleted.
[1249] 'wch' inserted; 'cittie' deleted.
[1250] 'whoe hath a sumptuous tombe over him' inserted.
[1251] 'daye' deleted.
[1252] 'we' inserted; 'I' deleted.

The xxxth daye we travellead[1253] by the cittie Regium [Reggio Emilia] where wee sawe apicture of or Ladies wch worckethe many[1254] wonderfull myracles as the inhabytants thereof do testifie[1255] and soe over a ryver called Les[h]e where is ye devition (192) of the Dukedom of Parma and Farara, [*The dukedum of Parma*] from thence[1256] to Parma. in the said[1257] Cittie[1258] is a monestarie of Benedictans verie ritchly adorned the revenues of it come[1259] to 25000 crownes yearly:

The firste daye of November we iorniead[1260] to Ferenzola [Fiorenzuola d'Arda]. The second[1261] throwe the cittie of Placentia [Piacenza] nighe unto the wch runnethe the famous ryver of Poe wch we passed over wth a strange device of boates chained together, and soe by myrandal [Mirandola], [*The Dukedum of Millan*] wch is six myles from Placentia where is the devition of the Dukedoms of Parma and Millan and frome thence[1262] to Cassala [Casalpusterlengo].

[*Millan ye greate*] The thirde[1263] by the cittie of Lodi[um] [Lodi] to Millan wch is the greateste[1264] in Itally, there is a lardge cathedrall churche wherein liethe many Sts bodies, allso[1265] a newe churche of St Celsa verie somteously adorned; in one of the altars whereof is kepte wth great reverence apicture of or Ladies wch is constantlie reported[1266] hathe wrought strange[1267] myracles, the altar is ritchly sett out havinge foure pillers of Silver verie great and lardge, and in the backe of it a cubbord wch hathe leaves of silver imbossed wth golde; there is lyinge in a fayere churche of the Domynicanes the body of St Peter martire; in the same alsoe weare buried the three kinges wch offred gyftes unto or Savior Jesus Christe, whose corpes[1268] weare

[1253] 'we travellead' inserted.
[1254] 'myracles' deleted.
[1255] 'as the inhabytants thereof do testefie' inserted.
[1256] 'from thence' inserted; 'and soe' deleted.
[1257] 'said' inserted.
[1258] 'of Parma' deleted.
[1259] 'comethe' – 'the' deleted.
[1260] 'we iorniead' inserted.
[1261] 'day' deleted.
[1262] 'soe' deleted; 'frome thence' inserted.
[1263] 'daye' deleted.
[1264] 'cittie' deleted.
[1265] 'allso' inserted; 'there is' deleted.
[1266] 'is constantlie reported' inserted.
[1267] 'strange' inserted.
[1268] 'corpes' inserted.

removed from thence, and nowe are at Collyne [Cologne]. In this cit-tie[1269] is the place where Saint Ambrose christned Saint Augustin and where they did singe Te deum. moreover[1270] a monesterie[1271] of Benedictans, wherein liethe the bodies of Saint Ambrose Saint (193) Gervatious and prothatious, over the wch[1272] is an altar wch hathe an antependium of beaten gold all sett wth pretious Stones of inestimable vallewe we sawe[1273] there[1274] a churche dedicated[1275] to[1276] Saint Frances under whose highe altar, liethe the bodie of St Barnaby the apostle, in itt[1277] is to be seene[1278] St Mathewe his heade and many other relickes;

We tooke note of a[1279] mightie castle of invincable force wheare the kinge of Spaine alwayes kepethe nyne hundred men in Garrison this fortres[1280] maye comaunde the whole cittie if occation be offered.[1281] at my beinge in Millan[1282] I mett by chaunce wth an Itallian gent. whoe verie kindly saluted me, and understandinge my want wente wth me and bespeake me[1283] a coatche,[1284] desiringe the coatchman to use me well for that I was as he saide a deere frende of his, this was a rare curtesie in a man wch befor that tyme never had seene me; at Millan I parted wth the companie of those wch I travelled in from Rome, amongst the wch one Father Battie[1285] was a man of great vertue and my speciall frende,

There is in that cittie fortie Nunries and at leaste as many monesta-ries of friers and monckes beside the cathedrall and parishe churches,

---

[1269] 'In this cittie' inserted; 'there' deleted.

[1270] 'moreover' inserted; 'there is' deleted.

[1271] 'monesterie' inserted; 'churche' deleted.

[1272] 'wch' inserted; 'there' altered to 'the; 'bodies' deleted.

[1273] 'we sawe' inserted.

[1274] 'is' deleted.

[1275] 'dedicated' inserted.

[1276] 'of' altered to 'to'.

[1277] 'in itt' inserted; 'There' deleted.

[1278] 'to be seene' inserted; 'alsoe' deleted.

[1279] 'We tooke note of a' inserted; 'There is a' deleted.

[1280] 'fortres' inserted; 'castle' deleted.

[1281] 'if occation be offered' inserted.

[1282] 'in Millan' inserted; 'there' deleted.

[1283] 'me' inserted.

[1284] 'for me, and did' deleted.

[1285] Reginald Bates (b.1569), entered English College, Rome, in June 1591; ordained there March 1594; was sent to England, 22 Oct. 1597, and was working in Newgate in 1612. Godfrey Anstruther, *The Seminary Priests: A Dictionary of the Secular Clergy of England and Wales 1558–1850*, I: *Elizabethan 1558–1603* (Ware and Durham, [1969]), 26. In the inter-nal college dispute of 1595, Bates and Piers were among the minority who sided with the Jesuit administration, Foley, *Records*, VI, 3.

The fifte daye to the cittie Pavia, five myles shorte of it is a monestarie of Carthusians verie ritch and fayere, wch is aplace of great hospitallitie, it is vallewed to be worthe CX thowsande crownes by the
yeere, in the saide cittie liethe in a monestarie of Augustine fryers,
the bodies of St Augustin and of Snt Severyanus Boetius, there are
two colleadges (194) one made by Pope Gregorie the thirteinthe
and the other by Cardinall Boromeo[1286] who was Archbishopp of
Millan, beinge a man induead wth great virtue and lerninge.[1287]

[*The Dukedum of Ianua*] The vith[1288] thorowe the river Gravanall and
soe to Sarevall [Serravalle]

[*Ianua ye proude*] The vii[1289] over the Apenyne montaines to Janua
[Genoa], where I mett wth som of ye Englishe scollers wch weare
sent by Father Parsons from Rome to Spaine; In the cathedrall
churche of Ianua are the ashes of Saint John Baptiste wheare they
are wth great reverence kepte in a cheeste of Silver in an altar of
his owne chappell, In the benedictans monasterie[1290] liethe the
bodye of venerable Beade,[1291] This cittie is builded harde by the
Sea side in a vallewe havinge mightie montaines adioyninge unto
it, There lande there is verie barrene, There montaines beare noe
woode, the sea there yealdethe litle fishe and yet by reason of
there trafficke wth other contries, it[1292] is become one of the ritchest
in the whole worlde, and there cittisens[1293] absolutly the moste high
sperited people[1294] in Itally in testemonie whereof[1295] I have seen
amongst other things of note[1296] the welthie merchants and ther
wives and reclininge carried when they goe abroade in statly

[1286] Carlo Borromeo (1538–1584), created cardinal in 1560. Miranda, *The Cardinals of the Holy Roman Church*, http://www2.fiu.edu/~mirandas/bios1560.htm#Borromeo, accessed 2 Dec. 2017.

[1287] 'beinge a man induead wth great virtue and learninge' inserted.

[1288] 'daye over' deleted; 'thorowe' inserted.

[1289] 'daye' deleted.

[1290] 'monasterie' inserted.

[1291] Bede [St Bede, known as the Venerable Bede] (673/4–735), monk, historian, theologian; author of *Historia ecclesiastica gentis Anglorum*; was buried at Jarrow, but his remains were said to have been removed in early 11th century to Durham; his tomb there was desecrated in 1541 but its contents are believed to be interred in Galilee chapel of Durham Cathedral, *ODNB*.

[1292] 'it' inserted; 'That cittie' deleted.

[1293] 'there cittisens' inserted.

[1294] 'moste high sperited people' inserted; words deleted.

[1295] 'testimonie whereof' inserted; 'soe muche as' deleted.

[1296] 'amongste other things of note' inserted in margin.

chariotts, [from one] streete to another[1297] They are governed there by a Duke whoe houldethe his place only for fowre yeere, at the experation of wch tyme the cheefe cittizence doe electe another in his place; by the lawe of Ianua. he is to be imprisoned and fyned wch wearethe any weapon as sworde daggar knyffe or suche other; heere[1298] the cheeftaine of the kinge of Spaine his Gallies dothe dwell and (195) hathe[1299] builded adioyninge unto it avery fayre Pallace, here also dothe moste of the kinges Gallyes harbor wch are allwayes in aredynes for the resistinge or invadinge of the Turckes Gallyes wch yeerely doe many roberies wthin that straight, I had my passadge free from Ianua to Spayne by meanes of Cardinall Penelle[1300] his letters sent by me to his brother in Ianua.

[*The dukedum of Savoy the kingdum of Corsica*] The xxiith day of November we tooke shippinge from Iannua in a vessell of at the leaste seaven hundred tonne the wch was laden wth munition and paper, and passed by the montaines of Apenia and the costes of Savoy; [*Provance in frannce*] by a Towne called Villafranca [Villefranche-sur-Mer] leavinge Corseca on the lifte hande and soe we Sayled by Provance in France, The Iles of Ire [Ile d'Hyères] and Marcellus wch border uppon the same, [*the kingdum of Mayorke*] and from thence[1301] throughe the gulfe of Lyons to mayorke [Majorca] wch wee lefte on the lifte hand, here a flae of wynde had almoste overthrowne or Shipp in the wch was at that tyme Itallians Spanyards Englishmen frenchemen som of or owne contrie men, and of the Dutche Nation there weare also in hir two Turckes and as it was thought certaine Jewes wch because they were passinge into Spayne wente disguised for that[1302] they are prohibited to resorte thether. but wthout doubt we weare the rather delivered out of this danger for that[1303] we had in or companie som godly Fathers of the Societie of Jesus and two Domynican Friers wch used great praier and meditation did preache unto us by turne and cathekysed all the youthes that[1304] weare in the Shipp; and soe leavinge mynorcke

---

[1297] '[from one] streete to another' inserted.

[1298] 'heere' inserted; 'in this cittie' deleted.

[1299] Change of ink, from brown to black; continues to top of p. 199 of text.

[1300] Domenico Pinelli (1541–1611), native of Genoa, created cardinal 18 Dec. 1585; from 1592 a leading figure in the Roman Inquisition, *Dizionario Biografico degli Italiani*, http://www.treccani.it/enciclopedia/domenico-pinelli_(Dizionario-Biografico), accessed 6 Dec. 2017.

[1301] 'sayled' deleted.

[1302] 'that' inserted.

[1303] 'that' inserted.

[1304] 'wch' deleted.

[Minorca] on the (196) right hande we sayled[1305] by the costes of Cateloona [Catalonia] wthin the sight of Solay[1306] Barcelona lyeath[1307] on the right hand therof[1308] and so dothe[1309] Mount Serata [Montserrat] a place of great devotion to our blessed lady; and frequented by the whole worlde in pillgreemadge where the sacred[1310] virgin worckethe infinitt and strange myracles, not far from thence on the side of the hill thereunto adioyninge (as it is, credibly informed) there dwellethe a devoute hermitt whoe for the carriadge of vittles[1311] for his relife unto him hathe an asse whoe soe[1312] sone as the hermitt dothe[1313] laye upon him his vessells and bagges wherein his almes are[1314] putt dothe of himself goe to the monestarie before named, and there beinge loden wth suche provition as in charitie is bestowed upon his master, dothe take the same way backe againe unto the hermitage wch is[1315] a thinge verie rare in a resaonlesse creature; From thence throughe the Gulfe of Valentia passinge by Cape Martine, [*The kingdum of Valentia*] and soe wee aryved on the xith of December at Alecant [Alicante], a cittie in the kingdom of Valentia in Spaine.

In it is to be seene a faire and lardge marckett place, adioyninge unto the wch standeth a churche, on whose outside are made, of a good height, two smale chappells in the wch there is masse usually saide on the marckett dayes wch is a great commoditie for the poorer sorte, for that they maye wthout any hinddrance of their other busines, use there devotion, it also causethe men wch have any care of theire consciences to be the more warie in there dealinges (197) when they see the royall presence of the Sonn of god, wch is the only beste motive, for to stur up good Christians unto upright carriadge in their actions, In this cittie a man may have a quart of verie stronge wyne for iid. a pounde of reasinges for a [ ][1316] d in that towne I tasted the moste cleere and nurishinge water that ever I sawe in my life; From Alecante we tooke iorney to Avent on the

---

[1305] 'sayled' inserted; 'passed' deleted.
[1306] 'we lefte' deleted.
[1307] 'lyeath' inserted.
[1308] 'hand therof' inserted; 'hand' deleted.
[1309] 'so dothe' inserted.
[1310] 'sacred' inserted; 'blessed' deleted.
[1311] 'unto' deleted.
[1312] 'soe' inserted.
[1313] 'dothe' inserted.
[1314] 'are' inserted; 'is' deleted.
[1315] 'is' inserted.
[1316] Symbol unclear; possibly '1/2'.

xiii of the same, these vents are Innes of verie hoomly intertainmt, In this kingdom of Valentia I have seene great fieldes of rosemary gro- winge as thicke as firres doe in other contries, and in those parts it servethe them for fewell,

[*The kingdum of Casteele*] The xiiiith day by Malona wch devidethe the kingdom of Valentia from Casteele; this place is six leages from Alecante, and soe wee iornied to Avente.

The xvth daye by sea to a Vent

The xvith to a villadge called Semyihilla [Chinchilla]

[*One Spanishe Leage conternalethe three Englishe myles*]

The xviith by Alnacete [Albacete], to Civeta

The xviiith to Fercana

The xixth to Provincia [El Provencio]

The xxth to Belmonte

The xxith to Villanova [Villanueva de Alcardete]

The xxiith to Lagnardia [La Guardia]

The xxiiith to Novanswies [Aranjuez] where the kinge hathe a house by wch runnethe the ryver Tagus

In any of the villadges beforenamed wch stande betwixt Alycant and Madride, I sawe not any matter worthy of greate note, for that they be townes of noe[1317] accounte savinge that I did observe that there were in them (198) many olde men and agreat sorte of yonge boyes, but verie fewe able men, whereby it dothe appeere that the kinge of Spaine his occations for imployinge of[1318] men are soe dyvers that moste of his ordinarie subiectes are as soone as, they come to any sufficient yeers of adge sente to doe his ma[jes]ties service either in the Indies or in som other kingdom or territorie, subiecte to his comaunde,

---

[1317] 'great' deleted.
[1318] 'them' deleted.

The xxiiiith daye we travelled to madride and were as we passed thether verie kindely intertained in a Colledge wch belongethe unto the Jesuits

At or comminge to madride we happely chaunced to meete wth mr Thomas firz harbard[1319] an Englishe gent. then pentioner unto the kinge of Spaine whoe gave us a corteous and frendly wellcom, He is a man verie zealous in religion sufficiently learned wonderfull lyberall and exceedingly well qualified as well in musicke as in other laudable sciences sithence the wch tyme as I have heard he wente to Rome and there tooke the holy order of priesthoode, where he hathe written dyvers learned bookes greatly lendinge to the good of god[e]s churche, and the comforte of well disposed christians.

The vth day of Jannuary I tooke iorney from thence by the Esquiriall [El Escorial][1320] to Guaderara [Guadarrama]; [*Oulde Casteel*] The vith over a montaine wch devidethe olde Castyell from them[1321] newe to Sta maria Nova [Santa Maria la Real de Nieva].

The viith to Valedelid [Valledolid] beinge a great cittie (199) where the Chauncery of Spaine is helde; in the benedictans churche called Reale is the right arme of Saint marke, and St Bennett his thighe bone. in this churche of the benedyctans is a crosse of Unicorne his horne and many other relicks. By this cittie runnethe the river Piswergie [Pisuerga], and two leages shorte of it passethe the ryver dewri [Duero] wch is verie famous in that countrie[1322]

[1319] Thomas Fitzherbert (1552–1640), writer; after the death of his wife in 1588 he moved from England to Spain, and received a pension from Philip II; in 1596 Fitzherbert became English secretary to Philip II; author of *A defence of the Catholycke cause, containing a treatise in confutation of sundry untruths and slanders, published by the heretics, in infamous libels as well against all English Catholicks in general, as against some in particular, etc., by T.F: With an apology of his innocence in a fayned conspiracy against her majesty's person, for the which one Edward Squyre was wrongfully condemned and executed in November, 1598, wherewith the author and other Catholykes were also falsely charged* (St Omer, 1602); he moved to Rome, and was ordained priest 24 Mar. 1602; served as Roman agent of the English clergy, resigned, and entered Society of Jesus in 1615; served as rector, English College, Rome, 1619–39, *ODNB*; Fitzherbert's cousin Nicholas Fitzherbert (1550–1612) was living in Rome in the 1590s, and thus Piers probably knew him, Nicholas Fitzherbert, *ODNB*.
[1320] 'E' partly erased.
[1321] 'them' inserted; 'Castyell' (after 'newe'), deleted.
[1322] 'in' deleted.

Heere or Englishmen have a verie faire colledge the wch is able to maintaine som fiftie scollers, in the wch I remained for the space of one fortnight and was verie kindly intertained by Father Creswell and the other Englishe Fathers there, In Valledelid I mett wth Bryan Mc Fargus o Ferrall whoe was[1323] a man of great[1324] learninge gravetie and good liffe, whose untymely deseace hathe bene an infinitt losse unto his native contrie

[*The discription of the Squiriall*] The xxth day I tooke my iorney backe againe to madride and did see the Squirall [Escorial] wch is a house of exceedinge great coste and rare worckmanshipp, the churche there is dedicated to Saint Lawrence, havinge over the intrance six statues of the good kinges of Isarel [Israel] verie faire and stately sett forthe[1325] there are some lx altars in the churche and chappells adioyninge thereunto verie ritchly adorned[1326] wth rare Imagerie, all there candlstickes being[1327] of Silver; there are xii lampes of silver worthe eache of them three score pounde or thereaboute[1328] the highe altar hathe xii steppes of Jasper Stone ascendinge unto it, they are thirtie footte everie of them at leaste in leinthe, it is moste curiously sett out with (200) Imagerie to the rooffe of the churche; on the one side of it, are the statues of the Emperor Charles the fifte and his wives wth his armes over his heade; on the other side are the statues of the kinge of Spaine and his wives wth his armes, they are vallewed to have coste 200000 crownes, there are in the churche two paire of Organs verie fayer all of Silver, and[1329] many relickes of inestimable value. the Sacaristya is verie ritche of churche stuffe, all ther challices are of puer Silver and som of golde, there hange aboute it many costly pictures, the quier is wonderfull fayer havinge over it in the tope[1330] the Laste iudgmt excellently painted in itt[1331] are Seats verie curiously carved beinge one hundred and fortie in number, the bookes only for the quire are valued at six thousande crownes,

---

[1323] 'was' inserted; may be identified with 'Bernard O Ferail' described as *sacerdotem theologum* at Valladolid in 1601 for 'seven continuous years', he studied letters at the University of Valladolid where he spent a further four years studying theology. On 14 Dec. 1601, Hugh O'Neill and Red Hugh O'Donnell recommended O Ferail to Philip III for the vacant see of Meath, Benjamin Hazard, *Faith and Patronage: The Political Career of Flaithrí Ó Maolchonaire, 1560–1629* (Dublin, 2010), 172–173.

[1324] 'great' inserted.

[1325] 'sett forthe' inserted.

[1326] 'adorned' inserted; 'sett out' deleted.

[1327] 'being' inserted; 'are' deleted.

[1328] 'or thereaboute' inserted.

[1329] 'there' deleted.

[1330] 'of' deleted.

[1331] 'in itt' inserted; 'there' deleted.

The lyberarie is som lxxx paces in leinthe beinge all of moste rare worckmanshipp the deskes and presses where there bookes lye are all of strange Indian tymber verie conninglye carved, the paintinge over the lyberarie did coste as is reported[1332] som xii thousande crownes; at the[1333] one ende are drawen the foure doctors of the Latin Churche, at the other the fowre great Philosophers Arist. [and] Plato etc[1334] and right over there heades are the seven sciences in forme of women; in the seconde degree are the pictures of all the famous men wch invented sciences; the refectory is lardge and fayer the chapter house ritchly hanged wth costly (201) pictures, the cheefe cloister is verie lardge havinge rounde aboute it the whole historie of or Savior exceedingly well painted from ye conception of or blessed virgin unto the last iudgmt, the convent, is som hundred and thirtie Jeromyles,[1335] there is also a colledge where are som fortie monkes whereof dyvers doe reade divinitie and Pholosophy;[1336] and wthin the same circuite is the kinge his pallace wch dothe yeelde corespondence unto the reste;[1337] the churche and Pallace of the Squiriall are made in the forme of a Greedierone, the wch kinge Phillipe did builde in satisfaction of a churche of Saint Lawrence wch he burnt in Fraunce when the warres was[1338] betwene Charles the[1339] fifte his Father and the Frenche kinge, it is saide for certaine that the buildinge of that place did coste the kinge som xxxtie millions.

The xxiiith daye I came to madride here I hard of the deathe of my mother[1340] the wch was an extraordinarie corys[ad]e unto my harte and the rather was my sorie increasede for that I was not present at hir departure for hir inclynation towards Catholicke religion was suche as I doe not doubt but[1341] shee woulde willinglie have bene reconsiled unto ye churche had there bene meanes procured for hir to that effect,[1342]

[1332] 'as is reported' inserted, different hand.

[1333] 'the' inserted.

[1334] Aristotle; 'etc' inserted.

[1335] Monks of a religious order more commonly known as 'Hieronymites', or the Order of St Jerome; Philip II assigned them the monastery he built at El Escorial.

[1336] *Recte* 'Philosophy'.

[1337] 'of' inserted, but in faint ink.

[1338] 'was' inserted.

[1339] 'thirde' deleted.

[1340] Ann Houlte (or Holt) was buried in Christ Church Cathedral, Dublin, beside her husband Captain Pearse (or Piers), 12 Feb. 1596–1597, National Library of Ireland, Genealogical Office, MS 64, fo.11r.

[1341] 'but' inserted.

[1342] 'to' inserted; 'for' deleted; following 2 lines erased: 'but I am in full hope that god hath [acc]epted of hir good intent and inward resolution'.

In madride were divers great processions[1343] sett forthe in suche sorte as those were wch I sawe in Rome but especially in the holy weeke amonge the wch there came one from Saint Fraunces his churche in the wch there were noe (202) fewer then a thowsande disciplynants wch did severly punishe themselves wth many stripes,

In Saint Andrewe his churche wch is in that towne liethe the body of Saint Iseder [Isidore] whoe was a laboringe man and borne in madride his liffe and myracles are wonderfull strange; in madride is a monsterous beaste called the Ringnoscerus he is covered all over his body wth a kinde of a shell wch abidethe muskett shott, he had a horne growinge in his forehead wch was[1344] cutt of, as also his eyes weare[1345] put out, leaste he shoulde breake[1346] forthe and kill the inhabitantes there abouts, there are divers other monsters in the said towne.[1347] One licke agoate in his fore partes in[1348] his hinder partes licke a deere, there is a horse in the kinges Stable wch is an hermofreditt and divers other monsterous beastes; at the removinge of a picture of or blessed Lady of Totche [Atocha] (wch hathe don great myracles) was a sompteous processione, there ye[1349] cloister was hanged all wth clothe of golde and tisshue wherein weare portrayed the victories of Charles the fifte;

at my beinge in madride I gatt (by Father Creswell)[1350] his assistance a Shipp perteininge to Mr Weston of Dublin[1351] released wch was seased to the kinges use; and did procure favor for one Comerfoord a merchant of Waterfoorde,[1352] there occation of trouble

[1343] 'wch' deleted.
[1344] Altered from 'is' to 'was'.
[1345] Altered from 'are' to 'weare'.
[1346] 'oute' deleted.
[1347] 'in the said towne' inserted.
[1348] 'in' inserted.
[1349] 'ye' inserted.
[1350] Joseph Creswell SJ (1556–1623), joined Jesuits 1583 in Rome; rector, English College, Rome, c.1589–1592; went to Spain in 1592 as collaborator of Robert Persons, and for years lobbied at the royal court for funds for the English colleges in Valladolid and Seville, becoming informal agent with crown for the English in Spain; moved to Flanders in 1615, *ODNB*; on Creswell's Spanish career, see Albert Loomie, *The Spanish Elizabethans: The English Exiles at the Court of Philip II* (New York, 1963), 182–229.
[1351] Probably Nicholas Weston (d.1617), a leading Dublin merchant who by 1589 was engaged in shipping with Spain, and in 1597–1598 served as mayor of Dublin, *DIB*, sub nomine; on Weston, see Lennon, *The Lords of Dublin in the Age of Reformation*, 275; for a case study of an Irish merchant in the war years of the 1590s, see Ruth Canning, 'Profits and patriotism: Nicholas Weston, Old English merchants, and Ireland's Nine Years War, 1594–1603', *Irish Economic and Social History*, 43 (2016), 85–112.
[1352] In the 1580s and 1590s, Comerford family members were prominent in the civic life of Waterford, serving as sheriff and mayor, Niall Byrne (ed.), *The Great Parchment Book of Waterford: Liber Antiquissimus Civitatis Waterfordiae* (Dublin, 2007).

was for that they weare accused by som of the Irishe that favored the[1353] late comotion here in Ireland wch informed the states there that the citties from whence they came did not favor (203) there proceedinges, but assisted the Queens forces againste them; In madride are fiftie three churches, it is exceedinge populous. Upon my departure from thence Father Creswell procured for me som crownes for the furtheringe of my iorney.

The ixth day of Aprill I travelled in the companie of certaine Spaniards from madride to Illescas

In this towne is a picture of or[1354] Lady wch doth many miracles

The xth[1355] to Ardosse that day wee passed throughe Tolledo wch is the metropollitant sea of all Spaine, the cathedrall church there is verie fayre beinge som hundred and forty paces in leinthe, and lxx [ ][1356] in bredthe, there are beside the Archbisshopp and digneties belonginge to that churche forty cannons one hundred rationeroes and forty chaplynes, the Bisshoppricke is valued at three hundred and three score thousande ducketts by the yeere, the revenues of the whole churche dothe amounte to more then half a million yeerly; In itt[1357] are lyinge the bodyes of Snt Elutherio and Engenus, there is to be seene[1358] one arme of St Alfonso and many other ritche relickes, it is saide for certaine that the churche stuffe there for ritches and somtuesnes is not matchable in the whole worlde,[1359] Also a stone where our blissed lady did tread upon when shee appeered (204) to Saint Alfonso; the ryver Tagus runethe by Tolledo, from the wch the water is conveyed wth great arte and coste unto the Bishopp his house wch standethe on agreat height above it,

The xithe to malaga [Malagón] throughe the duke[1360] of medena cely [Medinaceli] his contrie. here aboutes doth begine the Sherra [Sierra] Morena,[1361]

[1353] 'that' deleted; 'the' inserted.
[1354] 'or' inserted.
[1355] 'day' deleted.
[1356] Last character uncertain; possibly 'x' i.e. 80 paces.
[1357] 'In itt' inserted; 'There' deleted.
[1358] 'to be seene' inserted; 'also' deleted.
[1359] 'There is' deleted.
[1360] 'dom' deleted.
[1361] Following line erased.

The xiith daye to Almalona by the river Gandama wch runnethe fifteene myles under grownde, and issuethe forthe againe wth great violence. and so[1362] throughe the cittie realle [Ciudad Real], nighe unto
wch is a place of execution where a bad and periured[1363] woman was
myraculously strucken into ashes by a thunderboulte.

The xiiith to Conquesta [Conquista],

The xiiiith to Dameu[s] [Adamuz].

The xvth day by a bridge nighe unto wch runnethe the ryver of
Civill, here endeth the Syerra Morena wch is a barren montaine con-
try of som xxiiiitie leagues in leinthe. also in this place is the divition
of [*Andelosia*] Casteele and Andelosia [Andalucia].

The same daye I travelled throughe Cordua [Córdoba] wherein is a
wonderfull great cathedrall churche, here liethe the bodies of Saint
Alfonso whoe was kinge of Spaine and of his Sonn whoe also was
a Sainte, besides manie other[1364] martires bodies;[1365] The
Bisshoppricke therof[1366] is valued to be worthe one hundred and fiftie
thousande ducketts yeerly; (205) and soe we went forward to the
Posa[d]os [Posadas]

The xviith[1367] to Avent som three leages shorte of Sivill [Seville], that
day we passed over the ryver[1368] wch runnethe by ye same[1369]

The xviiith day to the ritche cittie of Civill, here I was intertainede
verie kindly by Father Walpoule,[1370] agrave and learned Jesuit, and
was admitted as convictor in the Englishe Colledge there. where I
studied methaphisicke for the space of half ayeer, and went in prieste
aparrell. at my comminge thether there was a merchant of Galwaye
named Richard Skerrett whose goods were seased upon to the kings
use, for the same cause that those merchaunts of Dublin and
Waterford (as before I named) were trobled, but upon my intreatie

---

[1362] 'so' inserted.
[1363] 'and periured' inserted.
[1364] 'besides manie other' inserted; 'here are [an] infinitt' deleted.
[1365] 'besides' deleted.
[1366] 'thereof' inserted.
[1367] 'day' deleted.
[1368] 'of Civill' deleted.
[1369] 'which runnethe by ye same' inserted.
[1370] Richard Walpole SJ ([1564]–1607), prefect of studies at the English College in Seville
in late 1590s, *ODNB*.

Father Walpoole soe used the matter wth the regent of Civill as he was restored to his owne,[1371] and about the same tyme one Valentine blake[1372] a merchaunt of the same towne had his Shipp and goods confistated to the kings use and him self committed to prison, where he endured alonge tyme to his great chardge and hinderance these and many other the licke precedents (wch might be named,) being considered[1373] doe prove evidentlie that the merchants of Irelande wch trafficke for Spaine were then in a verie harde case; for there they weare for (206) the moste parte suspected of heresie, and reputed for spies. heere in Ireland vexed and ill thought of for beinge papists, and mistrusted as intelligencers for the Spaniards.

Civill is the welthieste cittie of all Spaine there the kinge hathe a mente house wherein is coyned daylie when they doe worcke one hundred thousande ducketts at leaste, This coyninge house is not far from the kinges Pallace; which is verie faire and lardge, nighe unto wch is in buildinge an exchange house of Stone verie spatious and costlye, and adioyninge almoste unto the same is the cathedrall churche wch[1374] in greatnes dothe everie way excell that of Tolledo. in[1375] itt as is constantly affirmed, is apicture of oure blessed lady wch was made by Angells and in the chappell where this picture is placed lie three kinges of Spaine interred. in the chappell of or lady called Antiqua is an antient picture of[1376] the blessed virgin before wch are continuallye burninge fiftie Silver lampes of divers greatnes, there is another chappell wherein there relickes[1377] are kepte wth wonderfull reverence, amongste wch is the heade of Saint Leander and an arme of St Bartholomewe ye apostle ritchly sett in Silver and golde as the reste are, this churche is exceedingly well (207) served, as well in respecte of there musicke as alsoe in regarde of[1378] stately ceremonies and sumptuous[1379] churche stuffe, The archbusshopp of Civill is comonly a cardinall, his revenues dothe amount at leaste to one hundred and fiftie 1000 ducketts yeerely; the dignities and cannonries are verie good and great som of them amountinge to eight thowsande ducketts by the

---

[1371] 'owne' inserted; 'goods' deleted.
[1372] Sir Valentine Blake (1560–1635), created baronet 1622, *DIB*; for Piers's contacts with Irish merchants in Spain, see above, Introduction, pp. 31–34.
[1373] 'it' deleted; 'doe prove evidentlie' inserted, smaller script.
[1374] 'is' deleted.
[1375] 'this churche' deleted; 'itt' inserted.
[1376] 'oure' deleted.
[1377] 'the' altered to 'there'; 'of the churche' deleted.
[1378] 'there' deleted.
[1379] 'sumptuous' inserted.

yeere, there are noe lesse then five[1380] hundred masses daily saide in it,[1381]

In Civill is a churche of Saint Fraunces wch hathe a cloister wherein is curiously painted[1382] his liffe wth the pictures and names of soe many kinges and noble men as have been of that order, there is also in Civill a picture of or blissed lady called devalia wch hathe done great myracles, besides many other chourches monestaries and colleadges; the river wch[1383] runethe by itt[1384] somtymes dothe soe over flowe his banckes as it drownethe muche land and a great parte of the cittie; in this common wealthe as also in all Spaine, the kinge hathe paied unto his cofers the tenthe peny of all suche comodities as are bought or sold, wch amontethe to an infinitt som of mony by the yeere; the governmt of cevill[1385] for[1386] cheefeste matters of warre or busines of state is managded[1387] by an assistant soe named who is a man of great honor and reputation[1388] for the kinges (208) excheates and hearinge of many other causes, is a regent and a courte of audientia,[1389] for the kings revenues and matters of treason againste his ma[jes]tie the house of contractation, for enquirie of heresie and punishinge of heretickes, the holy house of inquisition, For desydinge matters of lesse importance are fowre and twenty in maner of Aldermen called there vintie quato.[1390]

The xiith daye of September I wente to a fayre wch was in[1391] a towne called Entrero [Utrera] five leagues from Civill where is apicture of or Lady wch dothe great myracles, and iorniead[1392] backe againe[1393] theether[1394] on the 14 of the same; in the almeda of that cittie[1395] stande two pillers wch are certainely affirmed to be those wch in olde tyme were called Hercules pillers, upon wch are written non

[1380] '5' placed above 'five'.
[1381] 'that churche' deleted.
[1382] 'St Fraunces' deleted.
[1383] 'river wch' inserted; 'there' altered to 'the'.
[1384] 'itt' inserted; 'Civill' deleted; 'wch' deleted.
[1385] 'of cevill' inserted.
[1386] 'the' deleted.
[1387] 'busines of state is managded' inserted; 'other wise' deleted.
[1388] 'who is a man of great honor and reputation' inserted.
[1389] 'di' inserted betweeen 'u' and 'e'.
[1390] Abbreviation; unclear.
[1391] 'in' inserted.
[1392] 'iorniead' inserted.
[1393] 'againe' inserted.
[1394] 'to Civill' deleted; 'againe theether' inserted.
[1395] 'that cittie' inserted; 'Civill' deleted.

plus ultra.[1396] In the subards therof[1397] is an hospitall De sangre, soe called only for women, verie fayere and lardge, the reveneus thereof come[1398] to 1400 ducketts by the yeere,

[*A wonderfull costlye hearse*][1399] at my beinge in Civill there was in makinge ahearse for the kinge lately deseaced[1400] of wonderfull coste and worckmanshipp, beinge built wth three heights reachinge to the topp of ye cathedrall churche in the higheste height was sett forthe the orders of Spaine, in the Seconde the kinges proper heires, and in the theerde his fowre wives statues wth many other pictures and rare imagerie of divers sortes it was thought that it woulde coste eare itt were finishead[1401] above 24000 ducketts and that[1402] the artificers wadges would[1403] come to no less then[1404] 1500,[1405] (209) the wax candles and tapers wch sett it out coulde be noe fewer then three thowsande; when the kinge died all those wch weare able did mourne in blacke as well strangers as others;

upon my departure from the colledge I changed my self unto laye apparell, and one the verie same daye one Captene Hawkins[1406] an Englishe gent. wch had bene longe prisoner in Civill did finde the meanes to escape, and for that I did use in my other attyre to visitte Mr Blake wch laye in the same prisone I was suspected to be accessarie unto his departure and for as muche as I was then upon my cominge for Irelande I bought som wyne fruite and banketinge stuffe wth entent therwth to paie my waye unto the Fathers and Scollers of the colleadge, wch at that daye weare recreatinge themselves in the venyarde nighe adioyninge unto the cittie and soe passinge wth this provision throwe the streetes accompanied wth certaine gent. of this contrie, it was thought that I wente to relieeve Hawkins,

---

[1396] The standard form is 'ne plus ultra' [Lat. 'no more beyond']; denoted the uttermost limit of navigation in the ancient world, A.J. Bliss, *A Dictionary of Foreign Words and Phrases in Current English* (London, 1966), 256.

[1397] 'ther' inserted; 'Civill there' deleted.

[1398] 'comethe' altered to 'come'.

[1399] Different ink.

[1400] Philip II died 13 Sept. 1598.

[1401] 'eare itt were finishead' inserted.

[1402] 'and that' inserted.

[1403] 'would' inserted.

[1404] 'no less then' inserted.

[1405] 'ducketts' deleted.

[1406] Sir Richard Hawkins (*c.*1560–1622), English naval officer; was captured June 1594 by the Spanish at San Mateo, off coast of present-day Chile; was held in Lima for almost three years and in 1597 was transferred to a prison in Seville. In Sept. 1598 he attempted to escape but was recaptured and transferred to a prison in Madrid. In 1602 he was released after eight years in captivity. On his return to England he was knighted in 1603. *ODNB.*

[*An unlooked for trouble*] and thereupon I was apprehended by an officer and carried to the house of contractation, where I was imprisoned and examyned, upon the wch examination, notwthstanding my inocency; I was sent to the rackinge house and had bene racked the next day in the morning, had not Capten Hawkins that night beene founde, whom they wch persued him overtooke in a venyard som two leages from Civill, This Hawkins had before that tyme (210) bene taken by the Spaniards at sea and was converted and reconsiled in the prison wherein he laye[1407] (by Father Richard Wallpoll) whoe in his nede lente him som two hundred crownes the wch he[1408] himself confessed when he was examyninge me. whereupon the iudges did mistruste that he did sett downe the plotte for Hawkins his escape to the ende that thereby the Englishe Jesuits might gett the greater favor in Englande supposinge that I was his instrument for effecting that busines[1409] but after they had fully examyned Capten hawkins upon his returne and wth exacte diligence[1410] looked into the matter, understanding as well by Father Wallpoll as by divers others of the maner of my behaviour and the places of my residence sithence my departure from Ireland, theie at lenight founde me cleere of the cryme wch was laid to my[1411] chardge and delivered me out of prison

But I muste confesse that these presumptions beinge soe many and pregnant did give them great occation to condemne me[1412]

Wee maye by this accidente and suche others of that nature consider howe carefull and sircumspecte iudges ought to be in ther proceedings espetiallie when theye sitt for matter of life and deathe, for somtymes the innocent man is putt awaye by meanes of suspitious licklyhoods and often it fallethe oute, that moste wicked offenders are saved by craftie sleights and deceitefull practises.

Aboute the same tyme I heard from Irelande of the deathe of divers of my frends and of (211) the burninge wastinge and prayinge of my land, these casuall mischaunces[1413] concurringe together were great crosses unto me, yet did I as patiently as I coulde endure them,

---

[1407] 'wherein he laye' inserted; 'of Civill' deleted.
[1408] 'he' inserted; 'Father Wallpoll' deleted.
[1409] 'supposinge that … busines' interlined; different hand.
[1410] Margin, erased: 'Another burdene of affliction'.
[1411] Changed from 'me' to 'my'.
[1412] Changed from 'my' to 'me'.
[1413] 'mis' inserted.

knowinge that my sins had deserved greater punishments then these were;

In Civill the Jesuits have a good colledge where they doe use to reade divinitie and Philosophie theie have also there a professe house wch is verie faire and ritchly adornede, but the greateste coste is bestowed upon there churche, the wch is curiously made and furnished exceedinge costlye, nighe unto the colledge of the Jesuits is a fayere Pallace belonginge unto the Duke of Medena, Scidonia,[1414] adioyninge unto the wch standethe the Englishe Colledge, the wch was builded as I p[ar]tely touched befor, by the meanes of Father Parsons whoe procured divers as well noble men as others to contribute to the setting up of the same, but the greateste benyfactor of the Englishe there was a widdowe in Civill,[1415] wch gave unto Father Parsons for makinge up of[1416] a churche for the Colledge, (wherein shee hirself shoulde be buried and daily praied for), the som of forteene thowsand crownes, and after the churche was builded wch was finished at my beinge there, shee bestowed three thowsande crownes for makinge of churche stuffe for the same, right before the highe altar is hir buriall (212) place, under the wch is a vaute wch is covered wth a verie fayre tombe stone, where is ingraven hir name and armes, the colledge hathe in it som twentye chambers, a verie fayre hale and divers howses of office requisite for suche a building,

I have harde Father Parsons saye that the daye before that this great some of 14 thowsande crownes was bestowed (as before is resited) there came to enquire for him (he beinge then at the duke of Medena Sidonia his house) a poore widdowe wch had earnestly sought for him wth whom when he had talked shee protested unto him that the cause whye shee came to speake to him was[1417] for that shee harde the prieste of ye parishe wherein shee dwelled exortinge of his parishioners to extende there beste helpe towardes the settinge up of a colledge for the Englishe nation, affirming howe meritorious a thinge it weare to gyve meanes of mainteniance unto suche laborers as shoulde worcke in Englande, for ye purginge and rootinge out of suche weedes of heresie as were grown in it, by reason of the innyquitie of these later tymes, and therefor imitatinge[1418] the poore

---

[1414] Duke of Medina Sidonia.

[1415] Dona Ana de Espinosa, widow of Don Alonso Flores Quiñones, captain-general of the Fleet of the Indies, Martin Murphy, *St Gregory's College, Seville, 1592–1767*, Catholic Record Society, 73 (1992), 141.

[1416] 'of' inserted.

[1417] 'was' inserted.

[1418] Capital 'I' before 'imitatinge' – sense unclear.

widdowe spoken of in the Scriptures[1419] shee presented him wth a shil-
linge the wch Father Parsons verie thanckefully receaved not doubtinge but that god wch did move that poore woman to yelde hir
benevolence accordinge hir smale habillitie,[1420] woulde also move
greater persons to bestowe franckly accordinge to there welthe and
substance the wch answerably unto his expectation, was the next
day after performed by the ritche (213) widdowe, wch before I
made mention of, This colleadge maye finde three score Scollers
besids there teachers and[1421] servants,

[*A sudden affliction*] From the tyme of my departure out of the Colledge
untill that I was ready to take my Jorney for Ireland I laie at a
Frenche mans house nighe unto the great churche of the cittie and
did happen then to be exercised wth more trouble, for I was suddenly
areasted in my hoste is house by two officers wch carried me to the
regent of Civill whoe was informed that I determyned to carrye
awaye an Englishe youthe wch was his page into Ireland. and thereupon sente me to prison, comaundinge that I shoulde be well loaden
wth Irones. at the wch tyme I delivered unto him my pasports wch I
brought from Rome, the wch after he had perused he sente
backe againe for me and tould me[1422] that he perceaved by thos writtinges that I was agood Christian and therefor perswaded himself
that I was wrongefully accused. but before he had vewed those cer-
tificatts of my behavior, he did mistruste that I was a Lutheran or
of[1423] som other newe secte and that my intente of[1424] the supposed
takinge awaye of his Servante[1425] was to perverte him in religion,
and soe beinge fully satisfied of me he gave me verie good wordes
and cryed me mercy for that he had[1426] used me soe hardly; assuringe
me that from that tyme forthe he woulde stande my good frende to
the uttermoste of his power and therwthall[1427] he[1428] verie corteously
dismissed me.

[1419] In the New Testament, regarding those giving to the temple treasury, the widow 'out
of her poverty put in all she had to live on', Luke 21:1–4.
[1420] 'h' inserted in front of 'abillitie'.
[1421] 'teachers and' inserted.
[1422] 'me' inserted.
[1423] 'of' inserted.
[1424] 'takinge' deleted.
[1425] 'by me' deleted.
[1426] 'had' inserted.
[1427] 'therwthall' inserted.
[1428] 'did' deleted.

I departed from Civill on[1429] the xxviithe[1430] of October, by barke pas-singe harde by Careo [Coria], where there (214) is searche made of all wch passe for prohibited ware, and landed at Saint Lucar [Sanlucar de Barrameda] the xxixth of the same, this towne belongethe to the duke of Medena Sidonia it is in the mouthe of the river of Civill; the duke his revenue amounts as I was informed[1431] to three hundred 1000 ducketts yeerly; here is a resi-dence for Englishe pristes whose[1432] churche there is dedicated to Saint George.

The xxxth daye to herrishe [Jerez];[1433] upon the land of this cittie the beste wynes in Spaine are made, here I mette wth Sabastine Fleming[1434] a merchant of Drogheda wch lente me mony for dis-chardginge of my debts in the colleadge and furnished me for my passadge into Irelande I was by him verie frendlye and kindely used, The second daye of November I went backe againe to Saint Lucar.

The fourthe[1435] I tooke horse for Civill. in my travell I was benighted and was fayne to lye in a Fearmou[rs] house, of one of the ritche merchants of Civill I did observe the allowance of meate gyven unto his plowmen, wch was only breade oyle and Garlick; and there drincke water, they did cooke there meate in this sorte follo-winge, firste they boyled som water then they brake there breade into small peeces, and putt it into great boules and scalled it, there breade beinge soaken they caste oute the remainder of the water and sprinckled oyle upon it minglinge the same, wth good stoore of garlicke, and eate it, wth spownes, there wadges as they tolde me was ixd str a day; the Bailiffe of that place gave me parte of his meate, and his bedd far that (215) night wch was verie homely;

The vith daye I wente to Civill where I paied my debtes and tooke my leave of my frends there;

[1429] 'on' inserted.
[1430] 'daye' deleted.
[1431] 'as I was informed' inserted.
[1432] 'whose' inserted; 'the' deleted.
[1433] First letter deleted; thus starts with 'h'.
[1434] Perhaps the 'Bestian?' Fleming, Drogheda merchant, bond as debtor for £220 in June 1599, Ohlmeyer and Ó Ciardha, *The Irish Statute Staple Books*, 225.
[1435] 'day' deleted.

The xth[1436] I departed from thence and tooke horse for hereeshe [Jerez][1437] and laie at one Mr Flatcher,[1438] his house an Englishman wch had longe tyme dwelled there,

The xvith daye we did ride from thence to St Maria Porte [El Puerto de Santa Maria], there I mett wth Capten Cripes[1439] an Englishe gent. wch used me verie kindly; and gave me a faire bloodstone,[1440]

The xxiiith[1441] we wente by boate to Cales [Cadiz], wch cittie som yeere and a half before that tyme had bene sacked by the Earle of Essex,[1442] the inhabitants of Cales did cale him an honnorable ene- mye, for at this beinge there he suffred all the ladyes gentlwomen Nunnes and religious men to goe out of the cittie, untoutched wth as much welthe as they coulde carrye about them,

The xxviiith[1443] of november wee tooke Shippinge for Ireland in a Frenche vessell called the litle delphine of St Maloes the wch Sabastian Fleminge had fraighted, and ladded hir wth wynes, [*A con- tinuance of troblesom accidents.*] after we weare a shipboord, it was my happ not to departe wthout more trouble, for an officer of Cales borded us and woulde have areasted me affirminge that I was an Englishman, and a spie and althoughe I had there a sufficient testi- monye of my behavior and contrye yet was I fayne to recompence his paines, and to speake fayere while my hand was in the lyons mouthe.

(216) The xxixth daye we passed by Cape St Maria in the Condados, and not many dayes after that by Cape finis terre in Galitia, and soe we sailed forwarde leavinge the mountaines of Bisca called the Sturias [Asturias] on oure right hande; we were in

---

[1436] 'daye' deleted.

[1437] First letter erased; perhaps 'S'.

[1438] John Fletcher, English merchant with a wine business in Jerez, member of the Brotherhood of St George, the confraternity which administered the church of St George and adjoining entities in the port of Sanlucar until 1591, Albert Loomie, 'Religion and Elizabethan commerce with Spain', 40–41, repr. in A. Loomie, *Spain and the Early Stuarts, 1585–1655* (Aldershot, 1996).

[1439] One Captain Crisp, an Englishman, had been serving in the Spanish fleets since *c*.1594, Loomie, *Spanish Elizabethans*, 164, 247.

[1440] One of a category of precious stones, 'spotted or streaked with red, supposed in for- mer times to have the power of staunching bleeding, when worn as amulets', *OED*.

[1441] 'daye' deleted.

[1442] Robert Devereux (1565–1601), 2nd earl of Essex; led an expedition to Cadiz, and on 21 June 1596 destroyed a Spanish fleet there, landed troops, and stormed the city; Cadiz was plundered, burnt, and abandoned; Essex and his party returned to Plymouth, 8 Aug. 1596, *ODNB*.

[1443] 'daye' deleted; 'of november' inserted.

or passadge divers tymes pursued by Pyratts but while oure consarts
of Frenche men kept us companie we feared them not, upon theire
departure from us we were hoatly chaste two dayes together by
two Piratts and had bene endangered to have bene taken by them,
[*A Discription of a storme*] had not a soddayne storme parted us asunder
the wch continued verie forceably and boisterous for the space of
foreteene dayes, there might you have harde the tempeste descendinge from the hedious cloudes wch beinge full fraighted, wth uncon-
tainable whoorle wyndes, did burste out wth monsterous roaringes
menasinge to ship wracke the vessell wherein we weare embarcked,
wherewth the sea did swell wth pride torninge hyr smouthe waters
into swallowinge waves, and hoodge billoes of wrathfull displeasure,
these two great comaunders beinge at this deadly debate, did com-
pell oure shipp (upon whom they did exercise there unwelcom forces)
to vale bonett and stricke saile, beinge apatient of noe sufficient abillitie to enduer theactions of suche stronge agents, and therefor, was
gladd to submitt hi[r]self unto the mercye of those unmercifull com-
batistes, the one of them licke a lyon did roare threatninge ye rent-
inge of hir shroudes settinge wth his shrill (217) wislinge hir
rigginge and taucklinge on tenter hookes and threatninge wth his
angrie blastes the shiveringe asunder of hir mastes and splittinge of
hir keele, the other in a furious sodaine snatchinge wth violence
dothe carrie hir up unto the top of a montaine of seas, wch had mus-
tered themselves to gether as it weare of a sett purpose to throwe hir
weeread bulcke, into the thickeste cloods[1444] and then wth a hastie and
untamed moode dothe cast hir downe (in desperatt maner) into a
gapinge gulfe or hallowe cave of bremishe waters representinge the
deepeste dungion of hatefull pluto;[1445]

here if a man wth a spirituall consideration woulde meditat: image-
ninge the seas and winde to be the crosses and thowarts of this
worlde, the Shipp his body and the passanger his Soule, he would
wth more patience induer the miseries of this transetorie liffe and
not strive againste the streame of gods punishments, wch for the chas-
ticments of his sinne dothe runne upon him, but to expect wth will-
ingnes and humblenes the promise of god made by the mouthe of the
kinglye prophett David whoe saithe, [*psalm. 13.*] mansueti haeredita-
bunt terram et Delectabuntur in multitudine pacis. The milde and
patiente shall inheritt the land and be delighted wth abondance of
peace, for as he saithe [*Psalm. 33.*][1446] multae tribulationes iustorum

---

[1444] Probably 'clouds'.
[1445] Pluto: Greek and Roman god of the lower world.
[1446] Different hand; *recte* Psalm 36 (37):11; Psalm 33 (34):20.

et de omnibus his liberabit eos dominus. Many are the troubles of iuste men but god shall deliver them from all there aflictions, and then woulde not (218) man greve at the prosperitie of the wicked, but wth the same Prophett woulde expect god his leason untill he might saie, vidi impium super exaltatum sicut cedros libani et tranfruii, et ecce non erat, ques[i]vi eum, et non est inventus locus eius,[1447] I have seene the wicked man mightilye exalted and lifted up as the cedars of lybano, and I passed by but he was not had, I sought for him and his place was not to be founde, for althoughe that wicked men enioye ever soe muche pleasure in this worlde, yet as the same[1448] prophett saithe [*psalm. 33.*][1449] mors peccatorum pessima, the deathe of wicked sinners is moste wretched and myserable, and in another place he saithe. Semen impiorum peribit,[1450] the posteritie of the wicked shalbe rooted out, but of the iuste he saithe thus [*psalm. 36*][1451] Iunior fui et enim senui et non vidi iustum derelectum nec semen eius quaerens panem. I was yonge but nowe am olde, and yet did I never see a iuste man forsaken, nor his seede begginge there breade. This small digression I have made to encouradge this poore contrie [Ireland] to devotione and patience, exortinge those wch be well inclyned to induere these calamities and myseries (wch lately have hapened) wth patience and wth feare and milde spirites to expect the infallible promisses of god, for[1452] after the blasteringe storme of his iustice comethe the sweete calme of his mercye.

But nowe to retourne unto the matter, (we beinge tossed wth the outrageousnes of this storme, as I have discribed) and wthin seaven dayes after the beginninge of it we sawe[1453] fifteene great Shipps wch we suspected to be (219) Flemings, and had it not bene for the violence of the weather they had visited us to or great hinderance or overthrowe,[1454] we weare soe farr dryven out of oure course by this meanes, that when the wynde came fayre the maryners coulde not descerne what land or region. should be nigheste unto them, but at lenight upon the xxvith daye of december about midnight he wch kept the compas discried land and had it not bene for the

---

[1447] Psalm 36 (37):35–36; the correct wording is 'Vidi impium superexaltatum, et elevatum sicut cedros Libani …'
[1448] 'same' inserted.
[1449] Psalm 33 (34):22.
[1450] Psalm 36 (37):28.
[1451] Psalm 36 (37):25.
[1452] 'for' inserted; 'and' deleted.
[1453] 'we sawe' inserted.
[1454] Final letter 'n' erased.

cleerenes of the night we had bene indangered in runninge unadwares upon it, this lande was Cape Cleere,[1455] but theye stoode in doubt whether it was[1456] England or Ireland, after or discreeinge thereof we labored into the sea, and the next daye we passed by Kinsale and other havens of Monster and that night for estuinge of the growndes of Wexford we made towards the coste of England;

on the xxviiith daye in the eveninge we caste ancker a leage or more from the heade of houthe [Howth, Co. Dublin] and hoiste out or cocke boate, in the wch we wente to lande, but the mariners not knowinge the place landed us upon the rockes of houthe where wee weare faine to clyme upe agreat height, before we coulde gett to the tope of the hill; in all my travell I was never in greater danger of my life then I was in clymeringe up these rockes, and had not Sabastiane Fleminge taken me by the hand, when I was almoste in the tope of therof[1457] I had fallen downe wthout any hope of life or recovery (22i)[1458] recoverye, from this and manye other dangers hathe god hetherunto delivered me, for the wch and all other his great benefitts bestowed upon me I doe yeld him moste humble and hartie thanckes but espatially for directinge me in the pathewaye of true religion, and prostratinge my self at the footte of his divine ma[jes]tie doe wthall humillitie crave that it maie please him to gyve me perseverance in the same, duringe my life, and that his grace will soe directe me as I maye ever use all my beste indevors for the settinge forthe of the honnor and glorie of his name, but principallie in performinge of all suche offices and services, as are due unto his churche my Prince and contr[i]e; I will not here make mention of any of the troubles[1459] crosses or[1460] damadges wch I have sustained since I came into this land for that they are alreadye sufficiently knowen to moste of this contrie;

Laus Deo Beatissimaeq[ue] virgini mariae[1461]

[Blank page]

[1455] Co. Cork, Ireland.
[1456] 'was' inserted.
[1457] Change from 'the' to 'therof'; 'rocke' deleted.
[1458] *Recte* 220.
[1459] 'or' deleted.
[1460] 'or' inserted.
[1461] Different hand.

(222)

A table of the iust number of myles wch are betwixt the principall Cities townes and other places of account mentioned in the precedent Discourse.

From Dublin to Hilbrye	I C and twentie[1462] myles
from Hilbrye to Chester	xiiii
from Chester to Nantwich	xviii
from Nantwiche to Sedsall	xxii
from Sedsall to Darbye	x
from Darby to Lester	xx
from Lester to Northampton	xxiiii
from Northampton to Onborne	xxxviii
from Onborne to London	xxviii
from London to Graves ende and soe	
Rocester and Canterbery to margat	lvii
[*on dutche myle is three Engly[s]h myles*]	
From margatt by sea unto ye brill in holland	
three hundred twentie dutche myles	
from ye[1463] brill to Rotterdam	iii
from Rotterdam to midlbrooghe	xx
from midlbrooghe to flushinge	i
from flushinge to Ratterdam	xxi
from Ratterdam to Delff	ii
from Delff to Hage	iii
from hage to Ratterdam	iii
from Ratterdam to Dorte	vi
from Dorte by Ratterdam to Layden	ii
from Layden to Harlden	v
from Harden to Amsterdam	iii
[New page – unnumbered]	
from Amsterdam to Harlyn	xiiii
from Harlyn to Leverden	iii
[*A myle in westfalia is vi English myles*][1464]	
from Leverden to Groyninge	vii
from Groyninge to Emden	v
from Emden to westfalia to Ouldenboorge	viii
from Ouldenboorge to breme	v
from Breme to Termule	vii
from Termule to Stode	iii

[1462] 'ten' changed to 'twentie'.
[1463] 'ye' inserted.
[1464] Slight difference in ink.

[*a myle in loe Saxony and in all partes of highe Germanie dothe countervaile five Englyshe myles*] [1465]

from Stode to Hamboorge in loe Saxony	v
from Hamboorge to Lubicke	x
from Lubicke to Orsumboorge	vi
from Orsumboorge to Lunaboorge	iiii
from Lunaboorge to Ensye	x
from Ensye to Brumswicke	vii
from brumswicke to wolfumbeetle	ii
from Wolfumbeetle to Alverstate	vi
from Alverstate to Islevyn	vii
from Islevyn to musticke	v
from musticke to Ihena	iiii
from Ihena to Cala	ii
from Cala to Gravatoll	v
from Gravatoll to Nestatle	iiii
from Nestatle to Pambrocke	viii
from pembrocke to Nerumboorge	ix
from Nerumboorge to wissingboorge	vii
from wissingboorge to Donauert	xi
from Donauert to Lanceboorge	vi
from Lanceboorge to Ausboorge	viii
from ausboorge to metavell	x

(223)

from metavell to Stretchin	vii
from Stretchin to Solle	viii
from Solle to Numarde	vi
from Numarde to trente in Itally	viii
from Trente to Bassania	vii
from Bassania to mestris	vii

[*at mestris doe begine ye Italyan myles wch are Ccante soe great as Englysh myls*]

from mestris to the famous Cittie of Venice	iii
from Venice to Padua	xxv
from Padua to[1466] Ruiga	xxx
from Ruiga to ferrara	xx
from ferrara to St George	xx
from St George to Bolonia	x
from Bolonia to Scargulisan	xx
from Scargulisan to Scarperia	xvi
from Scarperia to Florence	x

[1465] Ink as in previous margin entry.
[1466] 'to' inserted twice.

from florence to Syenna	xxxii
from Syenna to Rhodocophone	xxviii
from Rhodocophone to monteflesca	xxvi
from monteflesca to Backanoe	xxxvi
from Backanoe to ye holy Cittie of Rome	xiiii
from Rome to Regnata	xxi
from Regnata to Terny	xxiii
from terny to Vercana	xxvi
from Vercana to torrentine	xxvi
from torrentine to marcerata	x
from marcerata to Loreta	xiii
[new page, no numbering]	
from Loreta to Ancona	xv
from ancona to Fano	xxxv
from fano to Arymyne	xxx
from arymyne to forumlyvy	xxx
from forumlyvy to Emulle	xx
from Emulle to Bolonia	xx
from Bolonia to modena	xx
from modena to Regium	xxx
from Regium to ferencezola to parma	xx
from parma by Lodium to millan	xxxii
from millan to pavia	xx
from pavia to Sarewall	xxxvii
from Sarewall to Janua	xiii
from Janua[1467] by province in fraunce throughe the gulphe of lyons soe by mayorke and myork to allecante in the kingdom of valentin in Spaine by sea	CC vii
from alecante to avent leages	iii
from that vente by molona to another vente leages	vii
from that vente by Eda to another vente	vii
from that vente to Senychilla	ii
from Senychilla[1468] by allecante to Scyveta	vi
from Scyveta to farcana	iiii
from farcana to provencia	iiii
from proventia to Bellmonte	iiii
from Bellmonte to Villanova	vi
from villanova to Lagnardia	vi
(224)[1469]	
from Lagnardia to maranfwies	v

[1467] 'to' deleted.
[1468] 'to' deleted.
[1469] Added, in pencil, '115' – modern.

from maranfwies to madride	vii
from madride to Guaderamma	ix
from Guaderamma to Sta maria nova	xi
from Sta maria nova to valedelyde	xii
from valedelide backe ye same[1470] waye by the Squiriall to madride	xxxiiii
from madride to Elescas	[v]i
from Elescas[1471] by tolledo to ardos	xi
from ardos to mallagan	x
from mallagon by the Cittie Reale to almalona	x
from almalona to Conquesta	x
from Conquesta to Damyus	ix
from Damyus by Cordua to ye Passados	ix
from Passados over ye river of Civill to avent	xiiii
from that vente to Civill	iii
from Civill by Corye to St Lucars	
from St Lucars to Sherishe	iii
from Sherishe to Sta maria porte	
from Sta maria porte to by water to Cales	ii
from Cales by Sta maria in the Condados	
Cape finis terre in Portingall and the Coste of Biscay by Sea to Dublin	
	CCxx
	iii iii x

[1470] 'day' deleted.
[1471] 'to' deleted.

SELECT BIBLIOGRAPHY

Printed Primary Sources

Abbott, Thomas Kingsmill, *Catalogue of the Manuscripts in the Library of Trinity College Dublin* (Dublin and London, 1900).

Robert, Bellarmine, *Disputationes ... De controversiis Christianae fidei: Tertia controversia generalis: De summo pontifice* ([Ingolstadt, 1587]).

Bowler, Hugh (ed.), *Recusant Roll No. 3 (1594–1595) and Recusant Roll No. 4 (1595–1596)*, Catholic Record Society, 61 (1970).

Byrne, Niall (ed.), *The Great Parchment Book of Waterford: Liber Antiquissimus Civitatis Waterfordiae* (Dublin, 2007).

Calendar of Letters, Despatches, and State Papers relating to English Affairs, 1587–1603: Preserved Principally in the Archives of Simancas (London, 1899).

Calendar of State Papers, Domestic Series, 1595–1597: Preserved in the Public Record Office (London, 1869).

Calendar of the State Papers relating to Ireland, 1571–1608: Preserved in the Public Record Office, 13 vols (London, 1867–2010).

Calthrop, M.M.C. (ed.), *Recusant Roll No. 1, 1592–3*, Catholic Record Society, 18 (1916).

Dasent, J.R. (ed.), *Acts of the Privy Council of England*, NS, 46 vols (London, 1890–1964).

Erck, John (ed.), *A Repertory of the Inrolments on the Patent Rolls of Chancery in Ireland* (Dublin, 1852).

Foley, Henry (ed.), *Records of the English Province of the Society of Jesus* (London, 1880–1882).

Francini, Girolamo, *Le Cose Maravigliose dell'Alma Città di Roma* (Venice, 1588).

Heffernan, David (ed.), *'Reform' Treatises on Tudor Ireland* (Dublin, 2016).

Henson, Edwin (ed.), *Registers of the English College at Valladolid 1589–1862*, Catholic Record Society, 30 (1930).

Historical Manuscripts Commission, *Calendar of the Manuscripts of ... Marquess of Salisbury*, 24 vols (London, 1883–1976).

Kelly, Wilfrid (ed.), *Liber Ruber Venerabilis Collegii Anglorum de Urbe*, I: *Annales Collegii Pars Prima: Nomina Alumnorum (1579–1630)* (London, 1940).

Klarwill, Victor von (ed.), *The Fugger News-Letters, Second Series (1568–1605)* (London, 1926).

Knolles, Richard, *The generall historie of the Turkes, from the first beginning of that nation to the rising of the Othoman familie: With all the notable expeditions of the Christian princes against them ... digested into one continuat historie until this present yeare 1603* (London, 1603).

Law, Thomas Graves (ed.), *The Archpriest Controversy: Documents relating to the Dissensions of the Roman Catholic Clergy, 1597–1602*, Camden Society, NS, 56, 58, (1896–1898).

McCann, Timothy (ed.), *Recusants in the Exchequer Pipe Rolls, 1581–1592*, Catholic Record Society, 71 (1986).

McCoog, Thomas (ed.), *Monumenta Angliae: English and Welsh Jesuits*, 3 vols (Rome, 1992–2000).

Martin, Gregory, *Roma Sancta (1581): Now First Edited from the Manuscript*, ed. George Bruner Parks (Rome, 1969).

Munday, Anthony, *The English Roman Life*, ed. Philip Ayres (Oxford, 1980).

Munitiz, Joseph, and Philip Endean (eds), *Saint Ignatius of Loyola: Personal Writings* (London, 1996).

Murphy, Martin (ed.), 'William Atkins, A Relation of the Journey from St Omers to Seville, 1622', in *Camden Miscellany*, XXXII (London, 1994), 191–288.

Ohlmeyer, Jane, and Éamonn Ó Ciardha (eds), *The Irish Statute Staple Books, 1596–1687* (Dublin, 1998).

Palladio, M. Andrea, *L'Antichità di Roma* (Venice, 1554).

Piers, Henry, 'A chorographical description of the county of Westmeath' [1682], published in Charles Vallancey, *Collectanea de Rebus Hibernicis* (Dublin, 1786), 1–126.

Relatione della Guerra d'Hibernia, tra la Lega de' Catholici di quel regno, e l'asserta Reina d'Inghilterra (Rome, 1596).

Steele, Robert, *A Bibliography of Royal Proclamations of the Tudor and Stuart Sovereigns … 1485–1714*, 2 vols (Oxford, 1910).

Tanner, Norman (ed.), *Decrees of the Ecumenical Councils*, 2 vols (London and Washington DC, 1990).

Torsellino, Orazio, *Lauretanae Historiae Libri Quinque* (Rome, 1597).

Secondary Sources

Anstruther, Godfrey, 'Owen Lewis', in 'The English Hospice in Rome', *The Venerabile Sexcentenary Issue* (May 1962), 272–294.

Anstruther, Godfrey, *The Seminary Priests: A Dictionary of the Secular Clergy of England and Wales 1558–1850*, I: *Elizabethan, 1558–1603* (Ware and Durham, [1969]).

Barnard, Toby, 'Sir John Gilbert and Irish historiography', in Mary Clark et al. (eds), *Sir John T. Gilbert 1829–1898: Historian, Archivist and Librarian* (Dublin, 1999), 92–110.

Black, Christopher, *The Italian Inquisition* (New Haven, CT, and London, 2009).

Bossy, John, *The English Catholic Community, 1570–1850* (London, 1975).

Braudel, Fernand, *The Mediterranean and the Mediterranean World in the Age of Philip II*, 2 vols (London, 1973).

Bray, Massimo, *et al.* (eds), *Enciclopedia dei Papi* ([Rome], 2000).

Canning, Ruth, 'Profits and patriotism: Nicholas Weston, Old English merchants, and Ireland's Nine Years War, 1594–1603', *Irish Economic and Social History*, 43 (2016), 85–112.

Carey, Vincent, ' "Neither good English nor good Irish": Bi-lingualism and identity formation in sixteenth-century Ireland', in H. Morgan (ed.), *Political Ideology in Ireland, 1541–1641* (Dublin, 1999), 45–61.

Casey, Denis, *The Nugents of Westmeath and Queen Elizabeth's Irish Primer* (Dublin, 2016).

Chaney, Edward, ' "Quo vadis?" Travel as education and the impact of Italy in the sixteenth century', in Edward Chaney, *The Evolution of the Grand Tour: Anglo-Italian Relations since the Renaissance* (London, 1998), 58–101.

Corthell, Ronald, Frances E. Dolan, Christopher Highley, and Arthur F. Marotti (eds), *Catholic Culture in Early Modern England* (Notre Dame, IN, 2007).

Crawford, Jon, *A Star Chamber Court in Ireland: The Court of Castle Chamber, 1571–1641* (Dublin, 2005).

Croft, Pauline, 'Trading with the enemy 1585–1604', *Historical Journal*, 32 (1989), 281–302.

Cross, F.L., and E.A. Livingstone (eds), *The Oxford Dictionary of the Christian Church*, 3rd edn, revised (Oxford, 1997).

Edwards, David, 'A haven of popery: English Catholic migration to Ireland in the age of plantations', in A. Ford and J. McCafferty (eds), *The Origins of Sectarianism in Early Modern Ireland* (Cambridge, 2005), 95–126.

Einstein, Alfred, *The Italian Madrigal* (Princeton, NJ, 1949).

Fenning, Hugh, 'Irishmen ordained at Rome, 1572–1697', *Archivium Hibernicum*, 59 (2005), 1–36.

Fiorani, Luigi, 'Processioni tra devozione e politica', in Marcello Fagiolo (ed.), *La festa a Roma: Dal rinascimento al 1870* (Turin, 1997), 66–83.

Fosi, Irene, 'Conversion and autobiography: Telling tales before the Roman Inquisition', *Journal of Early Modern History*, 17 (2013), 437–456.

Frank, Thomas, 'Elizabethan travellers in Rome', in Mario Praz (ed.), *English Miscellany: A Symposium of History Literature and the Arts*, 4 (Rome, 1953), 95–132.

Gillow, Joseph, *A Literary and Biographical History, or, Bibliographical Dictionary of the English Catholics*, 5 vols (London and New York, 1885–1887).

Girouard, Mark, *Cities and People: A Social and Architectural History* (New Haven, CT, and London, 1985).

Hamilton, Donna, *Anthony Munday and the Catholics, 1560–1633* (Aldershot and Burlington, VT, 2005).

Hamy, Alfred, *Documents pour servir à l'histoire des domiciles de la Compagnie de Jésus … [1540–1773]* (Paris, [1892]).

Hazard, Benjamin, *Faith and Patronage: The Political Career of Flaithrí Ó Maolchonaire, 1560–1629* (Dublin, 2010).

Hickey, Elizabeth, 'Some notes on Kilbixy, Tristernagh and Templecross and the family of Piers who lived in the abbey of Tristernagh in Westmeath', *Ríocht na Midhe*, 7 (1980–1981), 52–76.

Highley, Christopher, *Catholics Writing the Nation in Early Modern Britain and Ireland* (Oxford, 2008).

Holt, Geoffrey (ed.), *St Omers and Bruges Colleges, 1593–1773: A Biographical Dictionary*, Catholic Record Society, 69 (1979).

Hunt, Arnold, *The Art of Hearing: English Preachers and their Audiences, 1590–1640* (Cambridge, 2010).

Hyde, Douglas, and D.J. O'Donoghue (eds), *Catalogue of the Books and Manuscripts … of Sir John Gilbert* (Dublin, 1918).

Iske, Basil, *The Green Cockatrice* (Meath, 1978).

Kenny, Anthony, 'From hospice to college', in 'The English hospice in Rome', *The Venerabile Sexcentenary Issue* (May 1962), 218–273.

Koch, Ludwig, *Jesuiten-Lexikon* (Paderborn, 1934).

Lennon, Colm, *The Lords of Dublin in the Age of Reformation* (Dublin, 1989).

Loomie, Albert, 'Religion and Elizabethan commerce with Spain', repr. in A. Loomie, *Spain and the Early Stuarts, 1585–1655* (Aldershot, 1996), 28–51.

Loomie, Albert, *The Spanish Elizabethans: The English Exiles at the Court of Philip II* (New York, 1963).

Mac Craith, Mícheál, 'An Irishman's diary: Aspects of Tadhg Ó Cianáin's Rome', in R. Gillespie and R. Ó hUiginn (eds), *Irish Europe, 1600–1650: Writing and Learning* (Dublin, 2013), 63–84.

Macray, Gulielmus, *Catalogi Codicum Manuscriptorum Bibliothecae Bodleianae: Partis Quintae Fasciculus Tertius … Ricardi Rawlinson* (Oxford, 1893).

Mac Cuarta, Brian, 'Religious violence against settlers in south Ulster, 1641–2', in D. Edwards, P. Lenihan, and C. Tait (eds), *Age of Atrocity: Violence and Political Conflict in Early Modern Ireland* (Dublin, 2007), 154–175.

Mac Cuarta, Brian (ed.), 'Sir John Moore's Inventory, Croghan, King's County, 1636', *Journal of the County Kildare Archaeological Society*, 19 (2000–2001), 206–217.

McCoog, Thomas, *The Society of Jesus in Ireland, Scotland, and England, 1589–1597* (Farnham, Surrey, and Rome, 2012).

Martin, Francis Xavier, *Friar Nugent: A Study of Francis Lavalin Nugent (1569–1635), Agent of the Counter-Reformation* (Rome and London, 1962).

Milward, Peter, *Religious Controversies of the Elizabethan Age: A Survey of Printed Sources* (London, 1977).

Murphy, Martin, *Ingleses de Sevilla: El Colegio de San Gregorio, 1592–1767* (Seville, 2012).

Murphy, Martin, *St Gregory's College, Seville, 1592–1767*, Catholic Record Society, 73 (1992).

Murphy, Paul, 'Santa Casa di Loreto: Orazio Torsellini's *Lauretanae historiae libri quinque*', in T. Lucas (ed.), *Spirit Style Story: Essays honoring John W. Padberg* (Chicago, 2002), 269–281.

Murray, Molly, ' "Now I ame a Catholique": William Alabaster and the early modern conversion narrative', in R. Corthell *et al.* (eds), *Catholic Culture in Early Modern England* (Notre Dame, IN, 2007), 189–215.

Netzloff, Mark, 'The English colleges and the English nation: Allen, Persons, Verstegen and diasporic nationalism', in R. Corthell *et al.* (eds), *Catholic Culture in Early Modern England* (Notre Dame, IN, 2007), 236–259.

Nice, Jason, 'Being "British" in Rome: The Welsh at the English College, 1578–1584', *The Catholic Historical Review*, 92 (2006), 1–24.

O'Connor, Thomas, *Irish Voices from the Spanish Inquisition: Migrants, Converts and Brokers in Early Modern Iberia* (Basingstoke, 2016).

Ó Muraíle, Nollaig, 'An insider's view: Tadhg Ó Cianáin as eyewitness to the exile of Ulster's lords, 1607–8', in R. Gillespie and R. Ó hUiginn (eds), *Irish Europe, 1600–1650: Writing and Learning* (Dublin, 2013), 44–62.

O'Sullivan, William, 'A finding list of Sir James Ware's manuscripts', *Proceedings of the Royal Irish Academy*, 97, Section C (1997), 69–99.

Pattenden, Miles, 'Governor and government in sixteenth-century Rome', *Papers of the British School at Rome*, 77 (2009), 257–272.

Pritchard, Arnold, *Catholic Loyalism in Elizabethan England* (London, 1979).

Rak, Michael, 'Piazza Navona: Trionfi, feste da gioco, feste stellari', in Marcello Fagiolo (ed.), *La festa a Roma: Dal rinascimento al 1870* (Turin, 1997), 182–201.

Rossetti, Sergio, *Rome: A Bibliography from the Invention of Printing through 1899*, Vol. I: *The Guide Books* (Florence, 2000).

Schüller, Karin, *Die Beziehungen zwischen Spanien und Irland im 16. und 17. Jahrhundert: Diplomatie, Handel und die soziale Integration katholischer Exulanten* (Münster, 1999).

Schüller, Karin, 'Irish migrant networks and rivalries in Spain, 1575–1659', in T. O'Connor and M.A. Lyons (eds), *Irish Migrants in Europe after Kinsale, 1602–1820* (Dublin, 2003).

Schüller, Karin, 'Special conditions of the Irish-Iberian trade during the Spanish-English war (1585–1604)', in Enrique García Hernán *et al.* (eds), *Irlanda y la Monarquía Hispánica: Kinsale 1601–2001* (Madrid, 2002).

Tierney, Mark A., *Dodd's Church History of England*, II (London, 1839).

Trimble, William R., *The Catholic Laity in Elizabethan England* (Cambridge, MA, 1964).

Williams, Michael E., *St Alban's College, Valladolid: Four Centuries of English Catholic Presence in Spain* (London and New York, 1986).

Woolfson, Jonathon, *Padua and the Tudors: English Students in Italy, 1485–1603* (Cambridge, 1998).

Unpublished Sources

Frank, Thomas (ed.), '*An edition of A discourse of HP his travelles (MS Rawlinson D. 83), with an introduction on English travellers in Rome during the age of Elizabeth*', BLitt thesis, University of Oxford, 1954.

Miranda, Salvador, *The Cardinals of the Holy Roman Church*, a digital resource created and produced by Salvador Miranda consisting of the biographical entries of the Cardinals from 494 to 2015: http://webdept.fiu.edu/~mirandas/cardinals.htm.

INDEX

Achamatt, son of Haly Bassa 151
Acheron, river 68
Acquapendente, Italy 76
Acquaviva, Claudio, Jesuit general 25,
    80n, 103
Adamuz, Spain 205
Adrian VI, pope, held to be a Fleming 110
Adrianople, Selimus's court 150
Albacete, Spain 199
Alcala, duke of 30
Alexander Severus, thermae (baths of) 155
Alicante 27, 198
Allen, Gabriel, brother of Cardinal Allen
    22
Allen, William, cardinal 2n, 17–18, 23, 82–
    83, 108
Alps 67, 69
Alva-Cobham accord (1576) 32
Ambrose, St: church of, Milan 105; reli-
    gious order of 96
Ammer, river, Bavaria 67
amphitheatres, Rome 159
Amsterdam 56
Anabaptists 56–57, 64
Ancona, Italy 192
Anors, William, Frenchman in Seville 32
Antenor, of Troy 72
Antonius Pius, emperor 157–158
Annunciation, contemplation of the 185
Apenines, Italy 196
Appia, [Via] (the Appian Way) 115, 157
Aqua Marsia, aqueduct 158
aqueducts, Rome 158–159; Sixtus V 40
Aranjuez, Spain 199
arches, triumphant, in Rome 160–161
Ardosse, Spain 204
Ariosto, Ludovico, poet 73
armoury, in Venice 70–71
army, papal, against Ferrara 167–169
Arnemuiden, Netherlands 55
artillery, Castel Sant'Angelo 161; in
    Lüneburg 59
Ash Wednesday, Rome 114
Atocha, Madrid 203
Augsburg 66

Augustine, St 62
Augustinian friars 93; in Rome 109
Augustus, market place, Rome (the
    Forum) 160
Aurelius, emperor, thermae (baths of) 155
Aventine Hill, Rome 153, 157–158; ther-
    mae 155

Baronio, Cesare, cardinal 100
bandits, near Trent 69
baptism, of Constantine 166; of Jews and
    Turks, in Rome 166
baptistry, St John Lateran 166
Barbadicus, Agustinus, at Lepanto 151
Barnardinus John, of Cordua, at Lepanto
    151
Barrow, Henry, religious radical 7, 56
Bassa, Haly, Ottoman commander at
    Lepanto 147, 150; his sons 151
Bassa, Partan, at Lepanto 147, 150
Bassano [del Grappa], Italy 69
Bates, Reginald, priest 26–27, 195
Báthory, Sigismund 80n
baths, see thermae
Bavaria, duke of, and Loreto 191
Becket, Thomas à, see Thomas of
    Canterbury
Bede, the Venerable, body in Genoa 196
Benedictines: Ferrara 73; Genoa 196;
    Milan 195; Parma 194; Piacenza 82;
    Rome 90; Valledolid 200
Bellarmine SJ, Robert, cardinal 18;
    Controversies 167; *De summo pontifice* 117,
    131
Belmonte, Spain 199
bells, at Easter, Rome 123; Leiden 56
Belvider, gate, Rome 156; garden tower, in
    Vatican 88
Bible 50, 57; and Catholic Church 135–
    137; Vulgate 39; gospels 116; *see also*
    Jeremiah; New Testament; psalms
Biondi [Buindoe], Bartolomeo, ex-Jesuit
    103–104
Bizballius, Ferantes, at Lepanto 151
Blackwell, George, archpriest 9